GIANT BOOK OF MATH FUN

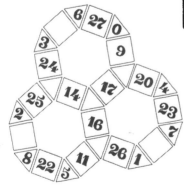

Raymond Blum, Glen Vecchione,
Kurt Smith, Steve Ryan &
Adam Hart-Davis

Sterling Publishing Co., Inc. New York

10 9 8 7 6 5 4 3 2 1
Published by Sterling Publishing Company, Inc.
387 Park Avenue South, New York, N.Y. 10016
Material in this collection was adapted from
Amazing Math Puzzles © 1998 Adam Hart-Davis
Math Challenges © 1997 Glen Vecchione
Math Logic Puzzles © 1996 Kurt Smith
Math Tricks, Puzzles & Games © 1994 Raymond Blum
Mathemagic © 1991 Raymond Blum
Mystifying Math Puzzles © 1996 Steve Ryan
Test Your Math IQ © 1994 Steve Ryan

Distributed in Canada by Sterling Publishing
c/o Canadian Manda Group, One Atlantic Avenue, Suite 105
Toronto, Ontario, Canada M6K 3E7
Distributed in Australia by Capricorn Link (Australia) Pty Ltd
P.O. Box 6651, Baulkham Hills, Business Centre, NSW 2153, Australia
Distributed in Great Britain and Europe by Chris Lloyd
463 Ashley Road, Parkstone, Poole, Dorset, BH14 0AX, United Kingdom

Sterling ISBN 0-8069-9465-7

Contents

MATHEMAGIC

CHAPTER ONE
ARITHMETRICKS

Arithmetricks

These amazing number tricks are fun to watch and even more fun to perform for others. They are easy to learn and, if you follow the steps carefully, they practically work themselves.

Practice a trick until you have successfully worked it through two or three times. Then you are ready to perform it for your friends. Be sure to work the trick *slowly* so that you don't make careless errors.

Remember, magicians never reveal their secrets. When someone asks you how you did a trick, just say, "Very well!" Also, don't repeat a trick for the same person. They might figure out how you did the trick if they see it a second time. Show them another trick instead and they will be even more amazed!

COIN CAPER

Your friend removes some coins from a bowl when your back is turned. After performing some number magic, you are able is disclose the number of coins that are hidden in her hand!

Materials

20 coins   A small bowl

Presentation   **Example**

    1. Put a bowl of 20 coins on the table, and then turn your back. Ask your friend to remove any number of coins from 1 to 9 and put them in her pocket.

She removes 7 coins

    2. Tell her to count the number of coins that remain in the bowl.

20 – 7 = 13 remain

    3. Ask her to find the sum of the digits of that number.

13 → 1 + 3 = 4

    4. Tell her to remove that number of coins from the bowl and put those in her pocket too.

She removes 4 more coins

    5. Ask her to remove any number of coins from the bowl and hide them in her *hand*.

She hides 6

6. When you turn around, take one of the coins out of the bowl. Hold it to your forehead and pretend to be in deep thought for a few seconds. Then reveal the number of coins that your friend is hiding in her hand!

How to Do it

When you turn around, secretly count the number of coins that remain in the bowl. Just subtract that number from 9. That difference is the number of coins that she is hiding in her hand!

9 – 3 coins in the bowl = 6 coins in her hand

An Exception

If your friend hides 9 coins in her hand and there are no coins left in the bowl, hold the bowl to your forehead.

The Secret

This trick uses a mathematical procedure called casting out nines. The first subtraction results in a number between 10 and 20. Any number between 10 and 20 minus the sum of its digits always equals 9.

A Variation

You can also tell her how many coins are in her pocket. It will always be 11!

Riddle Me

Why are 1980 U.S. pennies worth almost $20.00?

1,980 pennies = $19.80, which is almost $20.00!

NUMBER SPIRITS

Your friend randomly chooses any 3-digit number, and then works a few problems on a calculator. When the Number Spirits' magic dust is rubbed on your lower arm, his final total mysteriously appears!

Materials

A calculator   Paper and pencil
Ground cinnamon   A glue stick

Preparation

Put a small amount of cinnamon or any dark spice in a small container. This is the Number Spirits' magic dust.

Write the number 1089 on the inside of your lower arm with a glue stick. The number should be invisible yet remain sticky.

Presentation	Example
1. Tell a friend to write any 3-digit number on a piece of paper without letting you see it. Tell him that the first digit must be *at least 2 greater* than the last digit.	**831**
2. Ask him to reverse the 3 digits and write this new number (138) below the first number. Have him subtract the two numbers on a calculator.	**831** **– 138** **693**
3. Tell him to reverse this difference and add this new number (396) to the calculator total.	**693** **+ 396** **1089**

4. Remind your friend that he was free to choose any 3-digit number, and then ask him for his final total. Then summon the Number Spirits. Ask them to make your friend's final total magically appear as you sprinkle their magic dust on your lower arm. Perform some hocus-pocus as you rub the magic dust around. Blow off the excess dust and, like magic, the number 1089 mysteriously appears!

The Secret
It does not matter which 3-digit number your friend starts with. If he does the arithmetic correctly, the final total will always be 1089!

Mathematical Oddity

Which sum is greater?

987654321		123456789
87654321		12345678
7654231		1234567
654321	or	123456
54321		12345
4321		1234
321		123
21		12
+ 1		+1

Believe it or not, they both equal 1,083,676,269!

SUPERMAN

You can prove to your friends that you have the power to see through solid objects by adding the *bottoms* of 5 dice!

Materials
5 dice

Presentation

1. Tell your friend that you are going to look through the dice and find the sum of the bottom numbers.

2. Throw 5 dice on the table.

3. Pretend that you can see through the dice all the way down to the bottom numbers. (What you are really doing is finding the sum of the top numbers.)

4. Announce the total of the 5 bottom numbers. (Just subtract the sum of the top numbers from 35.) Then *carefully* turn over the 5 dice and add the bottom numbers. Your friend won't believe her eyes!

Example

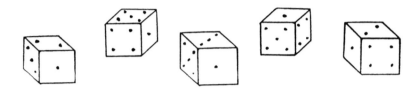

Sum of the top numbers = 13
35 − 13 = 22
So, the sum of the bottom numbers is 22!

The Secret

On any die, the sum of the top number and the bottom number is 7. So, if 5 dice are thrown, the total of all the top numbers and bottom numbers is:

5 x 7 = 35

Dice   Total

A Variation

Use a different number of dice and subtract the sum of the top numbers from a different number than 35. To find that number, just multiply the number of dice by 7.

YOUNG GENIUS

Your friends will think that you are ready for college when you add five large numbers in your head in just a few seconds!

Materials

Paper and pencil   A calculator

Preparation

Write this chart on a piece of paper

A	B	C	D	E
366	345	186	872	756
69	840	582	971	558
168	246	87	575	657
762	147	285	377	954
960	543	483	179	855
564	48	780	674	459

Presentation

While your back is turned, have a friend choose *one number* from each of the five columns and write them on a piece of paper. Tell her to add the five numbers using a calculator and write the answer underneath.

Example

        762
        246
        483
        674
      + 756
      2,921

Finally, ask her to read off slowly the five numbers in any order so that you can add them in your head. You will have the answer in seconds!

How to Do It

As your friend reads the five numbers, just mentally add the *five last digits*.

$$2 + 6 + 3 + 4 + 6 = \underline{21}$$

Mentally subtract this sum from 50.

$$50 - 21 = \underline{29}$$

Put the second number in front of the first number to get the sum of all five numbers!

$$\underline{2, 9}\ \underline{21}!$$

PHOTOGRAPHIC MEMORY

Your friends are really impressed when you show them that you have memorized fifty different 6-digit and 7-digit numbers!

Materials

50 index cards

Paper and pencil

Preparation

Copy these numbers onto index cards—one to each card. The card number appears in italics.

1	5,055,055	*11*	5,167,303	*21*	5,279,651
2	6,066,280	*12*	6,178,538	*22*	6,280,886
3	7,077,415	*13*	7,189,763	*23*	7,291,011
4	8,088,640	*14*	8,190,998	*24*	8,202,246
5	9,099,875	*15*	9,101,123	*25*	9,213,471
6	112,358	*16*	224,606	*26*	336,954
7	1,123,583	*17*	1,235,831	*27*	1,347,189
8	2,134,718	*18*	2,246,066	*28*	2,358,314
9	3,145,943	*19*	3,257,291	*29*	3,369,549
10	4,156,178	*20*	4,268,426	*30*	4,370,774

31	5,381,909	*41*	5,493,257
32	6,392,134	*42*	6,404,482
33	7,303,369	*43*	7,415,617
34	8,314,594	*44*	8,426,842
35	9,325,729	*45*	9,437,077
36	448,202	*46*	550,550
37	1,459,437	*47*	1,561,785
38	2,460,662	*48*	2,572,910
39	3,471,897	*49*	3,583,145
40	4,482,022	*50*	4,594,370

Example

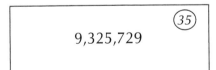

Presentation

Shuffle the deck of index cards so that they are not in order, and then hand them to your friend. Tell her that there is a different number written on each card and that you have memorized all fifty numbers. Ask her to choose any card. When she tells you the card number, you are able to tell her which 6-digit or 7-digit number is on that card!

How To Do It

1. When your friend tells you the card number, mentally add 4 and then reverse your answer. The result is the first two digits.

Example: Card #35
35 + 4 = 39 and 39 reversed is 93.

The first two digits are 93.

2. To get the next digit, mentally add the first two digits together. If this sum is less than 10, write it down. If it is 10 or greater, only write down the number that is in the ones place.

$$9 + 3 = 1\underline{2} \qquad\qquad 93\underline{2}$$

3. Continue adding the last two digits to get the next one until you have written down all seven digits.

3 + 2 = <u>5</u>	9325
2 + 5 = <u>7</u>	93257
5 + 7 = 1<u>2</u>	932572
7 + 2 = <u>9</u>	9325729

Answer 9,325, 729

Exceptions
If your friend picks a card number that ends in 6, the number on that card has only six digits.

Example: Card #36
36 + 4 = 40 and 40 reversed is 04
The number is 0,448,202

↑
(Don't say "Zero") ————┘

17

If your friend picks a card number from 1 to 5, mentally put a zero in the tens place before reversing your answer.

Example: Card #3
3 + 4 = 7 and *07* reversed is 70
The number is 7,077,415

A Variation
You can work the trick backwards. Tell your friend to give you the 6-digit or 7-digit number, and then you tell her the card number! When she tells you the number, reverse the first two digits and then subtract 4 to get the card number.

Example: The number is <u>1,2</u>35,831
<u>12</u> reversed is 21 and 21 − 4 = 17
The card number is 17.

An Exception to This Variation
If your friend gives you a 6-digit number, mentally put the zero back in front, and then work the trick backwards.

Example: The number is 336,954
(<u>0,3</u>36,954)
<u>03</u> reversed is 30 and 30 − 4 = 26
The card number is 26.

BRAIN POWER

Your friends will think that you are an amazing number magician when you find the sum of ten numbers in just a few seconds!

Materials

A calculator   Paper and pencil

Preparation

Write the numbers 1–10 on a piece of paper, one under the other.

Presentation

1. Tell your friend to write any 1-digit number on the first line and a different 1-digit number on the second line.

2. Ask him to add these two numbers together and write their sum on the third line.

$$5 + 9 = 14$$

3. Have him add line 2 and line 3 and write that sum on the fourth line.

$$9 + 14 = 23$$

4. Tell him to continue adding in this manner until there is a list of ten numbers. Make sure that he is adding correctly. Each number in the list (except the first two) must be the sum of the two numbers above it.

**Example
5 and 9**

1.   5

2.   9

3.   14

4.   23

5.   37

6.   60

7.   97

8. 157

9. 254

10. 411

When your friend writes down the last number, quickly look at his list and pretend that you are adding all ten numbers in your head. Secretly write your answer on a piece of paper, fold it several times, and put it aside. Ask your friend to slowly add all ten numbers, using a calculator.

(Example: 1,067)

He will be amazed when you unfold the paper and your answer matches his final total!

How to Do It

When ten numbers are added in this manner,

The Final Total = the seventh number x 11!

So when you look at your friend's list, just look at the seventh number. Multiply that number by 11 on your piece of paper to get the final total.

Here is a quick way to multiply by 11:

Multiply the seventh number by 10.   (97 x 10)   970

Add the seventh number to that answer.   +   97

1,067

Cross off your work so that your friend does not discover your secret. Make it look as if you have underlined your answer.

A Variation

Start with two 2-digit numbers and your friends will really be amazed!

MYSTERY POWDER

You and your friend write down five 4-digit numbers and add them using a calculator. When your secret mystery powder is rubbed over a piece of plastic, the correct answer magically appears!

Materials

A calculator

Paper and pencil

Glue stick

Ground cinnamon

Any piece of white plastic, such as the white lid from a plastic container

Preparation

Put a small amount of cinnamon or any dark spice into a small container. This is the mystery powder.

Write a number in the 20,000's on a piece of white plastic with a glue stick.

Example: 23,156

This is the Final Total. The number should be invisible yet remain sticky.

Figure out your *Key #*. First add 2 to the Final Total, and then cross off the first digit of your answer.

23,156
+ 2
23,158
Key #

Presentation

1. Ask a friend to write a 4-digit number on a piece of paper. The digits must be different and not form a pattern.

Example
8,351

2. You write the *Key #.*——————▶

3,158

3. Tell your friend to write a different 4-digit number below your number.

4,062

4. You write a 4-digit number so that the sum of the first and fourth numbers = 9,999.

1,648

5. You write a 4-digit number so that the sum of the third and fifth numbers = 9,999.

5,937

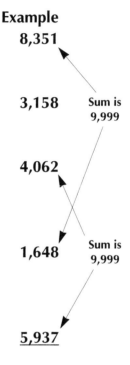

Sum is 9,999

Sum is 9,999

Give your friend the piece of paper and ask him to add the five numbers using a calculator.

(23,156)

Sprinkle your mystery powder over the piece of white plastic, and then perform some hocus-pocus as you rub it around. Blow off the excess powder and—like magic—the Final Total mysteriously appears!

An Exception

Your friend writes a 9 for the first digit of the first number or the third number.

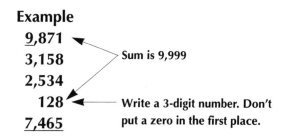

Example
9,871
3,158
2,534
  128
7,465

Sum is 9,999

Write a 3-digit number. Don't put a zero in the first place.

HAS ANYONE SEEN A GHOST?

This is a trick that you can do for a group of your friends or relatives. A prediction is put inside a shoe box and three random numbers are added using a calculator. When the shoe box is opened, your incorrect prediction has been mysteriously replaced by the correct answer!

Materials

A calculator
Shoe box
Marker
An index card
Pencil

A small spiral notebook that looks the same no matter which side is up.

Preparation

1. Write any 4-digit number on an index card with a marker, then cross it off. This is your prediction. Write a different 4-digit number (between 1000 and 2000) below the first number. Make it look like this number was written by a ghost. Put the card face down on the table.

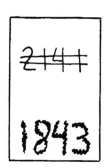

2. Open the notebook to the middle and write down three 3-digit numbers. Make it look as if each 3-digit number was written by a different person. The sum of these numbers should equal the ghostly number on the piece of paper. Turn the notebook over and put it on the table with the blank side up.

Performance

Give the calculator to a friend who is in the back of the room and tell him that you will need his help later.

Show your friends that there is nothing inside the shoe box, and then put your prediction and the marker inside. Put the top on the shoe box and give it to your friend to hold.

Ask another friend to come up to the table and write a 3-digit number on the blank page in the notebook. Repeat this with two other friends. Don't let anyone turn over the notebook.

When the third number is written down, pick up the notebook and take it to your friend with the calculator. As you are walking over to your friend, *secretly turn over the notebook.* Show him the top page (*your* three numbers) and ask him to add the three numbers using the calculator. Close the notebook so that no one sees the other side. Tell your friend to announce the answer.

When your friend says the answer, look disappointed and admit that your prediction in the shoe box is incorrect. Make up a story about a ghost who is a friend of yours and explain that he will assist you with the trick. Ask your invisible friend to enter the shoe box, pick up the marker, cross off your prediction, and write the correct answer underneath. Repeat the answer one more time and then ask your friend to remove the piece of paper from the shoe box. To everyone's surprise, your ghostly assistant has saved the day by writing the correct answer below your prediction!

THE HUMAN COMPUTER

You can astound your friends by adding five 6-digit numbers in just a few seconds!

Materials

A calculator   Paper and pencil

Presentation

1. Ask a friend to write a 6-digit number on a piece of paper. The digits must be different and not form a pattern.

2. Tell her to write a second 6-digit number below her first number.

3. Ask her to write one more number. This third number is your *Key #*. ⟶

4. You write a 6-digit number so that the sum of the first and the fourth numbers = 999,999.

5. You write a 6-digit number so that the sum of the second and fifth numbers = 999,999.

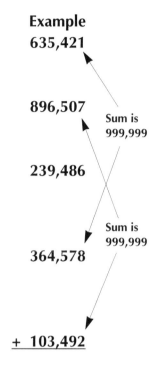

Example
635,421

896,507   Sum is
              999,999

239,486

             Sum is
             999,999
364,578

+ 103,492

Give your friend the piece of paper and ask her to add the five numbers using a calculator without letting you see the Final total—

(2,239,484).

When she hands you the paper, pretend that you are adding the five numbers in your head and quickly write down the Final Total!

How to Do It
When your friend hands you the paper, just look at the *Key #*, because the Final Total = 2,_____
            (*Key #* minus 2).

Example:
***Key #* is 239,486**
(*Key #* minus 2) = 239,484
The Final Total = 2,239,484

An Exception

Your friend writes a 9 for the first digit of the first number or the second number.

Example

$$
\begin{array}{r}
\underline{9}56,231 \\
623,178 \\
279,651 \\
43,768 \\
\underline{376,821}
\end{array}
$$

Sum is 999,999

Write a 5-digit number. Don't put a zero in the first place.

Variations

Seven 6-digit numbers:
   The Final Total = 3,_____
                        (*Key #* minus 3)

Nine 6-digit numbers:
   The Final Total = 4,_____
                        (*Key #* minus 4)

PSYCHIC PREDICTION

You are able to predict the sum of five 5-digit numbers before the trick begins! Also, when the digits of this sum are translated into letters, they spell your friend's name!

Materials

Paper and pencil   A calculator

Preparation

Write this chart on a piece of paper.

0	1	2	3	4	5	6	7	8	9
A	B	C	D	E	F	G	H	I	J
K	L	M	N	O	P	Q	R	S	T
U	V	W	X	Y	Z	.	,	!	?

Pick a friend who has three to six letters for a first or last name. (See *Variations* for more ideas.) The first letter must be a letter in the 2-column—C, M, or W.

Example: Cosby

Use the chart to translate your friend's name into a 6-digit number. This number is the Predicted Sum.

Cosby!
248,148

Figure out your *Key #*. Just add 2 to the Predicted Sum, and then cross off the first digit of your answer.

$$248,148$$
$$+ \qquad 2$$
$$\cancel{2}48,150$$

Presentation

Announce that you will write down the answer to a math problem before any numbers are given. Write the Predicted Sum on another piece of paper, fold it several times, and put it aside until later.

1. Ask your friend to write a 5-digit number on a piece of paper. The digits must be different and not form a pattern.

2. You write down the *Key #*. ——→

3. Ask him to write another 5-digit number.

4. You write a 5-digit number so that the sum of the first and the fourth numbers = 99,999.

5. You write a 5-digit number so that the sum of the third and the fifth numbers = 99,999.

6. Ask him to add the five numbers on a calculator.

Example

38,607

48,150   **Sum is 99,999**

76,231

61,392   **Sum is 99,999**

+23,768

248,148

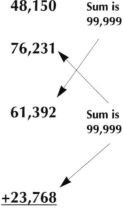

Finally, unfold your prediction and show your friend that it matches his answer! Then use the chart to translate his answer into letters and his name will magically appear!

248,148
COSBY!

Variations for Choosing a Name

Mr.C.!   **MS.G.!**   **MRBLUM**   **MSROTH**   **MRS.J.**

Other Variations

You could make words appear.

Example: MONDAY, MATH!!, MAGIC!, COLD!!, WEIGHT, etc.

Use your imagination! You could also rearrange the chart so that different letters appear in the 2-column. Then you could make many more names or words appear!

An Exception

Your friend writes a 9 for the first digit of the first number or the third number.

Example

$$92,761$$
$$48,150$$
$$49,135$$
$$7,238$$
$$+\ 50,864$$
$$248,148$$

COSBY!

Sum is 99,999

Write a 4-digit number. Don't put a zero in the first place.

CHAPTER TWO
CARD TRICKS

Card tricks are the most popular of all magic tricks. They can be performed anywhere and a regular deck of cards is all that is needed.

These card tricks are easy to learn and perform. No sleight of hand is required and, if you carefully follow the steps, they practically work themselves.

The tricks are organized from the easiest to the hardest, so choose those that are right for you. Even though the tricks are easy to learn, be sure to practice them by yourself first. When you have worked a trick through successfully two or three times, you are ready to perform it for others.

Never repeat a card trick for the same person or they might figure out the trick's secret. Perform a second trick instead, and everyone will have twice as much fun!

You will amaze your friends with your psychic powers when you look into the future and correctly predict the outcome of this card trick!

Materials

A deck of playing cards   Paper and pencil
An envelope

Preparation

Remove 9 red cards and 9 black cards from the deck.

Write "THERE WILL BE 2 MORE BLACK CARDS IN THE LONG ROW THAN RED CARDS IN THE SHORT ROW!" on a piece of paper and then seal it inside an envelope.

Presentation

1. Tell your friend that you have predicted the outcome of this trick and that you have sealed the prediction inside an envelope.

2. Hand him the 18 cards and ask him to shuffle them thoroughly.

3. Tell him to deal the cards face up in 2 rows in any order that he chooses. The first row should have 7 cards and the second row should have 11 cards.

4. Finally, remind your friend that he was free to choose the cards that were dealt into each row. Then open up your prediction and show him that it is correct. Your friend will think that you possess supernatural powers!

The Secret
The difference in the lengths of the rows determines the prediction. 11 − 7 = 4 and half of 4 is 2. So there will always be 2 more blacks in the long row than reds in the short row. Also, there will be 2 more reds in the long row than blacks in the short row.

A Variation
Start with 15 red cards and 15 black cards. Put 11 cards in the short row and 19 cards in the long row and see how your prediction changes.

There will be four more black cards in the long row than red cards in the short row.

Riddle Me

Why is it dangerous to do math in the jungle?

If you multiply 4 and 2 you will get 8 (ate)!

TREE OF CLUBS

You secretly predict which card will be chosen from the deck. It looks as if the "Number Spirits" have played a trick on you when your friend's chosen card doesn't match your prediction—or does it?

Materials

An envelope   Tape
A deck of playing cards with a Joker

Preparation

Photocopy the card on this page, cut around it and then tape or laminate it over the Joker. Seal this card inside an envelope.

Put the 3 of Clubs on top of the deck and put the 8 of Clubs in the ninth position down from the top of the deck.

Presentation

1. Tell your friend that he will randomly select a card from the deck and that the card in the envelope will match his selected card.

	Example
2. Ask him for a number *between* 10 and 20. (*Caution:* Between does not include 10 or 20.)	**17**

3. Deal that many cards into a small pile, one card at a time.

4. Ask your friend to find the sum of the digits of his number.	**17 → 1 + 7 = 8**

5. Return that many cards to the top of the big pile, one card at a time.	**Return 8 cards**

6. Put the rest of the small pile on top of the big pile.

7. Pretend to perform some supernatural hocus-pocus as you ask the "Number Spirits" for a sign that will tell your friend how many cards he should count down in the deck. Pretend that they tell you to turn over the top card. It will be the 8 of Clubs. This sign means that your friend should count down 8 cards in the deck and turn over the eighth card. It will be the 3 of Clubs.

8. Finally, remind your friend that he was free to choose any number. Then open up the envelope and pull out the Tree of Clubs. Act surprised and upset, and then blame the "Number Spirits" for switching cards and playing a mean trick on you. But wait! The trick worked after all!

The 3 of Clubs = The Tree of Clubs

The Secret
This trick uses a mathematical procedure called casting out nines. Any number between 10 and 20 minus the sum of its digits always equals 9.

LAST CARD

Your friend will be mystified when you correctly predict the number of cards that she secretly removes from the deck!

Materials
A deck of playing cards with a Joker
Tape

Preparation
Photocopy the card on this page, cut the card out and then tape or laminate it over one of the Jokers.

Put this card in the twenty-first position down from the top of the deck.

Presentation

1. Hand your friend the deck of cards. When your back is turned, ask her to remove from 1 to 15 cards from the *top* of the deck. Tell her to hide them in her hand.

2. Turn around and ask her to concentrate on the number of cards that she removed. Pretend that you are reading her mind as you *quietly* deal out 20 cards, one at a time, face down on the table. Put this pack of 20 cards in your hand and then set the rest of the deck aside.

3. Tell your friend to turn her cards over one at a time on the table. Every time she turns over a card, turn over the top card from your pack and put it face up on top of hers.

4. Continue turning over cards until hers are all gone. When she runs out of cards your next card will say, "THAT WAS YOUR LAST CARD!" It works every time, no matter how many cards your friend removes!

The Secret

When you count out 20 cards, their order is reversed. This puts the "THAT WAS YOUR LAST CARD!" card a certain number down from the top. That number will always equal the number of cards that your friend removes.

Favorite Number

Pick any number from 1 to 9. See what happens when you multiply that number by 259 and by 429. After you get the answer, clear your calculator. Then multiply 259 x 429 and you will see why it works.

YOUR SELECTED CARD IS...

Your friend secretly chooses a card from a deck of cards. When a magical phrase is spelled out, your friend's chosen card suddenly appears!

Materials
A complete deck of 52 playing cards with no Jokers

Presentation

1. Hand your friend a deck of cards, and tell her to shuffle them thoroughly.

2. Ask her to try to cut the deck into two equal packs. (It does not matter if the packs are equal, but each one should have between 20 and 30 cards.)

Example: 28 cards and 24 cards

3. Tell her to choose either pack and put the other pack aside until later.

4. Ask her to count the cards in her pack to see how close she got to 26. (If her pack does not have between 20 and 30 cards, ask her to start over and cut the entire deck again.)

5. Suppose your friend chooses the pack of 28 cards. Ask her to find the sum of the digits of that number.

28   2 + 8 = 10

6. Tell her to deal that many cards into a small pile, and then memorize the top card of that pile. Have her put the rest of her pack on top of this small pile.

7. Ask her to put her pack on top of the other pack that she did not choose, and then hand you the entire deck of cards.

8. Explain to your friend that you are going to spell out a magical phrase that will help you find her card. Deal cards from the top of the deck, one at a time, as you spell this phrase out loud: "Y-O-U-R S-E-L-E-C-T-E-D C-A-R-D I-S." Turn over 1 card for each letter of the phrase. The *next card* is your friend's selected card!

The Secret
This trick uses a mathematical procedure called casting out nines. Any number between 20 and 30 minus the sum of its digits always equals 18. This equals the number of letters in the magical phrase.

Riddle Me
What did the acorn say when it grew up?

Gee, I'm a tree (geometry)!

COME FORTH

Your friend will be astonished when you command his chosen card to come forth, and it rises up out of the deck!

Materials
A complete deck of 52 playing cards with no Jokers

Presentation

1. Have your friend shuffle the cards as many times as he wants. When he is finished, tell him to memorize the *bottom card.* **Example: Ace of Hearts**

2. Ask him to put the deck on the table and turn over the top 3 cards.

3. Tell your friend to deal cards face down below each of these 3 cards. He should start with the number on the face-up card (Aces = 1, Jacks = 11, Queens = 12, and Kings = 13), and then keep dealing cards until he gets to 15. For example, if the face-up card is a 9, he would deal 6 more cards to get to 15.

Example

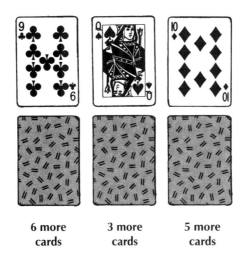

| **6 more
cards** | **3 more
cards** | **5 more
cards** |

4. Ask him to keep the 3 face-up cards on the table, and then put all the face-down cards on the *bottom* of the deck.

(12)

5. Have him find the sum of the 3 face-up cards (**9 + Q + 10 = 31**) Tell him to deal out that many cards, and then put them on the *bottom* of the deck.

6. Explain that you have supernatural powers and that you can force any card to come out of the deck on your command. Ask your friend for the name of his card so that you can command it to come out. He says, "It was the Ace of Hearts."

7. Pretend to do some hocus-pocus as you say, "Ace of Hearts, come forth!" Repeat your command, and then look pleased with the result.

8. Your friend, of course, won't see anything happen, but you insist that his card did come forth. Turn over cards off the top of the deck one at a time and say, "Here's the first card, here's the second, here's the third, and the Ace of Hearts comes FOURTH!" Turn over the fourth card and it will be your friend's card!

The Secret
Each face-up card + counting up to 15 + the value of the card = 16. So 16 x 3 face-up cards = 48. Then 48 + 4 (come fourth) = 52 cards in the deck.

WIZARD OF ODDS

You and your friend each select a card from your own deck of cards. The probability that you will select identical cards is 1 out of 2,704. But for some magical reason, you are able to beat the odds every time!

Materials

2 decks of playing cards without Jokers

Presentation

1. Have two decks of cards on the table, one for you and one for your friend.

2. Tell your friend to do exactly what you do. If you shuffle your deck, she should shuffle her deck. If you turn your deck around, she should turn her deck around, and so on.

3. This part of the trick is nothing more than a little hocus-pocus. Shuffle, double cut, turn, shuffle again, and triple cut your deck. Make sure that your friend does the same with her deck.

4. Flip your deck over, and then turn your deck clockwise and then counterclockwise 2 or 3 times. She should be doing the same with her deck. While you are doing this, it is very important that you *memorize your friend's bottom card*—this is your *key card*.

5. Turn your deck face down once again. Then pick out a card from near the center of your deck. Pretend that you are memorizing your card (but you only need to remember the key card on the bottom of your friend's deck) and then place it *on top of your deck*. Your friend does the same with her deck.

6. Each of you should cut your deck in half once so that the chosen cards are lost in the middle of their decks. This puts the key card on top of her chosen card.

7. Finally, exchange decks with your friend. Tell your friend to find her card and that you will find yours. Look through the cards until you see the key card. Your friend's chosen card will be the card *to the right* of the key card. Pretend that her chosen card is yours, remove it, and place it face down on the table. Your friend does the same with her card.

8. Explain to your friend that the probability of choosing identical cards is very small—1 out of 2,704 ($1/52 \times 1/52 = 1/2{,}704$). Your friend won't believe her eyes when you flip the cards over and they are identical!

ROYAL HEADACHE

Your friends will be amazed when you correctly predict which card will be chosen from the 20 cards on the table!

Materials

Paper and pencil
A deck of playing cards

An envelope

Preparation

Use 20 cards to make a figure 9 on the table. The values of the cards are not important but be sure that the suits are in the same order as shown in the diagram. Put the King of Hearts where the x is in the diagram.

Write "YOU WILL CHOSE THE KING WHO HAS A SWORD STUCK IN HIS LEFT EAR!" on a piece of paper and seal it inside an envelope.

Presentation

1. Tell your friend that you have predicted which card he will choose and that you have sealed the prediction inside an envelope.

2. Ask him to think of any counting number *between* 5 and 20. (*Caution:* This number must be greater than 5.) Tell him to start counting from the end of the 9's tail. (The first card is counted as number 1.) He should continue counting up and around counterclockwise until he gets to his number. Tell him to keep his finger on that card.

3. Remove the 5 cards from the 9's tail and put them aside, leaving only a circle.

4. Now ask your friend to count in the opposite direction—clockwise— around the circle until he gets to his number. (The card that his finger is on is counted as number 1.)

5. Remove the 5 Club cards from the circle.

6. Tell him to count 6 cards in either direction. (Again, the card that his finger is on is number 1.) No matter which direction he goes, he will end up on the King of Hearts!

7. Finally, remind your friend that he was free to choose any number. Then open up your prediction and show him what you wrote. He won't believe his eyes. He will think that you have E.S.P.!

The Secret
When you count one way around a circle and then count that same number in the opposite direction, you always end up in the same place. The 9's tail helps hide this secret.

IDENTICAL TWINS

Your friend randomly chooses any card on the table. He will be amazed when your prediction is opened and it matches his card!

Materials

Two decks of cards   A coin
An envelope

Preparation

Secretly seal an Ace of Hearts from a second deck in an envelope.

Place nine cards on the table in front of your friend. Be sure that they are in the *same order* as shown in the diagram.

Sit across the table from your friend, and put something between the two of you so that you cannot see the cards.

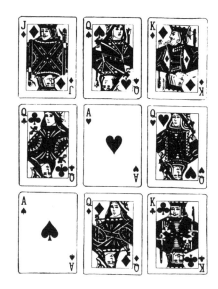

Presentation

Tell your friend that you have predicted which card he will choose and that you have sealed the prediction inside an envelope.

Ask him to place the coin on top of any of the four Queens. Tell him that he will be free to move that coin wherever he wants, but at the end of the trick, it will be sitting on your predicted card.

Explain that he can move the coin horizontally, vertically, forward or backwards, but *never diagonally*. Also, he cannot skip over cards. Make sure that the coin is on any Queen and then tell your friend to:

1. Move 6 times and then remove the Jack of Diamonds.

2. Move 3 times and then remove the Queen of Spades.

3. Move 2 times and then remove the Queen of Clubs.

4. Move 3 times and then remove the King of Diamonds and the Ace of Spades.

5. Move 2 times and then remove the King of Clubs.

6. Move 1 time and then remove the two red Queens.

If your friend followed your instructions, the coin will be on the Ace of Hearts!

Remind your friend that he was free to move the coin wherever he wanted. Then open your prediction and show him that the two cards are identical!

The Secret

There are only certain cards that you can land on when you move an even number or an odd number of times. Those cards that you *cannot* land on are removed. In the end, every card is removed except the Ace of Hearts.

SWITCHEROO

A deck of cards is divided into two piles. Your friend secretly takes a card from each pile and places it in the opposite pile. Even though each pile is thoroughly shuffled, you are able to find your friend's two cards!

Materials
A deck of playing cards without Jokers

Preparation
Put all the even cards in one pile (2, 4 ,6, 8, 10, Queen) and all the odd cards in another pile (Ace, 3, 5, 7, 9, Jack, King). Shuffle each pile so that it is well mixed.

Presentation

1. Have your friend shuffle each pile separately without looking at the cards. Spread both piles face down on the table.

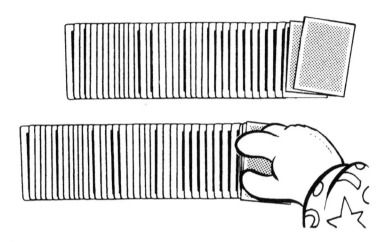

2. Tell her to choose one card from the group at the top, look at it, and place it in the group on the bottom. Then have her choose a different card from the group at the bottom, look at it, and place it in the group on the top.

3. Have her shuffle each pile, put one pile on top of the other, and hand you the deck of cards. Within seconds, you are able to reveal her two cards!

How to Do It
The odd card that is chosen will be surrounded by even cards, and the even card that is chosen will be surrounded by odd cards.

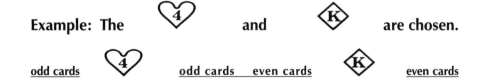

ELEVEN IN A ROW

Eleven cards are placed face down in a straight row on a table. After you leave the room, your friend moves some of the cards. When you return, you are able to tell how many cards were moved even though the row looks exactly the way it did when you left the room!

Materials
A deck of playing cards

Preparation
Take the following eleven cards out of the deck: Any Joker and any cards from Ace through 10. Place them face down on a table in order in a straight row.

J OKER	A	2	3	4	5	6	7	8	9	10

Left   Right

(All cards should be face down)

Presentation

1. Tell your friend that when you leave the room, he should move some cards from the left end of the row to the right end of the row, *one card at a time.* He may move any number of cards from 0 to 10.

2. Before you leave the room, move some of the cards yourself to show him how they should be moved. You are really doing this to get your *Key #.*

Example
You move 3 cards
(This is your *Key #*—remember it!)

J OKER	A	2	3	4	5	6	7	8	9	10	J OKER	A	2

Left   Right

3. Leave the room and have your friend move some of the cards.

Example
He moves 5 cards

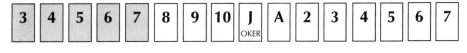

Left   **Right**

4. When you return, perform some hocus-pocus and pretend that the cards are speaking to you. Tell your friend that the cards will reveal the number of cards that he moved. Remember your *Key #* and count over that many cards from the *right end* of the row. Turn this card over and the number on that card will tell you how many cards your friend moved! (The Joker = 0 and Ace = 1.)

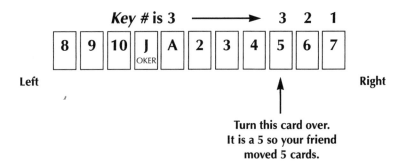

A Variation
Use a different *Key #* each time you perform the trick.

CRYSTAL BALL

Your calculator becomes your magical crystal ball when it mystically reveals a 2-digit number that is concealed inside a deck of cards!

Materials

A deck of playing cards   A calculator

Preparation

Remove all the 10s and face cards from a deck of cards so that your deck has only Aces through 9s.

Presentation

Ask your friend to shuffle the deck, remove two cards without looking at them, and place them face down on the table. The rest of the deck can be set aside.

Tell him to secretly look at either card and memorize its number (Ace = 1). Its suit is not important. You look at the other card, and then both cards are returned face down on the table. Put your card one inch to the right of your friend's card. Explain that the two cards represent a 2-digit number and that the calculator will be your crystal ball that will reveal that number.

Hand your friend the calculator and have him:

1. Enter the number of his card.   **9**

2. Multiply that number by 2.   **9 x 2 = 18**

3. Add 2 to that result.   **18 + 2 = 20**

4. Multiply that answer by 5.   **20 x 5 = 100**

5. Subtract the Magic Number.
The Magic Number is
    10 minus your card number.
    (10 – 3 = 7)   **100 – 7 = 93**

Finally, have your friend turn over the two cards on the table. The 2-digit number that is formed by the two cards will match the number that appears in the crystal ball!

INVISIBLE DECK

After your friend picks a card from your "invisible deck" and works a few problems on a calculator, you are able to announce the name of her invisible card!

Materials

A calculator   Paper and pencil

Preparation

Write these charts on a piece of paper.

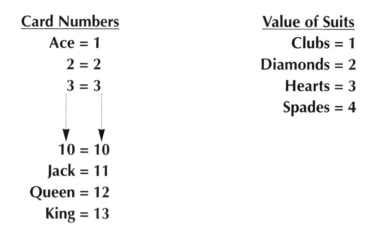

Card Numbers	Value of Suits
Ace = 1	Clubs = 1
2 = 2	Diamonds = 2
3 = 3	Hearts = 3
	Spades = 4
10 = 10	
Jack = 11	
Queen = 12	
King = 13	

Presentation

Pretend to have an invisible deck in your hands. Shuffle it thoroughly, and then ask a friend to pick a card from your "deck." Tell her to write the name of her card on a piece of paper.

Example: 7 of Hearts

Hand her the calculator and ask her to:

1. Enter the card's number.   **7**

2. Add the number that is one more than this number.
(7 + 1 = 8)   **7 + 8 = 15**

3. Multiply that result by 5.   **15 x 5 = 75**

4. Add the value of the suit to that answer.
(Hearts = 3)   **75 + 3 = 78**

5. Add 637 to that result.   **78 + 637 = 715**

Then, tell your friend to hand you the calculator with the final total. Just subtract 642 and her card will magically appear!

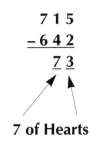

$$
\begin{array}{r}
7\ 1\ 5 \\
-\ 6\ 4\ 2 \\
\hline
\underline{7}\ \underline{3}
\end{array}
$$

7 of Hearts

An Exception
When your subtract 642 and get three digits, the first two digits are the card's number.

Example: <u>12</u> <u>4</u>

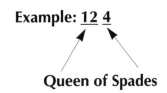

Queen of Spades

A Variation
Perform the trick with two or more friends at the same time. Before you announce their cards, pretend to +, −, x, and ÷ their totals so that they will think that their answers are somehow related to each other.

ABRACADABRA

You friend mentally chooses a card from a pile of 21 cards. When the magic word "ABRACADABRA" is spelled out, your friend's chosen card suddenly appears!

Materials
A deck of playing cards

Presentation

1. Shuffle the deck, count out 21 cards, and set the rest of the deck aside.

2. Deal out three piles of seven cards each, face down on the table. Deal the cards from left to right, one pile at a time, as if you were dealing to three players in a card game. There is no need for you ever to see the faces of any of the cards.

3. Ask your friend to choose one of the piles. Take the pile that he chose in your hand, fan out the cards towards him, and ask him to mentally select any card.

4. Put the pile that he chose between the other two piles so that you again have a pack of 21 cards in your hand.

5. Once more, deal out three piles of seven cards each, face down on the table. Taking up one pile at a time, fan out the cards towards your friend and ask him which pile has his chosen card. Again, put the pile that has his chosen card between the other two piles so that you have a pack of 21 cards in your hand.

6. Repeat Step 5 one more time.

7. Tell your friend that you are going to say the magic word "ABRA-CADABRA" and his chosen card will magically appear. Slowly spell "ABRACADABRA," turning over one card for each letter. The last card that you turn over will be your friend's chosen card!!

FOUR ACE BAFFLER

Three cards are randomly removed from the deck and they are all Aces! Then the "number spirits" are summoned and the fourth Ace mysteriously appears!

Materials
A deck of playing cards

Preparation
Put an 8 card in the eighth position down from the top of the deck and put the four Aces in the ninth, tenth, eleventh and twelfth positions.

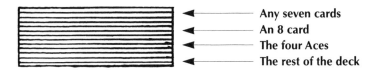

Any seven cards
An 8 card
The four Aces
The rest of the deck

Presentation

1. Ask a friend for a number *between* 10 and 20. (*Caution:* 10 will work, but 20 will not.)

Example
13

2. Deal that number of cards into a small pile one card at a time. Place the rest of the deck next to the small pile.

← 13 cards

3. Ask your friend to add the digits of that number.

13 � 1 + 3 = 4

4. Return that many cards to the top of the big pile one card at a time.

Return four cards

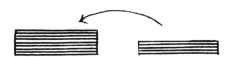

58

5. The top card of the small pile will be an Ace! Turn this card face up and show your friend.

6. Set the Ace aside and put the small pile on top of the big pile.

7. Repeat the six steps with two *different* numbers between 10 and 20 to remove two more Aces.

Finally, pretend to do some supernatural hocus-pocus as you ask the "number spirits" for a sign to help you find the last Ace. Pretend that they tell you to turn over the top card. It will be an 8. Count down eight more cards and the eighth card will the the fourth Ace!

MYSTERIOUS FORCE

You secretly predict which card will be chosen from the deck, and then the "number spirits" mysteriously force your friend to choose that card!

Materials

A deck of playing cards, complete with 52 cards plus two Jokers

Paper and pencil
A calculator, if needed

Presentation

1. Have your friend shuffle the cards as many times as she wants.

2. When she hands you the cards, say that you forgot to take out the Jokers. Turn the cards over, remove the Jokers, and sneak a peek at the bottom card. This is the "predicted card."

3. Secretly write the name of the "predicted card" on a piece of paper, fold it several times, and put it aside until later.

4. Tell your friend that a supernatural mathematical power will force her to choose your predicted card.

5. Deal out twelve cards face down from the top of the deck and spread them out on the table. Ask your friend to turn any four of these cards face up.

6. Put the other eight cards on the *bottom* of the deck.

Example

7. Hand your friend the deck and tell her to deal cards face down below each of these cards. She should start with the number on the face up card (All face cards = 10 and Aces = 1), and then keep dealing cards until she gets to 10. For example, if the face-up card is a 6, she would deal four more cards to get to 10.

60

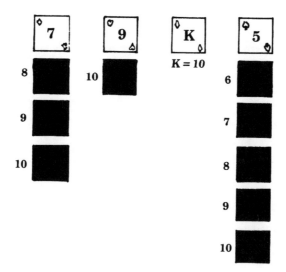

8. Tell her to keep the four face up cards on the table and put all the face down cards on the *bottom* of the deck.

9. Ask her to find the sum of the four cards:

(10)
7 + 9 + K + 5 = 31

10. Have her count down that many cards in the deck and turn the last card face up. (Turn card #31 face up.) This is her chosen card. Finally, unfold your prediction and show your friend that it matches her chosen card!

A Variation
If your deck of cards has no Jokers, sneak a peak at the bottom card after your friend hands you the deck.

POCKET PUZZLER

Your friend removes four cards from the deck and secretly puts one of them in her pocket. After performing some number magic on a calculator, you are able to reveal the card that is hidden in your friend's pocket!

Materials

A deck of playing cards   A calculator
Paper and pencil

Presentation

1. Ask your friend to write any 4-digit number on a piece of paper without letting you see it. Tell her that all four digits must be different.

Example
8756

2. Tell her to add the four digits together and write the sum below the first number. **(8 + 7 + 5 + 6 = 26)**

– 26

3. Have her subtract the two numbers, using a calculator.

8730

4. Hand her the deck of cards and ask her to secretly remove four cards that have the same numbers as the four digits. (Ace = 1 and 0 = King) Also, tell her that each card must be of a different suit.

Example
8 = 8 of Hearts
7 = 7 of Clubs
3 = 3 of Diamonds
0 = King of Spades

5. Tell her to put one of the cards *that is not a King* in her pocket, and then hand you the other three cards.

Example: She puts the 3 of Diamonds in her pocket and hands you the 8 of Hearts, the 7 of Clubs, and the King of Spades.

6. Mentally add the values of these three cards.

$$8 + 7 + 0 = 15$$

If your answer has more than one digit, add the digits together until there is only one digit.

$$15 \rightarrow 1 + 5 = 6$$

7. Mentally subtract this number from 9, and the value of the card that is in your friend's pocket will magically appear.

$$9 - 6 = 3$$

The card that is in your friend's pocket is a 3 and since the only suit that is missing is Diamonds, your friend's card is:

The 3 of Diamonds!

An Exception

When you mentally subtract from 9 and get 0, your friend's card is a 9—not a King.

CHAPTER THREE
CALCULATOR
CONJURING

Did you know that your calculator is a talented magician? If you enter the correct numbers, it will perform many magic tricks for you!

All of the magic tricks in this chapter are performed on an ordinary calculator. The tricks are organized from the easiest to the hardest, so choose those that are right for you. They are easy to learn and perform but you still need to practice them by yourself first. You should work a trick through successfully two or three times before you perform it for others.

You have to be very careful, however, and make sure you push the right buttons or the trick will not work. Perform each trick *slowly* so that you don't make careless errors.

Finally, remember that magicians never reveal their secrets. If someone asks you how you did a trick, just say, "Very carefully!" If they still question you, tell them to ask your calculator!

SEVEN-UP

You have the luckiest calculator in the world. No matter which number your friend enters, it is magically transformed into the lucky number 7!

Materials
A calculator

Presentation
Hand your friend the calculator and have her:

	Example
1. Enter any number that is easy to remember. (This number must be less than 8 digits.)	**123**
2. Double that number.	**123 x 2 = 246**
3. Subtract 16 from that answer.	**246 – 16 = 230**
4. Multiply that result by 4.	**230 x 4 = 920**
5. Divide that total by 8.	**920 ÷ 8 = 115**
6. Add 15 to that answer.	**115 + 15 = 130**
7. Subtract her original number from that result.	**130 – 123 = 7**

This trick can be repeated several times with the same friend. No matter which number she starts with, the final answer will always end up "lucky"!

The Secret
All of the tricks in this chapter were written using a branch of mathematics called algebra. In this trick, if all of the operations are carefully performed, your friend's original number is eliminated. Adding 15 in Step 6 guarantees that the final total will always be 7.

A Variation
Experiment by adding a different number in Step 6 and the final total will be a different number.

PAIR-A-DICE

Your friend rolls 2 dice when you are not looking. After he works a few problems on a calculator, you are able to reveal the two top numbers on the dice!

Materials
2 dice
Paper and pencil
A calculator

Presentation

When your back is turned, have a friend:

Example

1. Roll two dice.

2. Multiply the top number on the first die by 5, using a calculator or paper and pencil.

$$\underline{2} \times 5 = 10$$

3. Add 12 to that answer.

$$10 + 2 = 22$$

4. Double that total.

$$22 \times 2 = 44$$

5. Add that result to the top number on the second die.

$$44 + \underline{6} = 50$$

6. Add 15 to that answer.

$$50 + 15 = 65$$

Finally, ask your friend for his final total. Just subtract 39 and the top numbers on the dice will magically appear!

$$\begin{array}{r} 6\ 5 \\ -\ 3\ 9 \\ \hline 2\ 6 \end{array}$$

1st   2nd
die   die

The Secret

Multiplying by 5 and then doubling is just like multiplying by 10. This puts the number on the first die in the tens place. Adding the number on the second die puts that number in the ones place. Every other operation is mathematical hocus-pocus and adds an extra 39 to the total. Subtracting this 39 reveals the two top numbers on the dice.

68

SPECIAL FRIEND

Your friend will think that you possess supernatural powers when you correctly reveal the name that she has chosen from a list of her friends!

Materials

A calculator   Paper and pencil

Presentation

Ask your friend to make a list of at least five of her friends' names. Tell her to number each name.

Then ask her to:

	Example
1. Write the number of a "special" friend on a piece of paper without showing you.	**Friend #8**
2. Multiply that number by 5.	**8 x 5 = 40**
3. Add 5 to that result.	**40 + 5 = 45**
4. Double that answer.	**45 x 2 = 90**
5. Add 45 to that total.	**90 + 45 = 135**

6. Cross off the last digit of that answer.   13~~5~~

7. Add 44 to that result.   **13 + 44 = 57**

Finally, ask your friend for her final total. Just subtract 49 and the number of her special friend will magically appear!

$$
\begin{array}{r}
57 \\
-\ 49 \\
\hline
\end{array}
$$
Friend # 8 → **8**

The Secret

If all of the operations are carefully performed, the final total will always be 49 more than the special friend's number. Subtracting 49 reveals that number.

> ### BIRTHDAY SURPRISE

You will be able to divulge anyone's age and the year they were born by simply performing some number magic on a calculator!

Materials

A calculator

Presentation	**Example**
Hand someone a calculator and ask her to:	**Year Born: 1955**
	Age: 39
1. Enter the year that she was born, without letting you see it.	**1955**
2. Multiply that year by 2.	**1955 x 2 = 3,910**
3. Add the number of months in a year.	**3,910 + 12 = 3,922**
4. Multiply that total by 50.	**3,922 x 50 = 196,100**
5. Add her age to that result.	**196,100 + 39 = 196,139**
6. Add the number of days in a year.	**196,139 + 365 = 196,504**

Finally, tell her to hand you the calculator with the final total. Just subtract 965, and the year that she was born and her age will magically appear!

$$
\begin{array}{r}
\mathbf{196504} \\
\mathbf{-\quad 965} \\
\hline
\underline{\mathbf{1955}}\ \underline{\mathbf{39}}
\end{array}
$$

Year   **Age**
Born

Exceptions

If the person's age is less than 10, the tens place will be 0.

Example: 198905 = <u>1989</u> <u>05</u>, so age = 5

If it happens to be a leap year, add 366 in Step 6 and then subtract 966 from the final total.

The Secret

Multiplying the year by 2 and then by 50 is just like multiplying by 100. This moves the year over two and to the left of the hundreds place. Adding the age puts that number in the last two places. Every other operation is mathematical hocus-pocus and adds an extra 965 to the total. Subtracting this 965 reveals the year born and age.

LAST LAUGH

A card from a second deck is sealed in an envelope. You predict that this card will match your friend's chosen card. At the end it appears as though you have made a mistake, but you always end up getting the last laugh!

Materials

A calculator   2 decks of playing cards
An envelope

Preparation

Tear off the top half of the 10 of Diamonds from an old deck of cards so that only five of the ten diamonds are showing. Seal this card in an envelope.

Put the 5 of Diamonds in the eleventh position down from the top of the deck.

Presentation

Tell your friend that he will randomly select a card from the deck and that the card in the envelope will match his selected card.

Hand your friend the calculator and have him:

		Example
1. Enter his address or any other counting number that is easy to remember. (This number must be less than 7 digits.)		**41**
2. Multiply that number by 100.	**41 x 100 = 4100**	
3. Subtract his original number from that answer.	**4100 – 41 = 4059**	

4. Divide that total by his original number. **4059 ÷ 41 = 99**

5. Divide that result by 9. **99 ÷ 9 = 11**

Finally, remind your friend that he was free to choose any number. Then ask him for his final total. Have him count down that many cards in the deck and turn over the eleventh card, the 5 of Diamonds.

Open up the envelope and slowly slide out the 10 of Diamonds, being careful not to show the missing bottom. Your friend will think that you have made a mistake. Then slide the card all the way out and have him count the diamonds. Your prediction is correct after all because there are only 5 diamonds!

The Secret
Multiplying any counting number by 100, subtracting the number, and then dividing by the number always equals 99. Finally, dividing by 9 results in 11 for the final total.

DOUBLE TROUBLE

Pick any 1-, 2-, or 3-digit number. See what happens when you multiply that number by 7, then by 11, and finally by 13. After you get the answer, clear your calculator. Then multiply 7 x 11 x 13 and you will see why it works.

ORANGE ELEPHANT

Your friends are amazed with your mystical powers when you look into the future and reveal their deepest thoughts.

Materials

A calculator   Paper and pencil
An envelope

Preparation

Write "AN ORANGE ELEPHANT FROM FLORIDA" on a piece of paper and seal it inside an envelope.

Presentation

Tell your friend that you have predicted the outcome of this trick and that you have sealed the prediction inside an envelope.

 Then hand her the calculator and ask her to:

	Example
1. Enter any number that is easy to remember in the calculator without letting you see it. (This number must be less than 8 digits.)	**99**

2. Multiply that number by 4.   **99 x 4 = 396**

3. Add 25 to that result.   **396 + 25 = 421**

4. Double that answer.   **421 x 2 = 842**

5. Subtract 2 from that total.   **842 – 2 = 840**

6. Divide that result by 8.   **840 ÷ 8 = 105**

7. Subtract her original number
from that total.   **105 – 99 = 6**

Ask your friend to write her
final result on a piece of paper.   **6**

Tell her to number the letters of
the alphabet (A = 1, B = 2, C = 3, etc.)
and write down the letter that equals
her number.   **6 = F**

Ask her to write down the name of a
U.S. state that starts with that letter.   **F = Florida**

Tell her to look at the third letter
of that state and write down a basic
color that starts with that letter.   **o = orange**

Ask her to look at the last letter of that
color and write down the name of a very
large animal that starts with that letter.   **e = elephant**

Finally, open up your prediction. Unbelievably, it should match her 3
answers.

An **orange elephant** from **Florida!**

The Secret
If all of the operations are carefully performed, your friend's original number is eliminated and the final total will always be 6.

A Variation
Instead of making a prediction, have your friend concentrate on her three answers and then pretend that you are reading her mind.

CONCEALED COIN

This is a trick you can do for a group of your friends or relatives. When your back is turned, someone hides a coin in one of their hands. After you work some number magic, you are able to disclose who has the coin and which hand it is hiding in!

Materials

A calculator   A coin

Paper and pencil

Presentation

Pick one of your friends to be your assistant, and then number the rest of your friends starting with number 1. While your back is turned, have your assistant hide a coin in someone's hand. Tell him to write down that person's number and the hand that is hiding the coin. Tell everyone else to make fists with their hands.

Hand your assistant the calculator and have him:	**Example** **Friend #4** **Right Hand**
1. Enter the number of the person who has the coin.	**4**
2. Multiply that number by 5.	**4 x 5 = 20**
3. Add 13 to that answer.	**20 + 13 = 33**
4. Multiply that result by 4.	**33 x 4 = 132**
5. Add 88 to that total.	**132 + 88 = 220**
6. Divide that answer by 2.	**220 ÷ 2 = 110**
7. Add 4 if the coin is hidden in the left hand. Add 5 if the coin is hidden in the right hand.	**110 + 5 = 115**
8. Add 50 to that result.	**115 + 50 = 165**

Finally, ask your assistant to hand you the calculator with the final total. Just subtract 123 and you will be able to find that coin!

$$\begin{array}{r} 1\,6\,5 \\ -\,1\,2\,3 \\ \hline 4\,2 \end{array}$$

Person #4 ➤ 4 2 ◄— Hand
1 = left
2 = right

An Exception
When you subtract 123 and get three digits, the first two digits are the number of the person.

$$\begin{array}{r} 2\,7\,4 \\ -\,1\,2\,3 \\ \hline 1\,5\,1 \end{array}$$

Person #15 ➤ 1 5 1 ◄— Left Hand

The Secret
Multiplying the person's number by 5 and 4 and then dividing by 2 is just like multiplying by 10. This moves the person's number over two and to the left of the tens place. Adding the hand puts that number in the ones place. Every other addition is mathematical hocus-pocus and adds an extra 123 to the total. Subtracting this 123 reveals the person's number and the correct hand.

Riddle Me
Why did the math book go on a diet?

It had a lot of fractions to reduce!

BEWITCHED

Someone has placed an evil spell on your calculator. No matter which number your friend enters, it is ghoulishly transformed into the unlucky number 13!

Materials
A calculator

Presentation
Have a friend:

1. Enter in the calculator any number that is easy to remember—address, age, phone number, etc. (This number must be less than 8 digits.)	**Example** **77**
2. Double that number.	**77 x 2 = 154**
3. Add 15 to that answer.	**154 + 15 = 169**
4. Triple that result.	**169 x 3 = 507**
5. Add 33 to that total.	**507 + 33 = 540**
6. Divide that answer by 6.	**540 ÷ 6 = 90**
7. Subtract her original number.	**90 – 77 = 13**

This is a trick that can be repeated several times with the same friend. The final answer always ends up "unlucky"!

GIVE ME 5!

With your X-ray vision, you are able to see through the back of a calculator and reveal the number that appears in the display!

Materials
A calculator

Presentation
Have a friend:

1. Enter any number that is easy to remember in the calculator without letting you see it. (This number must be less than 8 digits.)	**Example** **365**
2. Multiply that number by 3.	**365 x 3 = 1,095**
3. Add 15 to that result.	**1,095 + 15 = 1,110**
4. Multiply that answer by 2.	**1,110 x 2 = 2,220**
5. Divide that result by 6.	**2,220 ÷ 6 = 370**
6. Subtract his original number from that total.	**370 – 365 = 5**

Finally, tell him to hold the *back* of the calculator towards you. Pretend that you have the power to see through solid objects, and then announce the total that appears in the display. No matter which number your friend chooses, the final total will always be 5!

Variations

When repeating this trick, change Step 3 and the final total will be a different number.

Step 3

Add	3	6	9	12	15	18	21	24	27	30 →
Final total	1	2	3	4	5	6	7	8	9	10 →

TALKING CALCULATOR

Your friend secretly selects two numbers, works a few math problems, and hands you the calculator. When you hold the calculator up to your ear, it whispers the two numbers that she chose!

Materials

A calculator   Paper and pencil

Presentation

Have a friend write down a 1-digit number and a 2-digit number on a piece of paper without showing you.

Then hand her the calculator and ask her to:

	Example 6 & 82
1. Enter her 1-digit number.	6
2. Multiply that number by 5.	6 x 5 = 30
3. Add 5 to that answer.	30 + 5 = 35
4. Multiply that result by 10.	35 x 10 = 350
5. Add 20 to that total.	350 + 20 = 370

6. Multiply that result by 2.   **370 x 2 = 740**

7. Subtract 8 from that answer.   **740 – 8 = 732**

8. Add her 2-digit number to that result.   **732 + 82 = 814**

Finally, ask her to hand you the calculator with the final total. Say that you are going to activate the calculator's talking mode by entering a special code. Subtract 132, push =, and your friend's two numbers will appear in the display.

$$\begin{array}{r} 8\ 1\ 4 \\ -\ 1\ 3\ 2 \\ \hline \underline{6\ 8\ 2} \end{array}$$

Sneak a peek at the two numbers as you put the calculator up to your ear. Pretend that the calculator is whispering to you, and then announce your friend's two numbers!

An Exception
When you subtract 132 and get only two digits, your friend chose 0 for the 1-digit number.

Example   159
0 & 27   – 132
                   27 = <u>0</u> <u>27</u>

SECRET CODE

Your friend thinks of an important date in his life, and then works a few problems on a calculator. When he is finished, you enter a magical secret code and his date suddenly appears in the display!

Materials

A calculator   Paper and pencil

Preparation

Write this month chart on a piece of paper.

1-Jan.	4-April	7-July	10-Oct.
2-Feb.	5-May	8-Aug.	11-Nov.
3-March	6-June	9-Sept.	12-Dec.

Presentation

Ask a friend to think of any important date in his life—his birthday, for instance, or a favorite holiday.

Hand him the calculator and tell him to:

	Example
1. Enter the number of the month from the month chart without letting you see it. (September = 9)	**Sept. 10**
	9
2. Multiply that number by 5.	**9 x 5 = 45**
3. Add 6 to that total.	**45 + 6 = 51**
4. Multiply that answer by 4.	**51 x 4 = 204**
5. Add 9 to that total.	**204 + 9 = 213**
6. Multiply that answer by 5.	**213 x 5 = 1,065**
7. Add the number of the day. (Sept. 10)	**1,065 + 10 = 1,075**
8. Add 700 to that total.	**1,075 + 700 = 1,775**

Finally, tell your friend to hand you the calculator with the final total. Just enter the secret code (minus 865 equals) and the important date that he thought of will magically appear! The first digit is the number of the month, and the last two digits are the number of the day.

$$1775$$
$$-885$$
$$910$$
$$\uparrow\ \uparrow$$

Sept. 10

An Exception

When you subtract 865 and get four digits, the first two digits are the number of the month.

Examples   **1031 = 10 31 = Oct. 31**
1205 = 12 05 = Dec. 5

FAMILY SECRETS

After a friend works a few problems on a calculator, you are able to divulge how many brothers, sisters, and grandparents she has!

Materials
A calculator

Example
4 brothers
3 sisters
2 grandparents

Presentation
Have a friend:

1. Enter her number of brothers in the calculator.	**4**
2. Multiply that number by 2.	**4 x 2 = 8**
3. Add 3 to that total.	**8 + 3 = 11**
4. Multiply that answer by 5.	**11 x 5 = 55**
5. Add her number of sisters to that total.	**55 + 3 = 58**

6. Multiply that answer by 10.   **58 x 10 = 580**

7. Add her number of grandparents
to that total.   **580 + 2 = 582**

8. Add 125 to that answer.   **582 + 125 = 707**

Finally, tell her to hand you the calculator with the final total. Just subtract 275 and her number of brothers, sisters, and grandparents magically appear!

$$
\begin{array}{r}
7\ 0\ 7 \\
-\,2\ 7\ 5 \\
\hline
\underline{4}\ \underline{3}\ \underline{2}
\end{array}
$$

brothers →   ← grandparents

↑ sisters

Exceptions
When you subtract 275 and get only two digits, your friend has no brothers.

Example: 12 = <u>0</u> <u>1</u> <u>2</u> so number of brothers = 0.

When you subtract 275 and get only one digit, your friend has no brothers and no sisters.

**Example: 2 = <u>0</u> <u>0</u> <u>2</u> so number of brothers = 0
and number of sisters = 0.**

POCKET MONEY

After your friend works a few problems on a calculator, you are able to reveal his favorite number and how much loose change he has in his pocket!

Materials
A calculator

Presentation
Have a friend:

Example
Favorite Number-25
Loose Change-47¢

1. Enter his favorite number in the calculator. (This number must be five digits or less.)

25

2. Multiply that number by 2.

25 x 2 = 50

3. Add 5 to that answer.

50 + 5 = 55

4. Multiply that result by 50.

55 x 50 = 2750

5. Add the loose change in his pocket. (This amount must be less than $1.00)

2750 + 47 = 2797

6. Multiply that total by 4.

2797 x 4 = 11188

7. Subtract 1000 from that answer.

11188 – 1000 = 10188

Then, tell him to hand you the calculator with the final total. Just divide that total by 400 and your friend's favorite number and his loose change will magically appear!

$$10188 \div 400 = \underline{25}.\underline{47}$$

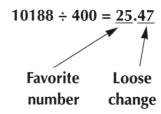

Favorite   **Loose**
number   **change**

Exceptions

If you divide by 400 and there is only one number after the decimal point, add on a 0 to get the loose change.

Example: 311040 ÷ 400 = 777.6 = 777.60
Loose change = 60¢

If you divide by 400 and there are no numbers after the decimal point, your friend has no loose change.

Example: 2800 ÷ 400 = 7. = 7.00
Loose change = 0¢

SUBTRACTION SORCERY

You ask a friend to work a subtraction problem on a calculator. After she tells you just one digit of the answer, you are able to divulge the entire answer!

Materials
A calculator
Paper and pencil

Presentation   **Example**
Ask a friend to:

1. Write any 3-digit number on a
   piece of paper without letting you
   see it. Tell her that all three digits
   must be different.   **427**

2. Reverse this number and write
   it below the first number.   **724**

3. Subtract the two numbers on   **724**
   a calculator. Tell her to enter the   **– 427**
   larger number first.   **297**

Finally, ask her to tell you either the first digit or the last digit of the total. You are now able to divulge the entire answer!

How to Do it

Here are all the possible answers when you subtract two 3-digit numbers as described.

99   198   297   396   495   594   693   792   891
(099)

Notice that the middle digit is always 9 and that the sum of the first digit and the last digit is 9. So just subtract what your friend tells you from 9 to get the missing digit.

Example

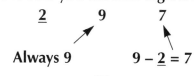

She tells you the first digit is 2.

<u>2</u>   9   7

Always 9   **9 – <u>2</u> = 7**

or

She tells you the last digit is 7.

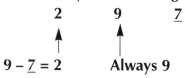

2   9   <u>7</u>

9 – <u>7</u> = 2   **Always 9**

An Exception

If your friend tells you that the first digit or last digit is 9, her answer will be 99.

CHAPTER FOUR
CALCULATOR
RIDDLES

The calculator that you own is a remarkable little machine. You've always known that it can perform mathematical calculations faster and with more accuracy than most humans, but did you know that it can also talk?

Yes, it's true! Your calculator will talk to you if you push the right buttons. For example, your calculator will tell you its name if you push clear and then *carefully* push **353 x 9 x 100 + 18 =** . Just turn your calculator *upside down*, and it will tell you!

Now that you and your calculator have been properly introduced, it's time to have some fun! Use the calculator alphabet below to help you find the answers to the math jokes and math riddles in this section. If you don't understand an answer, look at the explanation in the back of the book or just ask your calculator!

THE CALCULATOR ALPHABET

Upside-down numbers:	0	1	2	3	4	5	6	7	8	9
Letters:	O	I	Z	E	h	S	g	L	B	G

1. What is the only thing that gets larger the more you take away?

25,000 – 68 – 952 – 8,956 – 11,320 =

2. Which has fewer legs, a goose or no goose?

25.009 ÷ .001 + 10,000 =

3. Picture these U.S. coins: a nickel, a penny, and a dime. OK? Ellie's parents have 3 children. One is Nick and another is Penny. Who is the third?

.05 ÷ .01 ÷ .10 x 3 x 211 + 123 =

4. How many legs does a barbershop quartet have?

2 x 2 x 2 x 10 x 70 + 338 – .09 =

5. A pet store owner has 17 eels. All but 9 were sold. How many eels does the owner have left?

337.8 x 17 – 9 =

6. Who weighs more, Lee the 5-foot (152 cm) butcher or Bob the 7-foot (213 cm) wrestler?

5 x 7 x 10 – 13 =

7. A doctor gave you three pills and said to take one every half hour. How long will the pills last?

$$3 \times .5 + 2.6 =$$

8. Which would you rather have, an old one-hundred-dollar bill or a brand-new one?

$$100 \times 77 + 118.001 - 100 =$$

9. Bob and Bill took a dividing test in school. Bob wore glasses and Bill did not. Who got a higher score on the test?

$$10 \times 10 \times 10 - 200 + 8 =$$

10. How many seconds are in a year?

$$31{,}557{,}600 \div 1{,}000{,}000 - 26.3476 =$$

11. A barrel of water weighed 100 kilograms, but after somebody put something in it, it weighed only 25 kilograms. What was put in the barrel?

$$500 \times 100 + 4{,}000 - 300 + 4 =$$

12. Bill subtracted numbers for 20 minutes, Bess multiplied them, and Leslie added them.

Who was more exhausted when they finished?

9 + 57 + 868 + 7,920 + 93,208 + 215,475 =

Who went into debt when they were finished?

17,865 – 9,438 – 607 – 95 – 7 =

Who got the most work done in 20 minutes?

.3 x 2 x 2.6 x 20 x 7.1 x 25 =

13. What number did the math teacher bring the student who fainted?

222 x .2 ÷ 2 – .2 – 20 =

14. What is the largest number that will fit in your calculator's display?

99,999,999 ÷ 9 – 11,058,162 + 656,060 =

15. Bob says that only one month has 28 days. His boss says that there are more. Who is right?

28 x 29 x 30 + 31 – 18,882.486 =

16. What did seven do that made all the other numbers afraid of it?

$$7 \times .07 \div .7 \times 7 + 1.9 =$$

17. What number never tells the truth when it is resting?

$$223,314 \div 7 \div 2 \div 3 =$$

18. How much dirt is in a hole that is 5-feet (152.5 cm) deep, 2-feet (61 cm) wide, and 3-feet (91.5 cm) long?

$$5 \times 2 \times 3 - 30 =$$

19. Take two eggs from three eggs and what do you have?

$$9,992 \times .2 \times 3 - 2 =$$

20. What part of a lame dog reminds you of what happens when you start adding 37 and 26?

$$224 \times 25 - 25.486 + 37 + 26 =$$

MATH PUZZLES & GAMES

CHAPTER ONE
FANCY FIGURING

Get out your pencil. This chapter provides some old-fashioned arithmetic problems that call for serious ciphering. Now you can enjoy an assortment of brain-teasers that touch on such weighty mathematical concerns as *probability, recombinant shapes, number series,* and some just plain count-your-fingers figuring!

BULL'S-EYE

With your bow and arrow, shoot the following scores on the target using the smallest number of arrows: A. Shoot a 25. B. Shoot a 19. C. Shoot a 47.

JAWBREAKERS

Two jawbreaker-lovers stand at the vending machine with their pennies. The machine has 35 yellow jawbreakers and 35 blue jawbreakers. If they got a jawbreaker for each penny they put into the machine, how many pennies would they use before they had two jawbreakers of the same color?

Answers on page 238

ANTSY ANT

An ant decides to race along a ruler, starting at the 12-inch end. He runs from the 12-inch mark to the 6-inch mark in 12 seconds. How many seconds will it take him to reach the 1-inch mark?

A BURNED RECEIPT

This important receipt was badly burned in a fire. Can you reconstruct the missing digits so that the equation works?

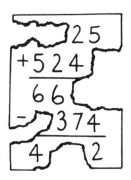

IN THE OLD CEMETERY

In the old cemetery, you stumble upon two tombstones. The dots indicate places where the stones are so worn that the dates have been erased. You find an old diary in the church and learn that both Mary and her brother John died in childhood and that the single missing digit in the bottom line of John's stone was one less than the single digit on Mary's. However, John lived *longer* than Mary. Calculate a possible birth year on Mary's stone.

Solution on page 238

MAGIC SQUARES

This ancient mathematical curiosity was once used as a charm to bring good fortune and protect against disease. Mathematicians now call it the *magic square*. It's magical because the square is constructed so that the numbers in each vertical column, horizontal row, and diagonal add up to the same number.

8	3	4
1	5	9
6	7	2

Third-Order Magic Square

16	3	2	13
5	10	11	8
9	6	7	12
4	15	14	1

Fourth-Order Magic Square

Magic squares can be of any order, beginning with a 3 x 3 square of nine numbers. In fact, any regular number sequence that you can place in a square (3 x 3, 4 x 4, 5 x 5, etc.) can be made into a magic square. The *magic constant* for a third-order square is 15. A fourth-order square has a constant of 34.

There are seven variations of a third-order (3 x 3) magic square, 880 variations of a fourth-order square, and over a million variations for a fifth-order square. Although it might seem difficult to construct anything larger than a third-order square, a French mathematician named Loubère came up with a trick for making any size of odd-order square. We'll use his method to build a simple fifth-order square.

A piece of large-grid graph paper comes in handy, since you'll be working on several squares at once, each one duplicating the original square.

Outline four neighboring 5 x 5 squares on your graph paper. You'll begin in the bottom left square. Write the number 1 in the top middle cell of that square. Write the number 2 diagonally above it to the right (in a new square), and repeat the number 2 at the bottom of that row (in the original square). Now write the number 3 diagonally to the right of the number 2, and repeat the number 3 above in the new square. Write the number 4 diagonally to the right of the number 3, and notice that another number 4 should appear in the first row of the original square, three cells from the top. When a cell is already occupied, place the next number in the cell directly below its preceding number, as in number 6.

Creating a Fifth-Order Magic Square

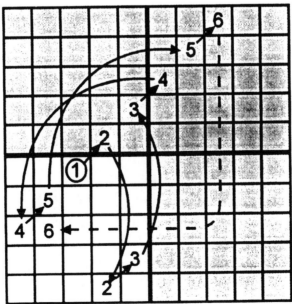

105

You should now begin to see a pattern emerge. Continue filling in the cells of your magic squares until you complete them. What is the magic constant for a fifth-order square?

17	24	1	8	15
23	5	7	14	16
4	6	13	20	22
10	12	19	21	3
11	18	25	2	9

Fifth-Order Magic Square

For a simple fifth-order square of this type, notice that the numbers proceed consecutively along the diagonal as the original square is duplicated.

You can perform all sorts of tricks with magic squares. Have a friend erase any number or series of numbers in the square and you can always replace them because you know the square's constant. Or have a friend completely rearrange all the numbers in a single row, column, or diagonal. Only you know the secret.

Solution on page 239

MORE MAGIC SHAPES

Similar to the magic square puzzles, these shapes rely on overlapping number relationships for their unusual qualities.

For the magic triangle, arrange the numbers 4 through 9 in the circles so that every side of the triangle equals 21.

For the magic daisy, place the numbers 1 through 11 in the circles so that every straight line of three circles totals 18.

For the magic star, place the numbers 1 through 12 in the circles so that each straight row of four circles adds up to 26. In this case, you may find more than one solution.

Magic Triangle

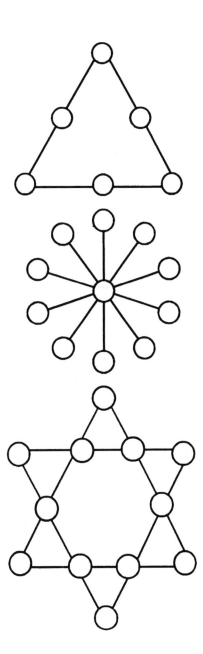

Magic Daisy

Magic Star

Solution on page 239

Ben Franklin's Wheel

Benjamin Franklin, the great American inventor, scientist, philosopher, and statesman, was also a maker of magic squares. He preferred to design them as wheels, however, and the one reproduced below represents one of his more elaborate designs. It was supposedly doodled one tedious afternoon when the young Franklin was a clerk at the Pennsylvania Assembly.

Knowing what you now know about magic squares, fill in all the missing numbers.

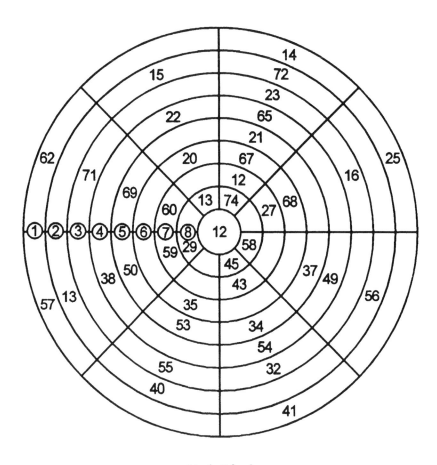

Magic Wheel

Solution on page 239

The Chimes of Big Ben

Big Ben, London's largest clock, calls out the time with loud chimes, one for each hour. If it takes Big Ben 3 seconds to chime three times at three o'clock, how long will it take Big Ben to chime six times at 6 o'clock?

Solution on page 239

Count the Streetlights

On opposite sides of a street, there are 45 streetlights, each one at a distance of 30 yards from the other. The streetlights on one side are arranged so that each lamp fills a gap between two other streetlights on the opposite side. How long is the street?

Weighing In

How many pounds does each cube, pyramid, and sphere weigh when each row has the combined weight indicated?

$$\square \; \square \; \triangle \; \bigcirc = 17$$

$$\square \; \triangle \; \triangle \; \bigcirc = 14$$

$$\square \; \triangle \; \bigcirc \; \bigcirc = 13$$

Solution on page 240

CHAPTER TWO
MATH LOGIC PUZZLES

Beginning Puzzles

Fishing

Four men went fishing. They caught six fish altogether. One man caught three, another caught two, one caught one, and one didn't catch anything. Which man caught how many fish? What did each of the fishermen use for bait?

1. The one who caught two fish wasn't Sammy nor the one who used worms.
2. The one who used the flatfish didn't catch as many as Fred.
3. Dry flies were the best lure of the day, catching three fish.
4. Torkel used eggs.
5. Sammy didn't use the flat fish.

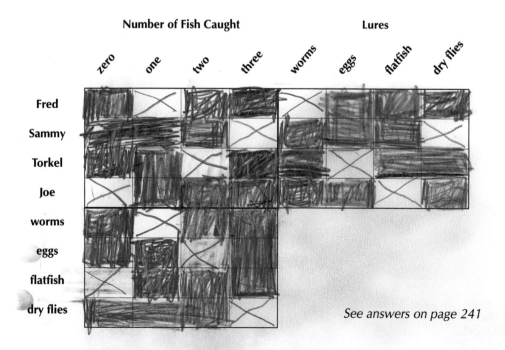

See answers on page 241

Jump Rope

Some kids were jumping rope (double Dutch) at the school break. They counted how many times each one jumped before missing. See if you can figure out how many jumps each kid made. (You may want to use a pencil and paper to do the adding and subtracting needed to solve this brainer.)

1. Gary jumped eight fewer times than Arnie.
2. Combined, Danielle, and Ruth jumped 37 times.
3. Jan jumped 8 more jumps than Danielle.
4. Gary and Danielle are separated by just three jumps.
5. Arnie's jumps number 5 more than Danielle.

	9	12	17	20	25
Danielle					
Gary					
Jan					
Arnie					
Ruth					

See answers on page 242

Pocket Change

Five boys went to the store to buy some treats. One boy had $4. One boy had $3. Two boys had $2, and one boy had $1. Using the following clues, determine how much money each boy started with and how much each had when he left the store.

The clues are:

1. Alex started with more than Jim.
2. Scott spent 15¢ more than Dan.
3. Duane started with more money than just one other person.
4. Alex spent the most, but he did not end with the least.
5. Dan started with 66% as much as Scott.
6. Jim spent the least and ended with more than Alex or Dan.
7. Duane spent 35¢.

	Started With				Ended With				
	$4	$3	$2	$1	1.65	95¢	70¢	40¢	10¢
Alex									
Scott									
Dan									
Jim									
Duane									

See answers on page 243

Temperature

A sixth-grade class project involved keeping track of the average temperature of the classroom over a two-week period in January. The results of the study showed that, at one particular time of the day, the temperature was always at its lowest point. Try to figure out when, during the day, the temperature was lowest, and the reason for it.

1. The automatic heating system in the school comes on at 6:00 in the morning.
2. No students arrive before 8:30. The first temperature reading takes place at that time.
3. The temperature is taken at half hour intervals from 8:30 until 3:00 in the afternoon, when the students go home.
4. The automatic heating system goes off at 2:00.
5. The highest temperature reading is at 10:00.
6. The 2:30 reading of the temperature shows a cooling off, but not the lowest temperature.
7. Morning recess is from 10:20 to 10:35.
8. Afternoon recess takes place from 1:45 until 2:00.
9. The highest temperature over the two-week period was 74 degrees F (23.3 degrees C).

So, when *was* the temperature at its lowest, and why?

See answer on page 243

Easy Puzzles

Coast to Coast

Jacques and Chi Chi rode bikes across the United States. They stopped at several major cities along the way. Figure out where they went and the order in which they visited the cities based on the coordinates given in the clues below. (The visited city is the one "closest" to the intersection of the coordinates.)

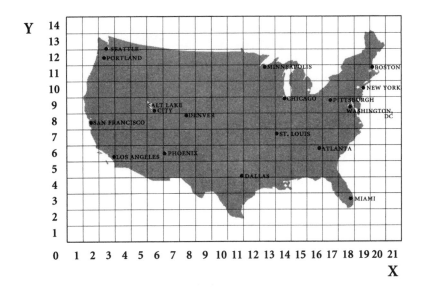

They started their journey at X6, Y5.5

Their first stop was at X3, Y5.5; then they rode on to X1.5, Y7.5.

Then they stopped off in the city at X2.5, Y11.5.

From there they rode to X5.5, Y8, and then to X7.5, Y8.

They stayed a few days at X11, Y4, and three days at X13, Y6.5.

From there they rode to X13.5, Y9, then to X16.5, Y9.

Finally, tired but happy, they ended their journey at X18, Y8.5.

Start to finish, what are the eleven American cities visited by Jacques and Chi Chi?

See answers on page 240

Coffee

A few friends meet each morning for coffee. For one of them, it is the only cup of coffee all day. For another, it's only the first of eight cups. Zowie!

Your challenge is to figure out how many cups of coffee each person drinks per day, how many sugar lumps they use per cup, and whether or not they put in milk.

1. Jan uses three times as many lumps as the person who drinks four cups.
2. Three people, including the one who uses four lumps, use no milk.
3. The one who drinks 1 cup a day (not Max) drinks his coffee black without sugar.
4. Doris uses both milk and sugar.
5. Max, who uses no milk, uses half as many sugars as the person who drinks twice as many cups as he does.
6. Boris drinks two more cups than Jan, but Jan uses two more sugars than Boris.

	Cups					Lumps of Sugar					Milk	
	1	4	5	6	8	0	1	2	4	6	Yes	No
Max												
Doris												
Blizzo												
Jan												
Boris												

See answers on page 240

Decimal Ruler

This ruler measures inches but, instead of measuring them in the usual way, in sixteenths, it measures them in *tenths.* In other words, the standard inch is divided into ten (decimal) units, rather than sixteen units.

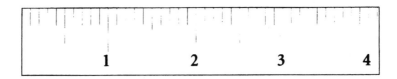

When we measure something with this decimal ruler, it is expressed as the number of inches plus the tenths. For example, the line just below measures 3.4 inches. Go ahead, check it out (mark the length on a straight piece of paper and then hold it next to the ruler).

Now, using paper and this ruler, measure these other lines:

a _____

b _____

c _____

d _____

e _____

f _____

g _____

Check your measurements in the solutions.

See answers on page 241

Destry's Missing Numbers

Destry has five boxes, shown below. Each is supposed to have a decimal number in it, but they're all empty! Help Destry find his missing numbers and put them back in their boxes.

Here are some clues to where the numbers should go:

1. One square (the sum of 11.09, 6.21, and 5.04) is to the left of a square with the difference between 13.27 and 1.34.
2. C is not 13.47 but another square is.
3. One square has a number larger than square B by 13.78.
4. The square with a sum of 13.62, 3.98, 7.00, and .57 is between B and E.
5. The smallest number is B; the largest is E.

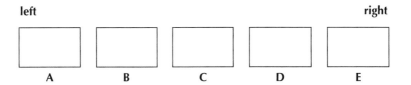

left   right

A   B   C   D   E

See answers on page 241

E.F. Bingo

Four girls—Lorraine, Michelle, Wanda, and Sheila—are in a serious game of E.F. Bingo (E.F. stands for equivalent fractions). The first one to fill in a line on her card (up-and-down, across, or diagonally) wins. To solve this puzzle, figure out which girl wins and gets to yell "Bingo!"

The fractions come up and are called in this order:

1. "Four twentieths"
2. "Eighteen twenty-seconds"
3. "Four tenths"
4. "Six tenths"
5. "Two eighths"
6. "Ten sixteenths"
7. "Twelve fourteenths"
8. "Four twenty-eighths"
9. "Six sixteenths"
10. "Six twentieths"
11. "Eight twelfths"
12. "Sixteen eighteenths"
13. "Four twelfths"

E.F. Bingo cards

$\frac{1}{4}$	$\frac{3}{8}$	$\frac{1}{8}$
$\frac{6}{7}$	$\frac{1}{3}$	$\frac{2}{10}$
$\frac{4}{5}$	$\frac{3}{5}$	$\frac{4}{10}$

Lorraine

$\frac{2}{5}$	$\frac{2}{3}$	$\frac{1}{6}$
$\frac{1}{7}$	$\frac{4}{5}$	$\frac{3}{8}$
$\frac{1}{2}$	$\frac{3}{9}$	$\frac{2}{6}$

Michelle

$\frac{5}{8}$	$\frac{2}{10}$	$\frac{2}{6}$
$\frac{6}{7}$	$\frac{8}{9}$	$\frac{3}{7}$
$\frac{1}{3}$	$\frac{1}{4}$	$\frac{9}{11}$

Wanda

$\frac{1}{2}$	$\frac{5}{8}$	$\frac{3}{10}$
$\frac{1}{4}$	$\frac{1}{3}$	$\frac{2}{12}$
$\frac{2}{6}$	$\frac{4}{10}$	$\frac{2}{3}$

Sheila

See answer on page 241

Famous Person

There's a famous person's name spelled out in the twelve boxes below. Using the coding provided, figure out the letters of the name and solve this puzzle.

A=1	G=7	N=14	U=21
B=2	H=8	O=15	V=22
C=3	I=9	P=16	W=23
D=4	J=10	Q=17	X=24
E=5	K=11	R=18	Y=25
F=6	L=12	S=19	Z=26
	M=13	T=20	

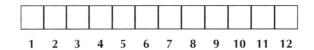

1 2 3 4 5 6 7 8 9 10 11 12

Clues:
   Boxes 7 and 10 are U – P
   Box 2 is C x E
   Boxes 4, 8, and 9 are the same letter: F + J – B
   Box 6 is Z – Y + J
   Box 12 is E^2
   Box 1 is O – E
   Box 5 is X ÷ D
   Box 11 is G x C – Q
   Box 3 is T + E + D

See answer on page 241

Flighty Decimals

Normally trustworthy and reliable, the decimals below got a little out of hand. They escaped from their geometric shapes and were scattered all over the place! Now the decimals are all lined up in two rows (below) in order from largest to smallest, but they really need to be put back into their proper geometric places. Your job is to do just that.

| 5.20 | 4.39 | 4.01 | 3.71 | 2.60 | 1.42 |

| 1.16 | 1.01 | .72 | .30 | .07 | .03 |

Here are clues to where the decimals are to go (four decimals in each shape) in the geometric spaces below:

1. 4.39 and 4.01 are supposed to be in the same figure; 5.20 (the ringleader) is supposed to be in a different one.
2. Decimals 3.71 and 1.01 are together in the rectangle.
3. The total in the circle, where .07 is supposed to be, is 6.46.
4. The smallest total comes from the rectangle, where .30 is supposed to be.
5. The difference between the totals of the square and the circle is 5.96.
6. Decimal 1.16 is supposed to be in the circle.

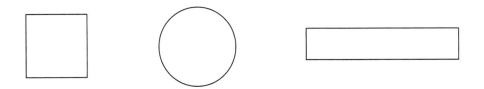

Add the decimals assigned to each shape and check your totals against the solution.

See answers on page 241

Heather's Garden

Heather's Garden is out of control! She planted it just so, and then went to surfing at a beach. When she got back from her trip, she found the turnips mixing with the cabbages, the pole beans mixing with the carrots, and the rows jumbled all over the place. Plus, field mice have gotten in and some of the garden is missing!

Heather had made a map so she would remember how much she planted where, but the mice got that too! See if you can reconstruct the garden's contents for her.

1. The most rows are neither spinach nor cabbages.
2. There are two more rows of carrots than turnips and two more rows of spinach than carrots.
3. There are four more rows of spinach than turnips.
4. There aren't as many rows of pole beans as "cukes" (cucumbers in garden talk).
5. There is one less cabbage row than spinach.
6. Heather doesn't like turnips so much, so she planted just one row (mostly to sacrifice to the mice, but they don't care all that much for turnips, either!).

Rows

	1	2	3	4	5	6
pole beans						
cabbages						
carrots						
cucumbers						
spinach						
turnips						

See answers on page 241

Mathathon

Several girls were trying to work some math problems. Several boys said they could help them find the solutions. The girls said, "Fat chance!". So there was a contest between the girls and the boys to see who was best at solving the problems. Check it out and see who won.

Each problem is worth 10 points if the answer is correct; −5 points if it is wrong.

Problem **1**   9 x .3 =
  The girls said 2.7, the boys said 2.7.
Problem **2**   1.06 + .089 + 11.2 + 6.34 =
  The girls said 18.689, the boys said 18.768.
Problem **3**   ½ + ¾ =
  The girls said 1¼, the boys said 1.25.
Problem **4**   13.88 − 6.96 =
  The girls said 6.92, the boys said 7.92.
Problem **5**   4.003 x 99 =
  The girls said 396.297, the boys said 386.297.
Problem **6**   2⅓ x ½ =
  The girls said 1.166, the boys said .765.
Problem **7**   .33 ÷ 3 =
  The girls said .11, the boys said 1.1.
Problem **8**   6.66 + 3.75 + 9.07 =
  The girls said 19.48, the boys said 19.38.

So, who was best at doing math — or at least at working these particular problems?

See answer on page 242

Mountain Climb

Dacon and his friends all went mountain climbing this summer, but not together. They climbed different mountains. Using the clues, see if you can figure out who climbed which mountain, and the heights of the mountains they climbed.

1. Dacon climbed higher than 4500 feet, but not on Goat.
2. Jake climbed higher than both Macom and the one who climbed Sleepy.
3. The mountain which is 9000 feet is not Old Baldy or Goat.
4. The shortest mountain was not climbed by Bacon.
5. Mirre is shorter than the mountain climbed by Macom, but higher than the one climbed by Drakon.
6. Sleepy is not the tallest, but taller than Goat.
7. Raleigh is taller than Goat, which is taller than the ones climbed by Drakon and Dacon.

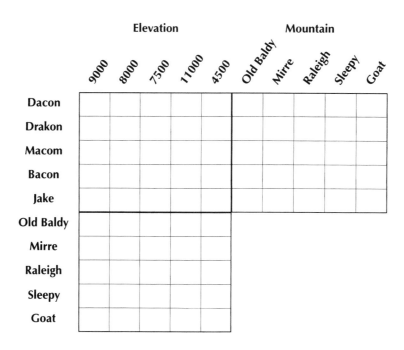

See answers on page 242

Mountain Race

Five people will race to the tops of mountains of different heights. To have a fair race, each person will carry a weight; the person climbing the lowest mountain, the heaviest backpack weight, etc.

Using the clues, figure out each person's full name, the mountain each will climb, and the weight to be carried in each backpack.

1. Paul's pack weighs 30 lbs.
2. Andy's mountain is 865 ft. higher than the one Brown is climbing.
3. Gerald's pack weighs the same as Dale's minus McGee's.
4. Stiller's pack is half as heavy as the person's climbing Mt. Morgan.
5. Jim's and Dorsey's packs combined weigh 60 lbs.
6. Anderson's pack is 20 pounds lighter than Dale's.

	Andy	Gerald	Dale	Paul	Jim	50	40	30	20	10
Anderson										
Brown										
Dorsey										
McGee										
Stiller										
Mt. Stewart (8989 ft)										
Mt. Morgan (8124 ft)										
Mt. Waring (7897 ft)										
Mt. McIntire (8876 ft)										
Mt. Picard (9125 ft)										
50					
40					
30					
20					
10					

See answers on page 242

Ned's Newspaper Route

Ned delivers papers in his neighborhood. In January he had 43 customers. He wanted to make a little more money, so he went door to door, and by April he had found five new customers. One new customer gets just a daily paper, two get just a Sunday paper, and two get both. What you need to do is figure out which of his new customers gets what, and the color of their houses (which helps Ned to keep track of things).

1. The Simpsons get both papers; their house is not white.
2. The Browns' house is neither gray nor the color of one of the houses that gets just the Sunday paper.
3. The customer's name who subscribes to just the daily paper begins with J.
4. The customer in the green house does not get a Sunday paper.
5. Mr. Johnson lives in the blue house.

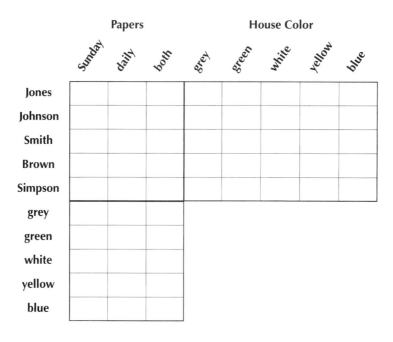

See answers on page 242

CHAPTER THREE
PENCIL PUZZLERS

BROKEN PENTAGRAM

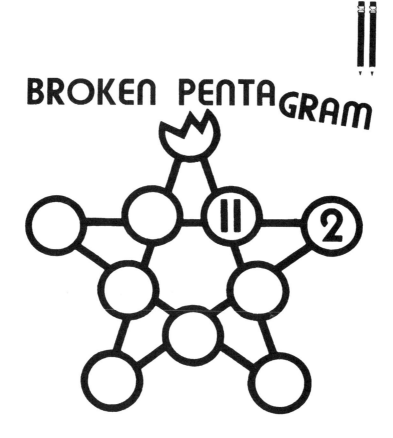

It's possible to position ten consecutive numbers on an unbroken pentagram of ten circles in such a way that each straight line of four circles totals exactly the same number. Here we issue the same challenge but with a little twist. Of ten consecutive numbers place nine in the nine unbroken circles in such a way that each straight line of three or four unbroken circles totals exactly twenty-four. Two numbers have been positioned for you.

Solution on page 244

(Need a clue? Turn to page 130.)

SQUARE SHOOTER

A standard checkerboard measures 8 squares by 8 squares and contains 32 black squares and 32 red squares. Exactly 139 other size checkerboards, ranging from 2 by 2 to 7 by 7 squares, exist on a standard checkerboard. How many of these smaller-size checkerboards can be found, that also contain an equal number of red and black squares.

Solution on page 244

THE
$10,000
PYRAMID

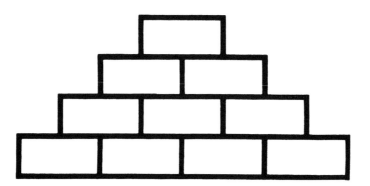

Using only the number four, place ten money amounts in the ten blocks of this pyramid to total $10,000.

Solution on page 244

Clue to the puzzle on page 128: Throw out the number five.

SITTING DUCKS

There are three different kinds of ducks in this puzzle. Position six more ducks on this two-dimensional pond so that each of the five horizontal and vertical rows will sport all three different kinds of sitting ducks.

Solution on page 244

CASE CLOSED

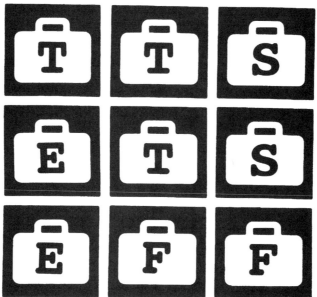

Before you are nine cases labeled with the letters "E", "F", "S" or "T". It is known that inside each case is a different number that begins with the letter seen on the outside of the case. Example: "T" could stand for two, three, ten, and so on. It is your challenge to determine all nine numbers to reveal a magic square in which each horizontal, vertical, and diagonal row of three cases totals exactly the same.

Solution on page 244

(Need a clue? Turn to page 135.)

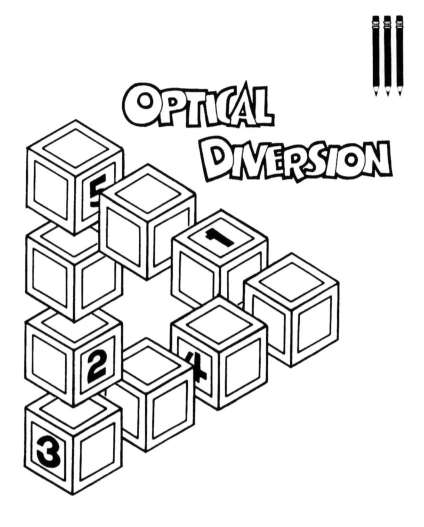

OPTICAL DIVERSION

Using the numbers one through nine three times each, number the remaining surfaces of the cubes in such a way that each cube totals exactly fifteen. In doing so, you must also assure that each row of four cube surfaces in a straight row and facing the same direction (up, left, or right) must total twenty. Example: The two cube surfaces three and four above are in a straight line, facing left. There are nine such rows to be completed.

Solution on page 244

Head 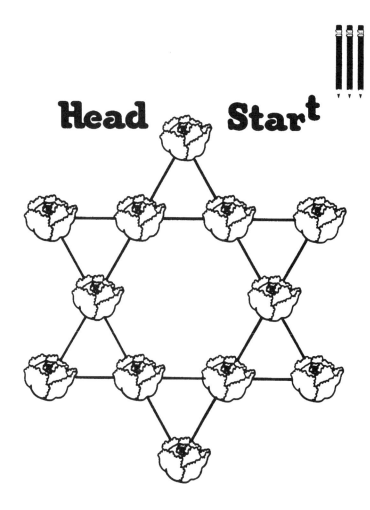 Start

These twelve heads of lettuce are planted in such a way as to create six straight rows each containing four heads of lettuce. Can you plant a garden using another configuration which fulfills these same requirements?

Solution on page 244

(Need a clue? Turn to page 136.)

FLOATING HEDGES #2

Draw a continuous line through this maze which connects the numbers one through eight consecutively. You may never travel the same passageway more than once.

Solution on page 244

Solution on page 244

Clues to the puzzle on page 132: Each row totals 36, the smallest number used is four.

135

Round Numbers #1

Position one letter in each of the five between-spoke openings on this wagon wheel. Do this in such a manner that three numbers are spelled out that total thirteen. Words may be written clockwise and counter-clockwise and, as in traditional crossword puzzles, individual letters may be shared. Example: On a larger wheel, four and five could be written: R-U-O-F-I-V-E.

Solution on page 244

Clue to the puzzle on page 134: Begin with a square four-by-four grid. Then eliminate four lettuce heads.

MAGIC WORD SQUARES

Each letter in this puzzle represents a different number from zero to nine. It is your challenge to switch these letters back to numbers in such a way that each horizontal, vertical, and diagonal row of three words totals the same number. Your total for this puzzle is 1515. It is known that "tab" is the highest scoring word and "raw" is the second highest scoring word.

Solution on page 245

(Need a clue? Turn to page 139.)

ARROWHEADINGS

In this maze, your course headings are predetermined and point values have been assigned to each passage. Starting from the bottom intersection, travel to each of the other five intersections and return to the beginning intersection with the lowest possible point score.

Solution on page 245

(Need a clue? Turn to page 141.)

Wicked Number

W I C K E D / 666

At present this puzzle really only totals 601. That's because three of the letters in "wicked" do not belong. You must eliminate the bogus letters and substitute the correct three letters to achieve the desired total.

Solution on page 245

Clue to the puzzle on page 137: DAD = 505.

EQUATOR XING

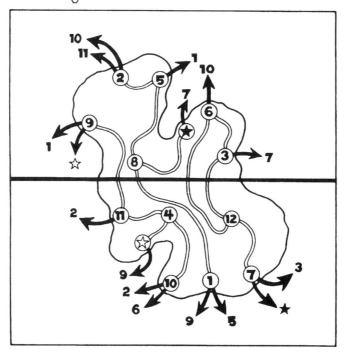

There are twelve numerical destinations (1 through 12) on this tiny tropical island. You must start your journey at one of the two stars and then travel to each number on the map and ultimately finish at the other star. At no time may any number be visited more than once. Throughout your journey you may only cross the equator a total of nine times: four by land, five by sea. Sea routes are illustrated by arrows which indicate your optional destinations.

Solution on page 245

MATCH WITS #2

At present we see an equation that incorrectly tells us that the Roman numeral nine is equal to the Roman numeral six. Can you add three additional matches to this equation to make both sides equal?

Solution on page 245

Clue to the puzzle on page 138 : Lowest score possible is forty-five points.

3 RING CIRCUIT

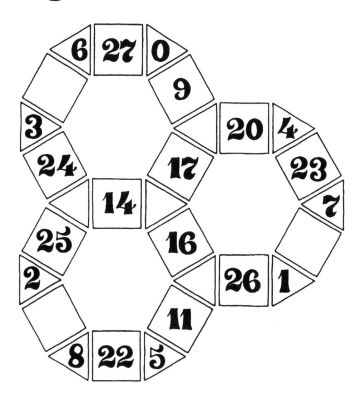

When this puzzle is completely solved, it will reveal the numbers zero through twenty-seven. All you have to do is position the remaining seven numbers to assure that each of the three rings of twelve numbers totals exactly the same number.

Solution on page 245

Key Decision #2

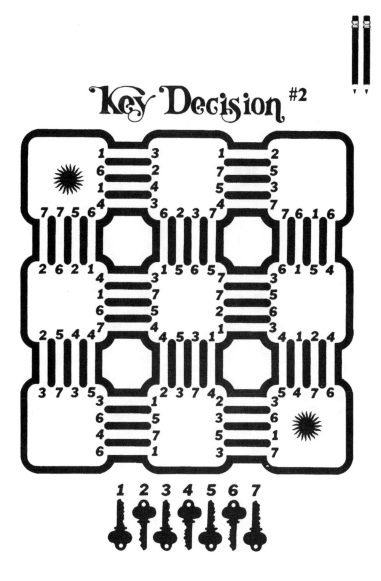

The numbered keys above correspond to the locked corridors in the puzzle. It is your challenge to select only three keys that will unlock the correct corridors and allow passage from one sunburst room to the other.

Solution on page 245

Trace Track

The numbers in this puzzle show the current position of four cars on this crisscrossing race track. As the three outer turnabout panels are currently arranged, only car 1 can cross the finish line. Rearrange three of the four turnabout panels around the center section of track to construct a single unending track that utilizes all road surfaces and will allow all cars to finish in the order 1,2,3,4. Cars may not pass one another on this final lap.

Solution on page 246

NUMERIC SHELVES

Rearrange the sixteen numbers in this puzzle to allow the two horizontal and two vertical rows of five squares to total the same number. There are twelve solvable totals. Your tasks are to construct the highest possible and lowest possible totals.

Solution on page 246

Lucky Lady

Nine pairs of dice are positioned in nine horseshoes in this puzzle. The pips are missing from all but two dice. From the illustrated sixteen dice you must add the pips to the blank dice to satisfy the following conditions: 1) Each horseshoe must total a different number. 2) Each horizontal, vertical, and diagonal row of three horseshoes must total twenty-one. 3) Doubles may not appear in any horseshoe.

Solution on page 246

Chapter 4
Grid & Dot Games

**Squiggling Snake • The Cop & the Robber
Springing Sprouts • Hare & Hounds • The Ratcatcher
Horse Race • Daisy Petals • Black & White**

All games are mathematical in that they present both a problem and a method for solving the problem. Board games like checkers or chess depend on the competing player's powers of calculation. Games that use playing cards, number wheels, or dice combine the player's skill with the laws of probabilty. Most games teach us about what mathematicians call *quantum operations*. This means that players must repeat small, uniform steps to reach a solution within a given framework of laws. So, playing a game of checkers isn't very different from solving a math puzzle.

SQUIGGLING SNAKE

In this game, players take turns joining dots by a line to make one long snake. No diagonal lines are allowed. Each player adds to the snake at either end, and a player can only add to his opponent's segment, not his own. The first player to make the snake close on itself loses the game.

Here's how an actual game might be played. To tell the two player's apart, one player draws straight lines, and the other player draws squiggly lines.

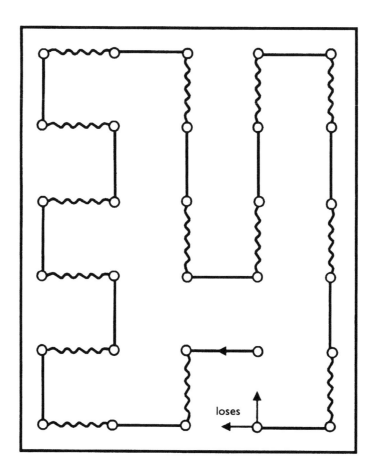

THE COP & THE ROBBER

On a piece of cardboard or construction paper, draw the game board below including the letters C (cop) and R (robber). This board represents a city grid of several blocks and streets, and the letters indicate the starting position of the cop and robber.

You need two different coins, one for the cop and one for the robber. Start with each coin on its letter. The cop always moves first. After that, robber and cop take turns moving. A player moves a coin one block only, left or right, up or down — that is, from one corner to the next. The cop captures the robber by landing on the robber in one move. To make the game a little more challenging, the cop must capture the robber in twenty moves or less, or the robber wins.

Hint: There is a way for the cop to nab the robber. The secret lies in the bottom right corner of the grid.

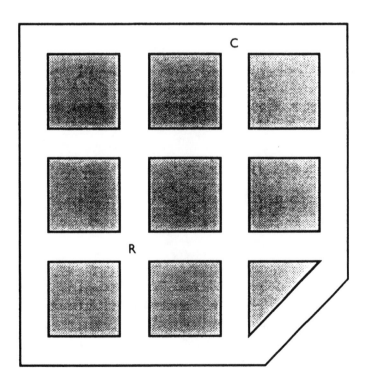

SPRINGING SPROUTS

Most mathematical games are played on grids, but some of the newer ones use *topology*, the geometry of flexible lines and surfaces, as a starting point. Springing Sprouts was invented in the 1960's by a mathematician at Cambridge University in England. Not only will you enjoy playing it, but your finished game makes an interesting piece of artwork!

The first player begins by drawing three spots (A). The second player must connect two of the spots with a line (remember, the line can be curved) and then adds a new spot somewhere along that line (B).

No lines may cross (C), but a player may connect a spot to itself in a loop — as long as he adds another spot (D).

A spot "dies" when three lines lead to it and no more lines can connect to it. To indicate a dead spot, darken it (E).

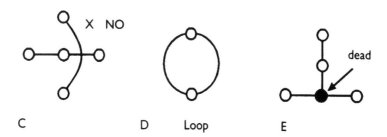

A player wins by drawing the last connecting line so that all the remaining spots are dead and the second player can no longer connect them. Here's a sample game, won by player A in seven moves.

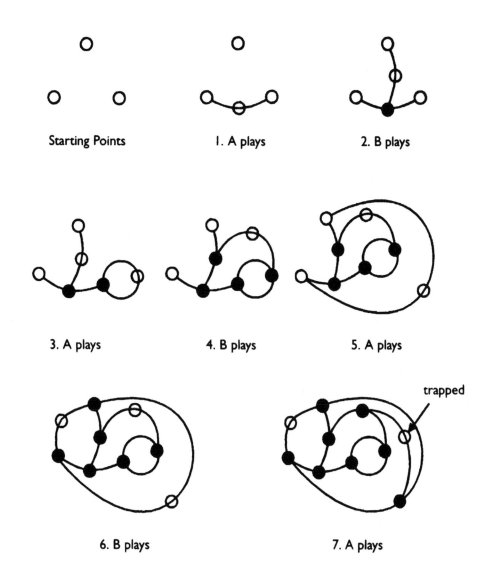

Starting Points

I. A plays

2. B plays

3. A plays

4. B plays

5. A plays

6. B plays

7. A plays

trapped

Mathematicians have tried to figure out how many moves it takes for either player to win Springing Sprouts. They've discovered, but not yet proved, that the number lies between twice and three times the number of spots you start with. Starting with three spots, for instance, the game can continue for six to nine moves. Starting with four spots, the game may last for eight to twelve moves, and so on.

HARE & HOUNDS

Many board games involve "hunting." This one was a favorite of Victorian schoolchildren. Games like this teach us about geometrical figures called trapezoids, which are four-sided figures with only two sides parallel. The corners of *trapezoids*, or *vertices*, also play an important part in this game.

Use a ruler to draw the board on a piece of paper or cardboard. At every place where the lines meet in a corner, draw a small circle. Draw a large A at the left side of the board and a large B at the right side.

Player #1 has one coin, representing the Hare, and Player #2 has three coins, representing the Hounds. The game starts with Player #1

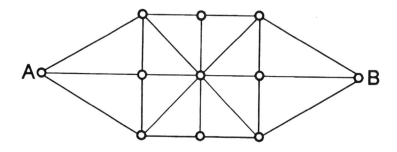

placing his Hare on circle A. Player #2 follows by placing one of his Hounds on any other circle. He will use the next two turns to place his other Hounds on circles, as the Hare moves from circle to circle, trying to escape.

The Hounds may move in any direction forward (that is, towards circle A) or up and down, but not towards circle B. The aim of the Hare is to reach the safety of circle B while the Hounds, of course, try to block his way and prevent him from moving.

THE RATCATCHER

This is another version of a strategic chase-and-capture game. One player has twelve Rats, and the other player is the Ratcatcher. The game starts with the thirteen pieces in the positions shown below, the white dot representing the Ratcatcher.

Both Ratcatcher and Rats can move in any direction onto an empty intersection of lines (*vertex*). The Ratcatcher can remove a Rat from

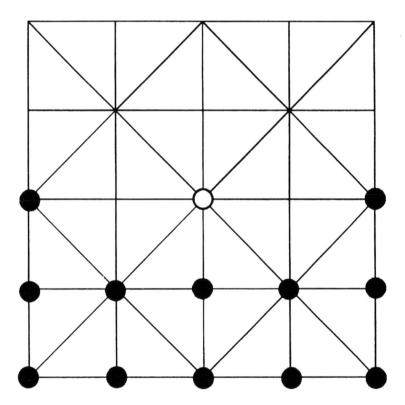

the board by jumping over him to an empty vertex on the other side. But the Rats can gang up on the Ratcatcher by surrounding him in such a way that he can neither move nor jump.

HORSE RACE

In this ancient Korean racing game, *nyout*, players throw one of a pair of dice (a die) to determine the number of moves, then race their buttons, or "horses," around the circular track illustrated below. Notice that the track has five large squares, sixteen smaller squares, and eight circles.

The players start at square A, and the first player to return to square A wins the game. When a player throws the die, he may only move up to five spaces; a throw of six must be thrown again. If a player's horse lands on one of the larger squares B, C, or D, the horse may take a shortcut through the circle to reach A.

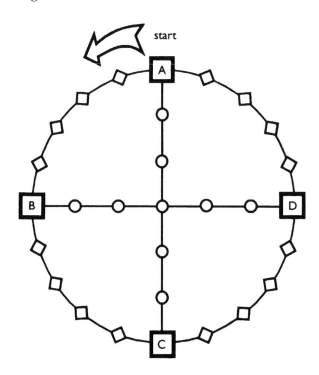

Each player may have up to three horses, but both players must have the same number of horses to ensure a fair game. A player may choose to add another horse instead of moving his original horse.

If one player's horse lands on a square already occupied by another of his own horses, both horses may move together in all the following moves. If one player's horse lands on a square occupied by his opponent's horse, the opponent's horse is removed and must reenter the race.

To win the game, a player must throw the exact number to get each of his horses back to A. It usually takes three or four times around the track before one player's horses win. And your fortunes may reverse at any time!

DAISY PETALS

On piece of paper or cardboard, construct a thirteen-petal daisy using crayons for the petals.

Two players take turns plucking either one petal apiece, or two neighboring petals apiece. The player who plucks the last petal wins the game.

Remember, a player can only take two petals if the petals are neighbors. The player who makes the second move can always win this game if he has a sharp eye and knows something about the principle of *symmetry*—that is, the balance of parts on opposite sides of a line or about a center point.

BLACK & WHITE

One player alone can enjoy this game, or two players can compete to see who can finish in the least number of moves.

Reproduce the board below with two 3-inch-square pieces of paper, joined at the corner and lined in a grid pattern. In squares on the left side of the board, place eight black pieces (buttons or pennies will do). In the squares on the right side of the board, place eight white pieces.

The object of the game is to exchange the positions of the black and white pieces in the least possible number of moves. You can move a piece by sliding it to a neighboring empty square, or by jumping over a neighboring piece of either color. This can be done in exactly 46 moves, but you can still consider yourself an expert if you finish in 52 moves or less.

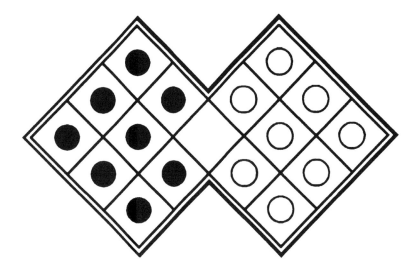

CHAPTER FIVE
MATH LOGIC PUZZLES

MEDIUM PUZZLES

Auction

The Clydesdale County Fair held its annual fund-raising auction last week. Five of the people who bought items are listed here.

Your challenge is to match the last names of the purchasers with their first names, identify which items each one bought, and figure out how much each one paid (the lowest amount that anyone paid was $3.50).

Here are a few clues:

1. Elroy is not Grey.
2. The man who bought the coffee paid the highest price, twice that of the fruit.
3. The cheese sold for $2.00 less than the coffee and was purchased by Black.
4. Ms. Green bought the pie for $2/3$ the cost of the cake.
5. White and Duane shared their cake and coffee.
6. The pie cost $0.50 more than the fruit.
7. Dan paid $6.00 for his item.
8. Neither Elroy, Denise, nor Black paid over $5.00.

Solution on page 240

Last Name | Purchase

	Green	White	Black	Brown	Grey	cake	pie	fruit	cheese	coffee
Irene										
Denise										
Duane										
Dan										
Elroy										
$										
$										
$										
$										
$										
cake					
pie					
fruit					
cheese					
coffee					

Hint: Start by working out the prices as early as possible.

Biology Class

Kristi and five of her friends have each adopted an animal in the biology class at their high school. Using the clues listed below, see if you can figure out which animal (the W's) belongs to which student (the K's).

1. Walter can fly; Willy can't.
2. Kristi's animal is 14 cm (6 in) long.
3. The ladybug is not a lady, nor the smallest.
4. Willy is 5 cm (2 in) shorter than the largest animal.
5. Kyle's animal is neither a fly nor a ladybug.
6. Walter is 10 cm (4 in) shorter than the bat, who's 3 cm (about 1 in) shorter than Wendy.
7. Wanda is the largest.
8. Kurt's animal is the smallest.
9. The hamster belongs to Kevin.
10. Willy is neither the rat nor the hamster.
11. Weldon, who is able to fly, belongs to Kristen.
12. Kate's adoption measures 18 cm (7 in).

Solution on page 240

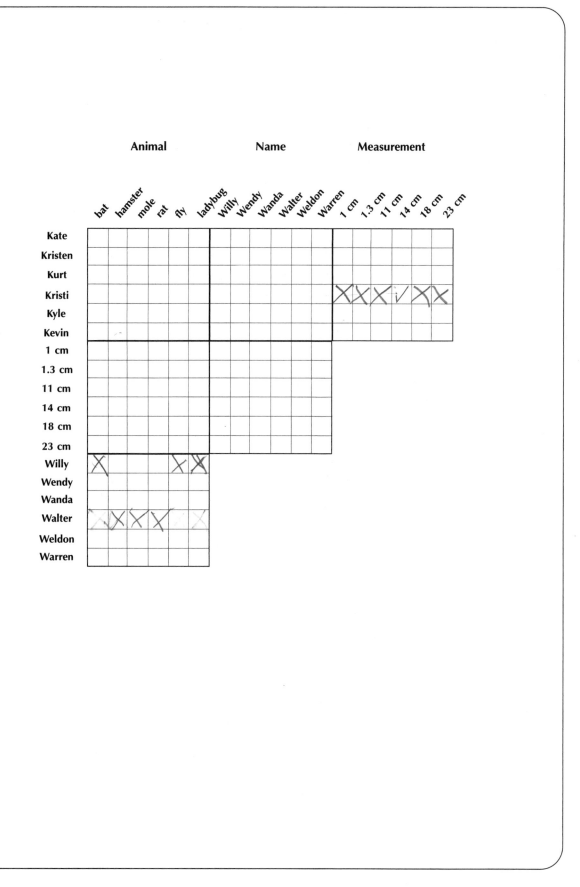

161

Chicken Mountain

At the top of Chicken Mountain live five chicken farmers. Each farmer thinks his chickens are the best. Farmer McSanders sas his chickens are best because they lay the most eggs. Farmer Saffola says his chickens make the best fryers.

See if you can figure out which farmer does have the best chickens, based on the following facts plus the formula provided to grade the chickens.

1. The chickens with the best feathers live on the McCombe farm. They sell for $0.73.
2. The chickens which sell for $0.64 produce 105 eggs per day. It's not the Poularde farm.
3. Farmer Saffola has 500 chickens.
4. The farm which produces 115 eggs per day sells its chickens for $0.71.
5. The smartest chickens live on the McPlume farm.
6. The best fryers get the most money.
7. Farmers McSanders and McPlume have 833 chickens between them.
8. The smallest farm produces the most eggs and the second-best price.
9. The biggest chickens produce 4.8 eggs per chicken on the Poularde farm.

Solution on page 240

	Amt. of Chickens (A)					Eggs per Bird (B)					Cost Price (C)				
	392	441	500	552	598	4.2	2.8	4.0	4.6	4.8	.73	.84	.94	.64	.71
Saffola															
McSanders															
McPlume															
McCombe															
Poularde															
140															
130															
125															
115															
105															
best feathers															
best fryers															
most eggs															
smartest birds															
biggest birds															

Eggs per Day (D)

Best Chickens on Chicken Mountain Grading Formula:

A ÷ B x C + D

Chocolate Chip Cookies

Five of the world's foremost chocolate chip cookie bakers arrived for the annual Cookie Fiesta. While the bakers all agreed on most of the ingredients that go into their famous chocolate chip cookies, they did not agree at all on the right number of chips per cookie or the amount of time they should be baked to come out perfect. Determine the full names of the five cookie bakers, the number of chips each puts in her cookies, and how long they leave them to bake.

Here are a few clues:

1. Ms. Strudel bakes her cookies for 17 minutes, 7 seconds.
2. Effie uses 2 chips fewer than Ruby does.
3. Ms. Applestreet bakes her cookies 51 seconds longer than Thelma does.
4. Ms. Spicer uses one less chip than Ms. Applestreet puts in her cookies.
5. Ms. Honeydew uses more chips than Ms. Spicer does.
6. Ruby isn't Ms. Honeydew.
7. Ms. Spicer bakes for less time than do either Miriam or Georgia.
8. The woman who bakes her cookies for 17 minutes, 7 seconds uses 7 chips.
9. Georgia bakes hers for 17 minutes and 8 seconds, 1 second longer than Ruby does.
10. The person using 5 chips isn't Ms. Spicer.

Solution on page 240

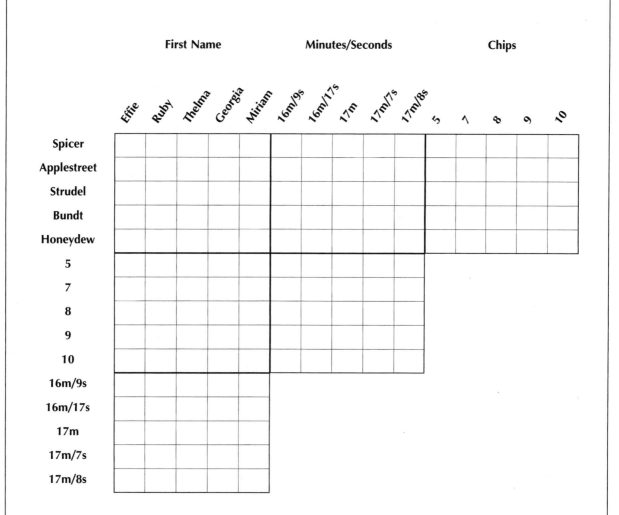

Dog Apartments

Six dogs live in the Airedale Apartments. Each dog lives on a different floor, eats a different amount of dog food (in pounds) each week, and takes a different number of baths each month. Using the clues below, figure out which floor each dog lives on, the amount of food each one eats, and the number of baths each one takes. Watch out for tricks!

1. The dog in 221 eats twice as much as the one who takes 1 bath a week.
2. MacTavish eats four pounds less than Spunky, but takes five more baths.
3. The dog that eats 32 pounds a month takes 3 baths a week.
4. Wilfred lives two floors above Spunky. Spunky lives two floors above Chico.
5. Taz and the dog on the 6th floor eat a combined weight of 80 pounds in a month.
6. The dog in 341 eats 24 pounds a month and bathes once a week.
7. The dog in 408 eats fewer pounds in a month than he takes baths.
8. The dog on the 5th floor eats 16 pounds a month and takes one less bath than Chico.

Solution on page 241

	Apartment No.						Food per Week						Baths per Month					
	103	221	341	408	512	609	2	4	6	8	10	12	2	3	4	6	9	12
MacTavish																		
Chico																			
Ivan																			
Wilfred																			
Taz																			
Spunky																			
Baths 2																			
3																			
4																			
6																			
9																			
12																			
Food 2																			
4																			
6																			
8																			
10																			
12																			

Lunch at Paul's

Paul invited some friends for lunch and asked each to bring two items. Everyone already had one item and they brought that, but they had to buy a second item at the store. Using the clues and the price list below, figure out who brought which items, and how much each person spent—including Paul, who bought the coffee.

Purchased Items	Price List
chicken	$6.40 pound
coffee	$5.50 pound
cheese	$4.80 pound
mayonnaise	$1.09 per 8-oz jar
bread	$1.39 loaf

1. Julie bought 9 ounces of one of her items, which cost her $2.70. She did not bring fruit.
2. The person who brought the salad also bought three loaves of bread.
3. Sandra bought two 8-ounce jars of mayonnaise but did not bring the fruit or the cake.
4. Paul needed pickles and salad. Wally brought one of them.
5. Diane's purchase was 12 ounces and it cost her $4.80.
6. The person who paid $2.75 for half a pound also brought the olives.

Solution on page 242

	Brought					Bought					Cost				
	pickles	salad	cake	olives	fruit	coffee	bread	cheese	mayo	chicken	$2.18	$2.75	$4.80	$2.70	$4.17
Paul															
Julie															
Sandra															
Diane															
Wally															
$2.18															
$2.75															
$4.80															
$2.70															
$4.17															
coffee															
bread															
cheese															
mayo															
chicken															

Multiplication Jeopardy

For a change, Dale and some friends studying for a multiplication test gave each other the problem answers (products) and tried to figure out the two numbers in the problem. From the clues, figure out each student's full name, the product each was given, and the correct multiplier and multiplicand. One of the products (where multiplicand and multiplier intersect) is 144.

1. Dale's multiplicand is 14.
2. Tina's last name is not Johns.
3. June's multiplier is 9.
4. Neil is neither James nor Jones.
5. Miss Jensen's product is 120.
6. The person whose multiplicand is 13 is not James, Jensen, or Mr. Johnson.
7. Tina's product is 143.
8. Neil's multiplicand is 18. His product is 126.
9. Johns's multiplier is 7.

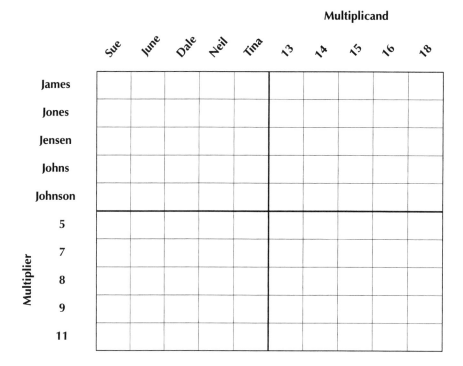

Solution on page 242

Old House

Six different families have lived a total of 88 years in an old house. The original owners lived there half the total number of years. A second family lived there a quarter of the years. The third family lived in the house half that. Then a family lived there five years. The fifth family lived there two years. And the sixth family still lives there.

Each family painted the house a different color. Right now, it is white. How long did each family live in the old house? What color did each family paint it?

1. The Smiths lived there eleven times longer than the Parkers.
2. The house was yellow for two years.
3. In all, the house was painted three different colors—blue, yellow, and white—for 11 years.
4. The color was changed from green to brown after the Carpenters moved.
5. The house was either brown or red for 33 years.
6. The Barneses lived there longer than the number of years the house was blue and white.
7. The house was yellow when the Warners moved in.

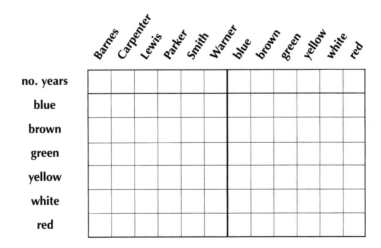

Solution on page 243

Play Ball

Toddy and some of her friends in a writing class had to bring a ball, representing their favorite sport, to class along with a composition that they had written about the sport. Toddy brought the ball weighing the least.

From the clues below, figure out who brought which ball, how much each ball weighed (in ounces), and what color it was.

1. The golf ball weighed less than the ball that Tanya brought, and also less than the brown ball.
2. Tom's ball weighed more than the red one.
3. The soccer ball, which was 14.5 ounces heavier than Teresa's ball, was not orange.
4. The person who brought the orange ball was not Teddie, whose ball weighed 15.2 ounces more than the Ping-Pong ball.
5. The ball that weighed more than all of them except for one was white.
6. The heaviest ball was the basketball, and the lightest one was yellow.
7. The 2-ounce ball was green, and smaller than the red one and the ball brought by Teddie.
8. The ball brought by Tillie was ten times heavier than the golf ball.

Solution on page 243

	orange	white	green	red	brown	yellow	1.5	.8	15	22	2	16
Teddie												
Teresa												
Toddy												
Tanya												
Tom												
Tillie												
Ping-Pong												
tennis												
golf												
soccer												
basketball												
football												
1.5												
.8												
15												
22												
2												
16												

Potato Chips

Everyone in Mr. Glitzwhizzle's classroom agreed that no one could eat just one potato chip, but decided to have a contest to see who could eat the most in three minutes. Five students, and Mr. Glitzwhizzle himself, entered the race. From the clues below, figure out the last names of the students and Mr. Glitzwhizzle's first name, and how many bags of chips (the small size) each one ate.

1. Witteyspooner and Gazelda together didn't eat as many bags as Elmo or Jones did.
2. Hubert ate twice as many bags as Grugenminer.
3. Sally's last name does not start with G.
4. Kettledrummel ate one-fourth as many bags as Hubert did.
5. Mr. Glitzwhizzle ate 18 bags. Gerald could eat only half that many.
6. Hubert ate as many bags as Elmo and Gazelda combined.

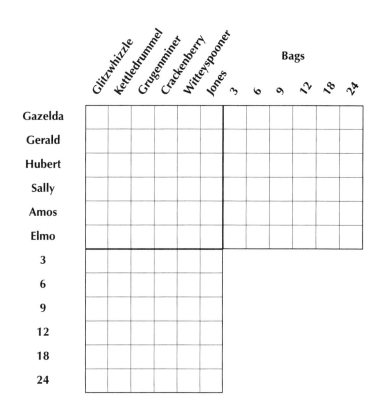

Solution on page 243

Queen Rachel's Bridge Toll

When the new Queen Rachel Bridge was built across the Queen Rachel River, Queen Rachel decided to charge a toll. Each person who crosses the bridge is charged .05 of the value of their shoes! So, if a person's shoes are worth $1.00, that person has to pay 5¢ in toll. With the information below, figure out how much each person has to pay to cross the Queen's bridge, and the color of their shoes.

1. Kurt's shoes are not green, nor is green the color of the shoes worth $3.60.
2. The person with the blue shoes must pay 36¢ toll.
3. Taber pays a higher toll then Cindy. Neither of them wears black shoes.
4. The person whose shoes are worth $3.60 is not Caleb.
5. One person, whose shoes are not green or red, pays an 18¢ toll.
6. The person with the red shoes pays 14¢ toll.
7. Caleb pays 24¢.
8. The person with the white shoes pays 38¢ toll.
9. Cindy's shoes are blue.

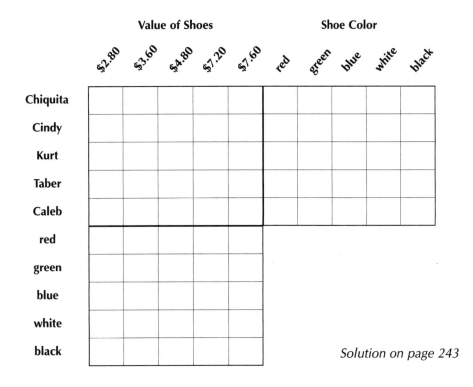

Solution on page 243

Skateboard Contest

Five kids in the finals of the Fossil Street skateboard contest ride their boards from home to the site for the event. From the clues provided, figure out the kids' full names, the number of blocks each has to ride to the contest, and the street on which they live.

1. Chestnut Avenue is 4 blocks farther away than where Roger lives.
2. Ms. Mander lives on Main Street, 8 blocks away from Lenny.
3. Cooper lives 3 blocks from Linden and 7 blocks from Kenny.
4. Chapman lives six blocks farther away than 11th Street.
5. Kenny, whose last name starts with "L", lives closer than Sally.
6. Jimmy lives on Elm Street.

Blocks from Fossil St.

	Jimmy	Sally	Lenny	Roger	Kenny	1	3	7	8	11
Linden										
Lyle										
Mander										
Cooper										
Chapman										
Elm St.										
Main St.										
Chestnut Ave.										
Acorn Dr.										
11th St.										
1										
3										
7										
8										
11										

Solution on page 243

CHAPTER 6
MIND-BENDING
MATH PUZZLES

Sox Unseen

Sam's favorite colors are blue and green, so it's not surprising that he has six blue sox and six green sox in his sock drawer. Unfortunately, they are hopelessly mixed up and one day, in complete darkness, he has to grab some sox to wear.

How many sox does he have to take from the drawer to make sure he gets a matching pair—either green or blue? (For some strange reason, his mother insists that his socks have to match!)

Solution on page 246

Add numbers to make squares:

1 =	1 = 1 x 1
1 + **2** + 1 =	4 = 2 x 2
1 + 2 + **3** + 2 + 1 =	9 = 3 x 3
1 + 2 + 3 + **4** + 3 + 2 + 1 =	16 = 4 x 4
1 + 2 + 3 + 4 + **5** + 4 + 3 + 2 + 1 =	25 = 5 x 5
1 + 2 + 3 + 4 + 5 + **6** + 5 + 4 + 3 + 2 + 1 =	36 = 6 x 6
1 + 2 + 3 + 4 + 5 + 6 + **7** + 6 + 5 + 4 + 3 + 2 + 1 =	49 = 7 x 7

Gloves Galore!

Gloria's favorite colors are pink and yellow. She has sox in those colors, of course, but she *really* likes gloves!

In her glove drawer, there are six pairs of pink gloves and six pairs of yellow gloves, but like Sam's sox, the gloves are all mixed up. In complete darkness, how many gloves does Gloria have to take from the drawer in order to be sure she gets one pair? She doesn't mind whether it's a pink or yellow pair.

(Hint: This may sound a bit like Sox Unseen, *but watch out! Gloves are more complicated than sox.)*

Solution on page 246

Birthday Hugs

"O frabjous day! Calloo Callay!"*

It's Jenny's birthday!

Jenny invites her three best friends Janey, Jeannie, and Joany to come to a party at her house, and when they all arrive they all give each other hugs.

How many hugs is that altogether?

*A special "gold star" if you can name the work and author of this famous line.

Solution on page 246

The last joint of your thumb is probably close to an inch long, measuring from nail to knuckle. The spread from the tip of your thumb to the tip of your forefinger is probably five or six inches. Measure them with a ruler–then you can use these "units" to measure the lengths of all sorts of things.

Sticky Shakes

For John's birthday celebration, he invites six friends—Jack, Jake, Jim, Joe, Julian, and Justin—to a favorite burger place where they order thick and sticky milk shakes: banana, chocolate, maple, peanut butter, pineapple, strawberry, and vanilla.

While they slurp the shakes, their hands get sticky. Laughing about "shake" hands, they decide to actually do it—shake hands with their shake-sticky hands. So each boy shakes hands once with everyone else. How many handshakes is that altogether?

Solution on page 246

The Wolf, the Goat, and the Cabbage

You are traveling through difficult country, taking with you a wolf, a goat, and a cabbage. All during the trip the wolf wants to eat the goat, and the goat wants to eat the cabbage, and you have to be careful to prevent either calamity.

You come to a river and find a boat which can take you across, but it's so small that you can take only one passenger at a time—either the wolf, or the goat, or the cabbage.

You must never leave the wolf alone with the goat, nor the goat alone with the cabbage.

So how can you get them all across the river?

Solution on page 246

Floating Family

Mom and Dad and two kids have to cross a river, and they find a boat, but it is so small it can carry only one adult or two kids. Luckily both the kids are good rowers, but how can the whole family get across the river?

Solution on page 247

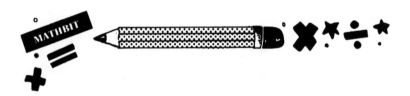

Did you know that most drinking glasses and cups have a circumference greater than their height? Test it out on some you have at home.

Take a piece of string and wrap it carefully once around a glass. You will almost always find the string is longer than the height of the glass. When is this not true?

Now you can amaze your friends by predicting this fun mathematical fact with one of their glasses before you measure it!

Slippery Slopes

Brenda the Brave sets off to climb a mountain which is 12,000 feet high. She plans to climb 3000 feet each day, before taking overnight rests. A mischievous mountain spirit, however, decides to test Brenda's resolve. Each night, Brenda's sleeping bag, with her soundly asleep in it, is magically moved 2000 feet *back down* the mountain, so that when Brenda awakes in the morning she finds herself only 1000 feet higher than she was the morning before!

Not one to give up, Brenda eventually succeeds. But how many days does it take her to reach the summit?

Solution on page 247

The Long and the Short of the Grass

Mr. Greengrass wants his lawn to be tidy and likes the grass cut short. Because he doesn't like mowing but wants to be able sit outside and read the paper on Sunday mornings and be proud of the smooth lawn, he decides to hire some good young mowers.

Two kids agree to mow Mr. Greengrass's grass on Saturdays for 15 weeks. To make sure they come every single Saturday, he agrees to pay them, at the end of the 15 weeks, $2 for every week that they mow it—as long as they will give him $3 for every week they miss.

At the end of the 15 weeks, they owe him exactly as much as he owes them, which is good news for Mr. Greengrass, but a rotten deal for the kids! How many weeks did they miss?

Solution on page 247

When drawing a graph, some people can never remember which is the x-axis and which is the y-axis. Here's a neat way to remember: say to yourself, "x is *a cross.*"

Sugar Cubes

The Big Sugar Corporation wants to persuade people to use lumps of sugar, or sugar cubes; so they run a puzzle competition. The first person to get the answers right (the puzzle is made up of three parts) wins free sugar for life! Here's the puzzle:

You have been sent a *million cubes* of sugar. Yes, that's right, 1,000,000 sugar cubes! Each cube is just half an inch long, half an inch wide, and half an inch high.

1. Suppose the cubes arrived all wrapped up and packed together into one giant cube. Where could you put it? Under a table? In the garage? Or would you need a warehouse? (*Hint: What you need to work out is: How many little cubes would there be in each direction? And how long, wide and high would the giant cube be?*)

2.Now, suppose you decide to lay the cubes all out in a square on the ground—all packed together but this time only one layer deep? How big a space would you need? Your living room floor? A tennis court? Or would you need a parking lot the size of a city block?

3.Now for the big one. Pile all the million cubes one on top of the other into a tower just one cube thick. (You'll need *very* steady hands and not a breath of wind!) How high will the pile be? As high as a house (say 25 feet)? As high as New York's Empire State Building (1472 feet)? As high as Mount Adams (12,000 feet) in Washington State or Mount Everest (29,000 feet)? Or will the pile of cubes reach the moon (240,000 miles)?

Solutions on page 247

Crackers!

Mad Marty, crazy as crackers, invites his friends to a cracker puzzle party. The puzzle he sets them is this: How many different kinds of spread can you put on a cracker?

Everyone brings a different kind of spread and Marty supplies a gigantic box of crackers. Then they all get down to business:

Marty has a cracker with mayo =   1 spread

Pete brings peanut butter; so now
they have: (**1**) mayo, (**2**) peanut
butter, (**3**) mayo and peanut
butter =   3 spreads

Jake brings jelly; so now they have
   (**1**) mayo, (**2**) peanut butter,
   (**3**) mayo and peanut butter,
   (**4**) jelly, (**5**) jelly and mayo,
   (**6**) jelly and peanut butter,
   (**7**) jelly and mayo and
   peanut butter =   7 spreads

Hank brings honey =   how many
                                                  spreads?

Charlie brings cheese =   how many
                                                  spreads?

Fred brings fish-paste =   how many
                                                  spreads?

Solution on page 247

Crate Expectations

You have six bottles of pop for a party, and you want to arrange them in an attractive pattern in the crate. Four will make a square . . .

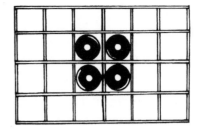

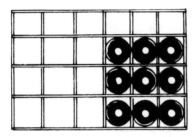

and nine will make a square. But six is a trickier number. How about an even number of bottles in each line?

Can you arrange them so that, in every row and in every column, the number of bottles is even (0, 2, 4, or 6)?

(Hint: This is quite tricky, and a fine puzzle to challenge your friends with. A good way to practice is to draw a grid on a piece of paper and use coins instead of bottles.)

Solution on page 247

Take It Away!

This is a game for two players. You will need someone to play against. It's a simple game, but the winning plan is really cunning. See if you can work it out just by playing the game.

You need about 12 or 15 small things—marbles, cookies, hard candies, pencils. It doesn't matter what they are, as long as they are all roughly the same size. Put them in a pile between the two players.

The first player takes either 1 or 2 things; then the second player takes 1 or 2 things, and they continue playing in this way. The winner is the player who takes the *last* thing.

For example, in a game starting with 14 pencils:

Player A takes 2	leaving 12
Player B takes 2	leaving 10
Player A takes 2	leaving 8
Player B takes 1	leaving 7
Player A takes 1	leaving 6
Player B takes 2	leaving 4
Player A takes 1	leaving 3
Player B takes 1	leaving 2
Player A takes 2 and wins	

OK, try it with a friend.

Solution on page 247

Oddwins

Here is another game for two players. You need 11 small objects—cookies, pebbles, paper clips.

Put the pile of objects between the players, and play alternately. First Player A takes either 1 or 2 objects. Then Player B takes 1 or 2 objects. Continue until all the objects have been taken.

The winner is the player who, at the end of the game, has an ODD number of objects—either 5 or 7.

Solution on page 247

Most people have a "wingspan" almost exactly equal to their height. So if you are 4 feet 10 inches high, then you will probably find that you measure 4 feet 10 inches from fingertip to fingertip with your arms stretched right out as far as they will go. Get a friend to help you measure your wingspan and check. Then you can use your wingspan as a measuring tool.

Witches' Brew

Three witches were mixing up a dreadful mathematical spell in their cauldron, and one of them—Fat Freddy—was reading out the recipe to the others.

Eye of newt and toe of frog
Wool of bat and tongue of dog

Suddenly they realized they needed some liquid—2 pints of armpit sweat. They had a bucketful of sweat, a saucepan that when full held exactly 3 pints, and a jug that when full held exactly 1 pint. How could they get exactly 2 pints?

(Hint: Try filling the pan, and then filling the jug from it.)

Solution on page 247

Witches' Stew

Many years later the same witches, now even older and more haggard, were mixing up a super-disgusting stew in their cauldron:

Adder's fork and blind worm's sting
Lizard's leg and howlet's wing...

And once again they needed to add the sweat, mixed this time with tears. They had a bucketful of liquid, and they needed to add exactly 4 pints, but all they had to measure it was a pitcher that held exactly 5 pints and a pot that held exactly 3.

How could they measure out exactly 4 pints?

Solution on page 247

Cookie Jars

Joe and Ken each held a cookie jar and had a look inside them to see how many cookies were left.

Joe said, "If you gave me one of yours, we'd both have the same number of cookies."

Ken said to Joe, "Yes, but you've eaten all yours, and you haven't any left!"

How many cookies does Ken have?

Solution on page 247

Fleabags

Two shaggy old dogs were walking down the street.

Captain sits down and scratches his ear, then turns to Champ and growls, "If one of yours fleas jumped onto me, we'd have the same number."

Champ barks back, "But if one of yours jumped onto me, I'd have five times as many as you!"

How many fleas are there on Champ?

Solution on page 248

Frisky Frogs

Across a stream runs a row of seven stepping stones.

On one side of the stream, sitting on the first three stones, are three girl frogs, Fergie, Francine, and Freda, and they want to get across to the other side.

There's an empty stone in the middle.

On the other side are three boy frogs, waiting to come across the other way—Fred, Frank, and Frambo.

Only one frog moves at a time. Any frog may hop to the next stone if it is empty, or may hop over one frog of the opposite sex on to an empty stone.

Can you get all the frogs across the river?

Solution on page 248

Leaping Lizards

Across a stream runs a row of eight stepping stones.

On one side of the stream, on the first five stones, sit five girl lizards—Liza, Lizzie, Lottie, Lola, and Liz—and they want to get across to the other side.

There's one empty stone in the middle.

On the other side are three boy lizards, waiting to come across the other way—Lonnie, Leo, and Len.

Only one lizard moves at a time. Any lizard may hop to the next stone if it is empty, or may hop over one lizard of the opposite sex onto an empty stone.

Can you get all the lizards across the river, and what's the smallest number of leaps?

Solution on page 248

Many spiders weave beautiful roundish webs, with a single strand spiraling out from the center. These amazing creatures keep the distances and turns so exact. Watch for webs on damp and frosty mornings and count the radial lines used in its construction.

Old MacDonald

Old MacDonald had a farm, EE-I-EE-I-OH!
And on that farm he had some pigs, EE-I-EE-I-OH!
With an *Oink oink!* here, and an *Oink oink!* there.
Here an *Oink!* There an *Oink!*
Everywhere an *Oink oink!*
Old MacDonald had a farm, EE-I-EE-I-OH!

Old MacDonald had some turkeys, too (certainly with a *Gobble gobble* here and a *Gobble gobble* there).

One day, while out feeding them all, he noticed that, if he added everything together, his pigs and his turkeys had a total of 24 legs and 12 wings between them.

How many pigs did Old MacDonald have? And how many turkeys?

Solution on page 248

Old Mrs. MacDonald

Mrs. MacDonald was a farmer too. She kept the cows and chickens. One day when she went out to feed them she counted everything up, and found that her animals had a total of 12 heads and 34 legs.

How many cows did she have? How many chickens?

Solution on page 249

Wiener Triangles

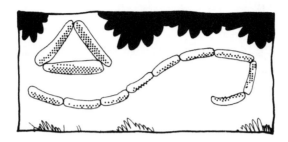

In the link-wiener factory in Sausageville , the wieners are made in long strings, with a link of skin holding each sausage to the next one. So, although the wieners are firm, you can bend the string of wieners around into many shapes. For example, you can easily bend a string of three wieners into a triangle.

Suppose you had a string of 9 wieners. Without breaking the string, how many triangles can you make?

Solution on page 248

If you use a combination lock, you can easily work out how long it will take a thief to try all the numbers and open it. If it has four dials with 10 digits on each, then there are a total of 10,000 different combinations. If the thief takes one second to try each, it will take nearly three hours to go through every number, since in three hours there are 3 x 60 x 60 seconds, or 10,800 seconds. On average, though, a thief will reach your secret number in half that time—say an hour and a half.

Tennis Tournament

You successfully arranged a "knock-out" tennis tournament, in which the winners of the first round meet in the second round, and so on. The little tournament had only four players, so arranging it was easy.

In the first round, Eenie played Meanie, and Eenie won. Miney played Mo, and Mo went through to the second round. In the second round—the final—Mo beat Eenie, and won the tournament.

The 3-game match card looked like this:

The match was so well organized, you've been asked to arrange another knock-out tennis tournament. This time 27 players enter. How many matches will have to be played to find the winner?

Solution on page 249

The Power of Seven

Far back in history, a lonely fort was being desperately defended against thousands of attackers.

The attacks came regularly at noon every day, and the defending commander knew he had to survive only three more days, for then would come the end of the attackers' calendar, and they would all go home to celebrate, giving time for his reinforcements to arrive.

He also knew that the attackers held an unshakable belief in the power of the number seven. So he always placed seven defenders on each wall of the fort. With three attacks to come, and only 24 defenders, he places 5 along each wall, and 1 in each corner tower.

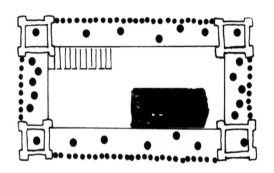

The attackers charge in from the north, and see seven defenders along that wall. Firing a volley of arrows, they wheel round in retreat, chanting "Neves! Neves!" meaning seven in their language. They charge from the west and again see seven defenders facing them. Firing a volley of arrows they retreat again. "Neves! Neves!"

From the south and then the east, again they charge. Each time they are met by exactly seven defenders. Each time they turn and flee, chanting "Neves! Neves!" And the attack is over for the day.

The commander mops his worried brow as the bugler blows the bugle to signal "Well done and all clear!" Then he learns the arrows have killed four of his men.

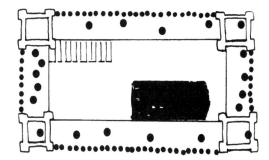

How can he rearrange the remaining 20 so that by noon of the next day there will still be 7 defenders on each side?

The Power of Seven continues

At noon on the second day the pattern of attack is different; the attackers come from the west, from the south, from the north, and then from the east. Each time they see seven defenders, fire a volley of arrows, and retreat, chanting "Neves! Neves!"

The attack is over, but five more men have been killed. Is it still possible for the commander to place seven defenders along each wall, now that he has only 15 altogether?

In other words, can they survive that third, final day of attack?

Solutions on page 248

CHAPTER SEVEN
SUM OF THE PARTS

Mathematicians have two ways of solving puzzles: piecing together small bits of information to understand larger problems and breaking down complicated ideas into simpler parts. For example, *geometry* helps them understand how to combine certain shapes to make larger shapes or how to reduce certain shapes into smaller shapes. *Fractions* help them understand the functions of whole numbers. In each case, breaking something down in order to put it back together again can lead to a valuable understanding of basic mathematical principles.

Stamp Stumper

Start with a sheet of 24 stamps. Following the diagram below, tear out two sets of three stamps, making sure the stamps of each set remain joined. Tear out a third set, then a fourth set. How many sets, total, can you tear from the sheet?

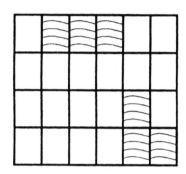

Broken Dishes

If you could put all the broken pieces back together in this drawing, how many dishes would you have?

Solutions on page 249

Cut the Pizza

A group of eight people walked into a restaurant and ordered a large pizza. The place was very busy, so when the pizza arrived, the waiter wanted to cut it up into eight even pieces as quickly as possible. He did this with only three straight cuts of his knife. Can you figure out how the waiter cut the pizza?

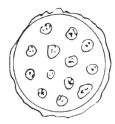

Solution on page 249

Fractured Fractions

In this puzzle, you must find two-thirds of three-fourths of five numbers.

Find 2/3 of 3/4 of 12.
Find 2/3 of 3/4 of 20.
Find 2/3 of 3/4 of 32.
Find 2/3 of 3/4 of 44.
Find 2/3 of 3/4 of 52.

Can you discover the trick to doing this quickly?

Divide the Time

By drawing only two lines, divide the clockface below so that the numbers in each section add up to the same sum.

Solutions on page 250

Parcels of Land

A landowner died and left a large, square piece of land to his wife and four sons. His wife received one fourth of the land (section A), and his sons had to parcel out the remaining three-fourths of land equally. Draw a picture showing how the landowner's sons divided the land. Remember, each of the four sections must be the same size and shape.

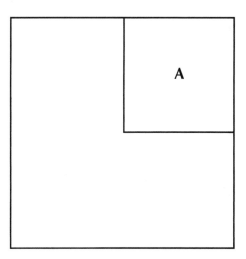

Four Lines in a Square

With a pencil and ruler, draw a square. Then draw four straight lines so that each line connects opposite sides of the square. Arrange your four lines so that you divide the square into as many sections as you can. Can you figure out the maximum number of sections you can make with only four lines?

Count the Blocks

Count the number of blocks in each arrangement. Assume that visible blocks rest on identically shaped hidden blocks, and that every arrangement is solid.

Solutions on page 250

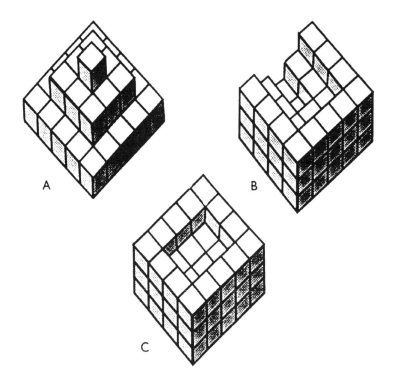

Sides, Edges & Corners

In the arrangement below, figure out how many blocks each numbered block touches. Blocks touch if any one of their sides, edges, or corners come in contact.

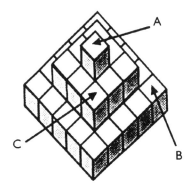

Solutions on page 250

Crayon Constructions

With 24 crayons, construct a large square. How many crayons does each side of the square contain?

Construct two squares of the same size. How many crayons are there to each side?

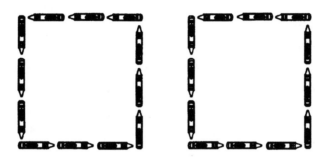

Now construct three squares of the same size. How many crayons are there to each side?

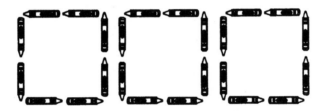

With one crayon to each side, you can make six identical small squares as shown.

1. How do you determine how many squares of the same size you can construct with 24 crayons?
2. Now construct squares of different sizes, using 24 crayons.
A. With three crayons to a side, how many smaller squares do you get?
B. Construct squares with two crayons, maximum, to a side to make seven squares of two different sizes.
C. Construct seven *identical* squares with one crayon to a side.
D. Also, with one crayon to a side, construct eight and nine identical squares. How many larger squares does each design contain?

Clue: Squares can overlap and there'll be some bigger squares containing smaller ones.

Box the Dots

Divide the hexagon below so that each dot is in its own rectangular "box." All the boxes must be the same size, and there should not be any spaces between the boxes.

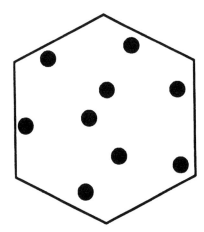

Hint: Think of the hexagon as a three-dimensional object.

Solutions on pages 250, 251

Logic Puzzles

At the root of all mathematical problem-solving is logical thinking. In fact, learning to think logically will help you solve nearly every kind of problem, mathematical or otherwise. Logical thinking begins with careful observation of the evidence, looking for consistent and inconsistent details, and then making a series of deductions that suggest a solution.

Tree-Chopping Contest

There was a race between six tree choppers to see who could chop down a tree first. Study the drawing below. Can you tell which chopper won first place in the contest? Which choppers won second, third, fourth, and fifth places? And finally, who came in last?

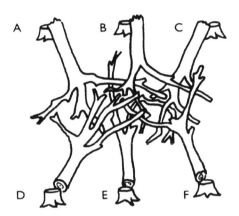

Filled Glasses

Of the six glasses below, three are filled with cranberry juice. By moving only one glass in the top row, make the top row resemble the bottom row.

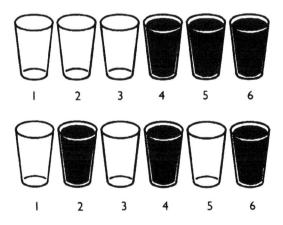

Solutions on page 252

Rare-Coin Thief

A shoplifter in a rare coin shop stole the oldest coin he could find, dated 260 B.C. If a rare coin is worth $30 for each year before Christ that it was minted, how much could the shoplifter get for his coin?

Fast Fishin'

If five fishermen catch five fish in five minutes, how long will it take fifty fishermen to catch fifty fish?

Solutions on page 252

Apricot Jam

After picking some apricots from your tree, you decide to make some delicious apricot jam. You cut up 10 pounds (4.5 kg) of apricots, blend them together, and place them on the stove. But suddenly you remember that you were supposed to add 1 teaspoon of lemon juice for every dozen apricots. Since you can no longer count the number of apricots in your mixture, how will you know how much lemon to add?

The Lumberjack's Brother

A lumberjack's brother died and left a million dollars to his only brother. However, the lumberjack never received any of the money even though it was legally paid out. How could this happen?

Chasing Shadows

Logical problem-solving always means a careful observation of the evidence. Look at the illustration of a tall tree seen from above and the shadow it casts at various times of day. Study the shadows carefully and identify four mistakes in the picture.

Solutions on page 252

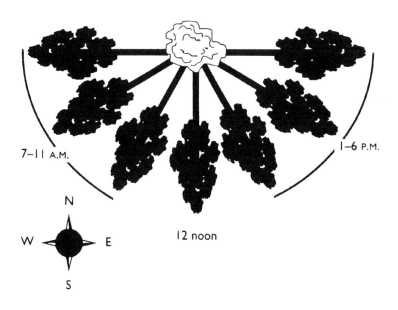

214

CHAPTER EIGHT
PENCIL-SHARPENING
MATH PUZZLES

IN TENTS

11	16	1	5
4	7	10	13
12	2	15	8
14	9	6	3

It is known that four officers are strategically located in four different tents that total thirty-two. Orders state that each horizontal, vertical, and diagonal row of four tents must quarter one officer. Which tents do the officers occupy?

Solution on page 252

THE THIRD DEGREE

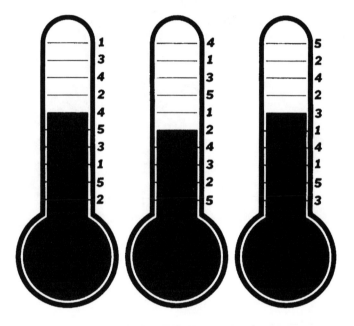

Your challenge is to balance the thermometers in this puzzle in such a way that they all read an identical number. For each unit rise in any thermometer, one of the other thermometers must fill one unit, and vice versa.

Solution on page 252

MAD HATTER'S CAP SIZE

Here is a puzzle in which your challenge is to eliminate fractions. Add two or more of the cap sizes together to produce a whole number.

Solution on page 253

(Need a clue? Turn to page 221.)

TRUE TO ONE'S COLORS

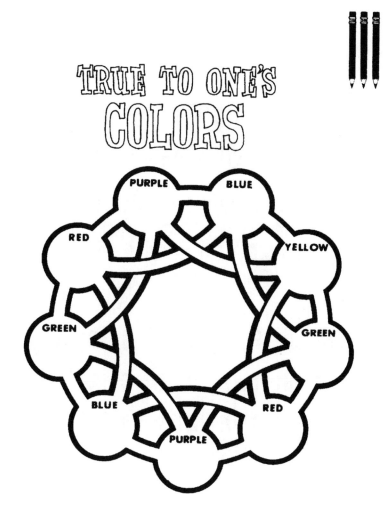

The interior lines of this puzzle crisscross but do not intersect. Place the numbers one through nine in the nine colored circles to fulfill the following requirements: 1) Any set of three numbers which totals fifteen (there are eight) must include three different colors. 2) Numbers of consecutive value may not be directly linked by any passage.

Solution on page 253

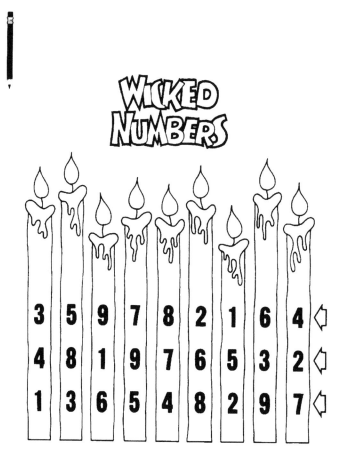

The numbers one through nine appear three times each in this puzzle. Your assignment is to blow out three candles which will total fifteen in each of the three horizontal rows. The three candles you select must carry the numbers one through nine. (No number may be used more than once.)

Solution on page 253

(Need a clue? Turn to page 224.)

NIGHTWALKER

DZOMPCEN

Position the eight remaining letters of the alphabet in the vacant squares of this puzzle to complete an alphabetical progression created by the moves of a chess knight.

Solution on page 253

Clue to the puzzle on page 218: Try "capsizing" on of the hats.

MAGIC
W☐RD SQUARES

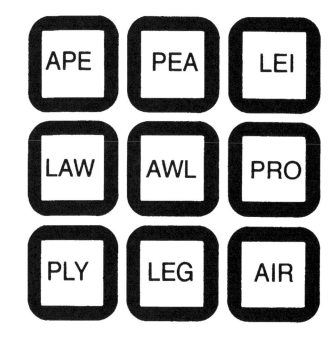

Each letter in this puzzle represents a different number from zero to nine. It is your challenge to switch these letters back to numbers in such a way that each horizontal, vertical, and diagonal row of three words totals the same number. Your total for this puzzle is 1446.

Solution on page 253

(Need A clue? Turn to page 225.)

TIC-TAC-TOPOLOGY

Here's a strategy game of topology for two players. Simply force your opponent to connect three or more states with their X's or O's and you win the game. Just as in tic-tac-toe, one player plays X and one player plays O. Players alternate positioning one of their marks per state until one player is forced to connect three or more states. In this sample game in progress, it is your move and challenge to position an O on the map in such a way that it will be impossible for your opponent to position an X without losing the game. Note: Only one X or O can be used to mark Michigan (a bridge is shown connecting both halves), but diagonally adjacent states, such as Arizona and Colorado, are not considered connected. You can enjoy playing this game with maps of other countries and continents.

Solution on page 253

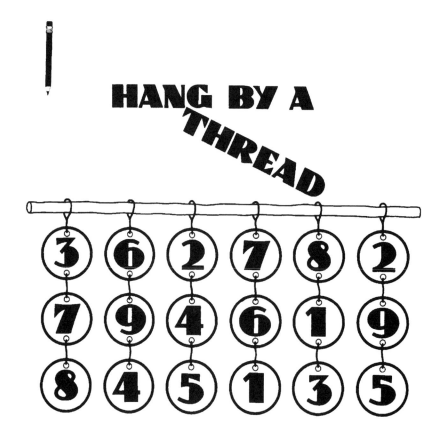

HANG BY A THREAD

Each of the numbers one through nine appears twice in the eighteen disks that are hanging by threads. Your task is to cut the least number of threads so as to drop one set of numbers and leave nine disks hanging that reveal the remaining set of numbers from one to nine.

Solution on page 254

Clue to the puzzle on page 220: Start by blowing out the middle candle.

PIG STYMIE

Put nine pigs in eight pens.

Solution on page 254

Clue to the puzzle on page 222: APE = 473

GEOMETRACTS

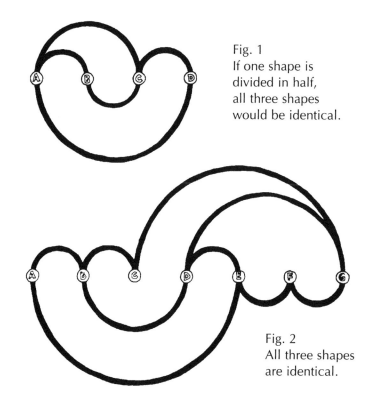

Fig. 1
If one shape is
divided in half,
all three shapes
would be identical.

Fig. 2
All three shapes
are identical.

Here are two distorted geometric figures. Both have been stretched in such a way that the original figure is unrecognizable at first glance. Your task is to straighten all the lines in each figure to reveal its original identity. The circled letters designate the intersection of two or more lines. Vital clues are given for each figure.

Solution on page 254

TIC-TAC-TOTAL

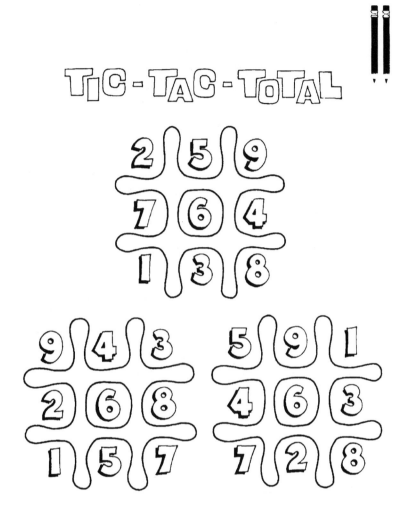

Your challenge in this puzzle is to circle a winning tic-tac-toe on each of the three game boards in the following manner: 1) One game must contain a diagonal win, one game must contain a horizontal win, and one game must contain a vertical win. 2) All numbers from one through nine must be circled in constructing these three winning lines.

Solution on page 254

PERFECT PERFECT VISION

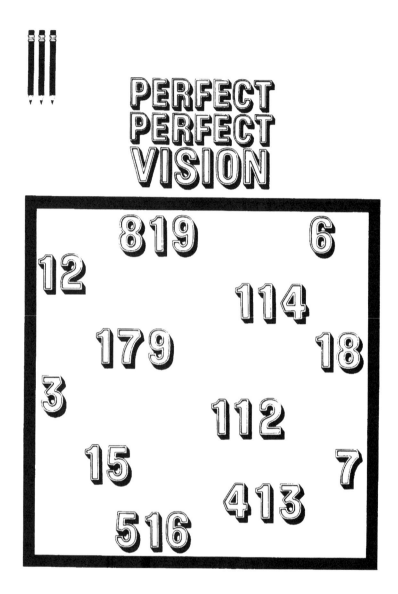

Using four straight lines, divide this square into nine pieces so that each piece totals the same number.

Solution on page 254

Chapter 9
Math Logic
Puzzles

Difficult Puzzles

Vegetable Soup Contest

Five people each bought 15 cans of vegetables for a soup contest. No one bought the same number of any kind, but 5 of one kind, 4 of another, 3 of another, and so on. Also, no vegetable was bought in the same quantity by any two people. Given all that, can you figure out how many cans of each vegetable each person bought and how much the purchases cost? Also, who won the contest for the tastiest soup?

1. The person who spent $6.43 bought 5 cans of asparagus and 3 cans of beans.
2. Lily spent the least amount of money, $1.66 less than T-bone. She bought 3 cans of carrots, 5 of peas, and 1 of corn.
3. Benny spent $1.20 on asparagus and $1.55 for corn and peas.
4. Joshua bought 2 cans of peas and spent $4.52 for his corn and carrots combined.
5. The person who won the contest bought 1 can of carrots and spent $7.42 total, 99¢ more than Benny.
6. T-bone spent the most. He bought 5 cans of corn, 4 of beans, and 1 of asparagus.

	corn	peas	carrots	asparagus	beans	amt. spent	winner
Benny							
Lily							
T-Bone							
Slim							
Joshua							

Shopping List	
corn	58¢
peas	39¢
carrots	44¢
asparagus	24¢
beans	64¢

See answers on page 243

Difficult Puzzles

Boxes

The sixteen boxes below are each worth the number inside. Their names are intersections of rows (letters) and columns (numbers), i.e., the lower left corner box is D-1 or 1-D. It is worth 9 points.

	1	2	3	4
A	11	6	15	3
B	5	8	12	10
C	16	1	14	7
D	9	2	13	4

Four boys playing a game are trying to make the most points by trading boxes. Everyone must have four boxes at all times. From the clues, how many points does each boy have at game's end?

1. Jeremy didn't own any of the boxes in the A row.
2. Boyd's highest number is A-3
3. B-2 and C-1 belong to the same boy, who isn't Bryce.
4. Bryce doesn't own any boxes in the 1 column.
5. On the last play of the game, Jeremy traded his 4-B for B-1.
6. D-2, A-2, and D-3 all belong to the same player.
7. C-1, B-3, and 4-D all belong to the same player.
8. Kevin's score was 4 higher than Boyd's.
9. Three of Boyd's boxes are in the A row.
10. Jeremy has just one box in the B row, which is B-1.

	1	2	3	4	5	6	7	8	9	10	11	12	13	14	15	16
Bryce																
Jeremy																
Boyd																
Kevin																

See answers on page 240

Foul Shots

Sometimes they make 'em, sometimes they don't! Using your excellent understanding of percentage, see if you can figure out the foul-shooting percentage for each of these six players this season. The highest is 83%. The lowest is 57%.

1. Player #34 had 102 successful shots, 30 fewer than the player who shot 71%.
2. The player with 57% (not #49 or #22) attempted 176 shots.
3. The player with 98 attempts shot 59%.
4. Player #27 shot 66%.
5. Player #12 had the fewest attempts and shot 80%.
6. The player with the highest percentage (not #18) made 38 fewer shots than #49.

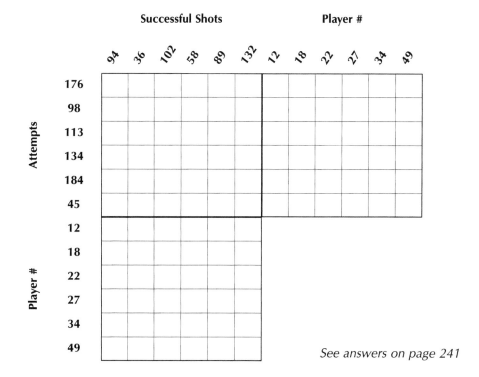

See answers on page 241

232

Garage Sale

Ms. Gaskin found a clothing item. A man who had searched for years bought an old dresser. All were happy to have saved money. Who bought what? What were the original and purchase prices?

1. The bicycle was bought at 50% off. The buyer's name starts with H.
2. Ms. Cullen bought the item priced at $15.00 for $4/5$ths that amount.
3. The tires sold for $1.00 less than the asking price.
4. The item that sold for $0.50 was an article of clothing.
5. Mr. Pazzini spent $4.00 less than Ms. Cullen.
6. Ms. Higgins paid for her dress with a $20.00 bill and received $19.25 in change.
7. Ms. Gaskin spent less for her item than Mr. Schmidt, who spent less than Mr. Pazzini.
8. The item originally priced the highest didn't sell for the highest price, nor did the lowest-priced item sell for the lowest amount.

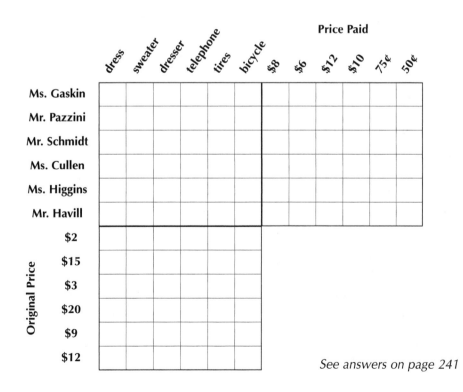

See answers on page 241

Great Pencil Sale

Four sixth-grade classes decided to sell pencils to raise money to go to a concert. Each class bought 500 pencils for $0.03 each (this cost must be deducted before any profit is made). They agreed that the class that made the most money (each class was allowed to charge any amount for their pencils) could sit in the front row at the concert.

Using the clues below, figure out how much profit each class made, and which class got to sit in the front row.

1. The least amount of profit was $11.30 less than the wining amount.
2. Mr. Pendip's class made $3.80 more in profit than the class that sold its pencils at 10 for 75¢.
3. The class that sold 219 pencils was not Mr. Pendip's.
4. Ms. Rimdrip's class sold its pencils for 7¢ more per pencil than Mr. Slimhip's class.

	Number Sold				Selling Price					
	219	375	413	500	5/40¢	10/75¢	10¢	15¢	$ profit	front row
Mr. Pendip										
Ms. Glenwhip										
Ms. Rimdrip										
Mr. Slimhip										

See answers on page 241

Hint: Use trial and error to determine the answer to clue #2 (the difference between Pendip's profit and Glenwhip's). Remember to deduct the original cost of the pencils from the profits when it is calculated.

Hidden Grades

Ms. Stonebelt told four of her best math students that their grades were hidden in the charts below. Using all the clues, see if you can figure out the grade each one received.

1. Dan's percentage is B + K - ½ C.
2. Bernard's grade is based on G + I + D – Dan's percentage plus sixty-five.
3. Jason earned a grade higher than Bernard. He scored 2E ÷ 3 + (½ J) – 2.
4. Dexter's grade, the only one of the four without a plus or a minus, was derived from:

$$(A + C - \{½\,F\}) \times 1/5\,G \div 10 + ½\,J$$

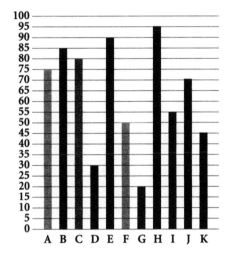

Grading System	
96-100	A
92-95	A-
89-91	B+
84-88	B
81-83	B-
77-80	C+
72-76	C
69-71	C-
62-68	D
0-61	F

See answers on page 241

Hundred-Miler

In a 100-mile bicycle race, Chet and his friends finished within 31 minutes of each other! From the clues, find each rider's last name, the bike color, the time each finished, and his average speed.

1. Both Dave and Seig rode over 6½ hours. Dave's bike is grey.
2. Day's bike, which beat Seig's green one, is blue.
3. The rider who rode for 6:32 hours was on a red bike.
4. Rick and the rider of the red bike both averaged under 16 mph.
5. The tan bike averaged 16.42.
6. The blue bike's rider is not Kurt, nor the one who took 6:40 hrs.
7. Brown, who rode in 6:09, is not Kurt or Bob.
8. Kurt's average beat Johns, who beat the green bike rider.

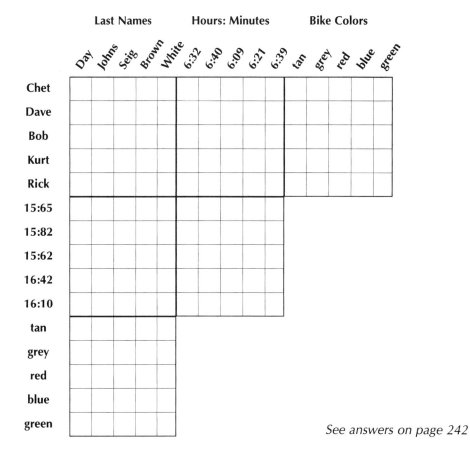

See answers on page 242

236

Motorcycle

Old Mrs. Frizzle needed a new motorcycle because her old one was worn out from so many trips to town. She summoned her five sons—Luke, Jake, Swizzle, Jeremiah, and Malcolm—and told them "Boys, I need a new motorcycle. It must be purple and it must have one extra tire. Also, I must have a new helmet, a new leather outfit, and new goggles. The one who finds me the best deal shall earn a handsome prize."

The sons met secretly and agreed that each would buy one of the five items and they would split the prize as follows: The one who bought the motorcycle would get 50% of the prize, the one who bought the tire would get 20%, the ones buying the outfit and the helmet would each get 12%, and the on e buying the goggles would get 6%.

See if you can deduce which son bought which of the five items, and how much Mrs. Frizzle gave as a prize.

1. Swizzle Frizzle did not buy the helmet.
2. Malcom earned 60¢ less than Jake.
3. Luke earned more than Jeremiah but less than Swizzle.
4 The one who bought the helmet—not Malcolm—Earned 90¢.

	Motor-cycle	Tire	Helmet	Outfit	Goggles	Prize Money
Luke						
Jake						
Swizzle						
Jeremiah						
Malcolm						

See answers on page 242

Hint: Start with clue #4, then go to clue #2.

Solutions

Bull's Eye

A. 16, 8, 1 (three arrows); **B.** 16, 2, 1 (three arrows); and **C.** 32, 8, 4, 2, 1, (five arrows).

You can form any whole number up to 63 on this target. Each number is a power of 2, which means that you can create any other whole number by combining numbers.

Jawbreakers

Three pennies. After the second penny, they would have either two yellow or two blue jawbreakers, or a yellow and a blue jawbreaker. A third penny would deliver a jawbreaker that had to match one of the colors.

Antsy Ant

Ten seconds. Since it takes the ant 12 seconds to cover the distance between 12 and 6 inches, it takes him 2 seconds to travel each inch. You can divide that distance into six 2-second time intervals.

Since it's a shorter distance between 6 inches and the 1-inch mark, you can divide that distance into only five 2-second intervals. So it takes the ant only 10 seconds to cover the remaining distance.

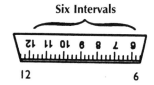

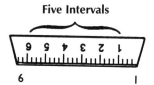

A Burned Receipt

$$
\begin{array}{r}
1425 \\
+\ 5421 \\
\hline
6666 \\
-\ 2374 \\
\hline
4292 \\
\end{array}
$$

In the Old Cemetery

Mary was born in 1896, 1897, 1898, or 1899.

For example, if Mary were born January 5, 1897, and died on her birthday, January 5, 1903, she would have died on the first day of her seventh year. The year 1900 was not a leap year, since it was centesimal (ending in 00); so, there were no leap years in Mary's lifetime. Thus, she lived exactly six years of 365 days each, or 2,190 days.

If her brother John were born January 5, 1903, and died the day before his birthday, January 4, 1909, it would have only been the last day of his *sixth* year. However, during John's lifetime there would have been two leap years, 1904 and 1908. Thus, although he lived six years minus one day, two years had an extra day, making his lifetime a total of 2,191 days—one day longer than Mary's.

For this to be possible, Mary must have been born no earlier than March 1, 1896, since her last year was expressed in a single digit.

Magic Squares

The magic constant for a fifth-order square is 65.

More Magic Shapes

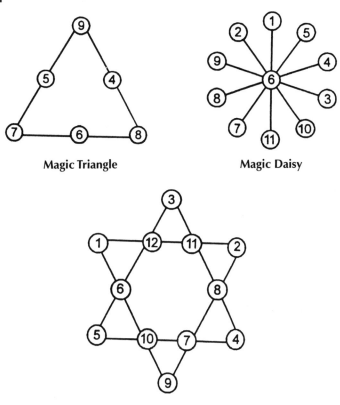

Magic Triangle

Magic Daisy

Magic Star

Ben Franklin's Wheel

Missing numbers, clockwise starting above the circled band numbers are: Band 1: 73, 30, 46 Band 2: 24, 47, 63 Band 3: 64, 39, 48 Band 4: 17, 70, 33 Band 5: 66, 18 Band 6: 19, 51, 36, 52 Band 7: 75, 28, 44 Band 8: 26, 61, 42.

The magic number that the rings add up to is 360, the number of degrees in a circle.

The Chimes of Big Ben

It takes 7½ seconds. You can illustrate the chiming of Big Ben like this.

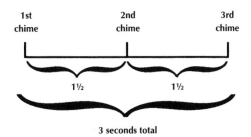

The first chime accounts for the interval from the first to the second chime. The second chime accounts for the interval from the second to the third chime and ends with the third chime. Therefore, you must divide the 3 seconds in half since only two intervals exist for three chimes, averaging 1½ seconds per interval.

At 6 o'clock, you would have five intervals totaling 7½ seconds as shown.

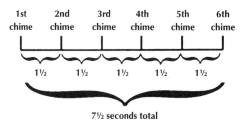

Count the Streetlights

It's 660 yards. There are 23 lamps on one side and 22 on the other side. There are 22 gaps between 23 lamps; therefore, the street is 22 times 30 yards long, or 660 yards.

Weighing In

The cube is 6 pounds, the pyramid 3 pounds, and the sphere 2 pounds.

Auction

Irene Black bought cheese ($5). Denise Green bought pie ($4). Duane Grey bought coffee ($7). Dan White bought cake ($6). Elroy Brown bought fruit ($3.50).

Biology Class

Kate adopted Willy, the mole (18 cm). Kristen adopted Weldon, the ladybug (1.3 cm). Kurt adopted Walter, the fly (1 cm). Kristi adopted Wendy, the rat (14 cm). Kyle adopted Warren, the bat (11 cm). Kevin adopted Wanda, the hamster (23 cm).

Boxes

Bryce had 2, 6, 10, and 13 for 31 total.
Jeremy had 1, 5, 9, and 14 for 29 total.
Boyd had 3, 7, 11, and 15 for 36 total.
Kevin had 4, 8, 12, and 16 for 40 total.

Chicken Mountain

Chicken-grading formula results: Saffola 242.5; McSanders 257.6 (winner); McPlume 172.2; McCombe 224.9; Poularde 196.6.

Chocolate Chip Cookies

Ms. Effie Bundt puts in 5 chips and bakes for 16 min 17 sec.
Ms. Ruby Strudel puts in 7 chips and bakes for 17 min 7 sec.
Ms. Thelma Spicer puts in 8 chips and bakes for 16 min 9 sec.
Ms. Miriam Applestreet puts in 9 chips and bakes for 17 min.
Ms. Georgia Honeydew puts in 10 chips, baking for 17 min 8 sec.

Coast to Coast

The route that Jacques and Chi Chi traveled took them in order to: Phoenix, Los Angeles, San Francisco, Portland, Salt Lake City, Denver, Dallas, St. Louis, Chicago, Pittsburgh, and finally to Washington, D.C.

Coffee

Max drinks 4 cups, with 2 sugars, no milk.
Doris drinks 5 cups, with 1 sugar, milk.
Blizzo drinks 1 cup, with no sugar, no milk.
Jan drinks 6 cups, with 6 sugars, milk.
Boris drinks 8 cups, with 4 sugars, no milk.

Decimal Ruler
The lengths of the lines are: **a** 3.3; **b** 1.3; **c** 3.9; **d** 2.8; **e** 0.6; **f** 3.8; **g** 1.8.

Destry's Missing Numbers
The square are: **A** 22.34; **B** 11.93; **C** 25.17; **D** 13.47; **E** 25.71.

Dog Apartments

Name	Apt. No.	Food/Week	Baths/Month
MacTavish	408	2 lbs.	9
Chico	103	10 lbs.	3
Ivan	609	8 lbs.	12
Wilfred	512	4 lbs.	2
Taz	221	12 lbs.	6
Spunky	341	6 lbs.	4

E.F. Bingo
Wanda won when the $^{16}/_{18}$ths fraction was called.

Famous Person
J O H N   F   K E N N E D Y

Fishing
Fred, using worms, caught one fish. Sammy, using dry flies, caught three fish. Torkel, using eggs, caught two fish. Joe, using flatfish, caught no fish at all.

Flighty Decimals

In the square:	4.39	4.01	2.60	1.42	total: 12.42
In the circle:	5.20	1.16	.07	.03	total: 6.46
In the rectangle:	3.71	1.01	.72	.30	total: 5.74

Foul Shots
Player #12 made 36 foul shots out of 45 attempts, for 80%.
Player #18 made 58 foul shots out of 98 attempts, for 59%.
Player #22 made 94 foul shots out of 113 attempts, for 83%.
Player #27 made 89 foul shots out of 134 attempts, for 66%.
Player #34 made 102 foul shots out of 176 attempts, for 57%.
Player #49 made 132 foul shots out of 184 attempts, for 71%.

Garage Sale
Ms. McGaskin bought the sweater for $0.50; original price $3.
Mr. Pazzini bought the tires for $8.00; originally $9.
Mr. Schmidt bought the dresser for $6; originally $12.
Ms. Cullen bought the telephone for $12; originally $15.
Ms. Higgins bought the dress for $0.75; originally $2.
Mr. Havill bought the bicycle for $10; originally $20.

Great Pencil Sale
Mr. Pendip sold 413 at 10¢ each for a $26.30 profit (front row seats).
Mr. Glenwhip sold 500 at 10 for 75¢, for a profit of $22.50.
Ms. Rimdrip sold 219 at 15¢ each, for a profit of $17.85.
Mr. Slimhip sold 375 at 5 for 40¢ for a profit of $15.00.

Heather's Garden
Heather has: 3 rows of carrots, 4 rows of cabbages, 1 row of turnips, 2 rows of pole beans, 5 rows of spinach, and 6 rows of cucumbers.

Hidden Grades
Dan scored 90 (B+); Bernard got 80 (C+); Jason got the highest grade, 93 (A–); Dexter got 87 (B).

Hundred Miler

Chet Brown rode the tan bike in 6:09 hours to average 16.42.
Dave Johns rode the grey bike in 6:39 hours to average 15.65.
Bob Day rode the blue bike in 6:21 hours to average 16.10.
Kurt White rode the red bike in 6:32 hours to average 15.82.
Rick Seig rode the green bike in 6:40 hours to average 15.62.

Jump Rope

Danielle made 12 jumps; Gary made 9 jumps; Jan jumped 20 times; Arnie jumped 17 times; and Ruth made 25 jumps before missing a jump.

Lunch at Paul's

Paul brought the olives and bought the coffee for $2.75.
Julie brought the cake and bought the cheese for $2.70.
Sandra brought the pickles and bought the mayonnaise for $2.18.
Diane brought the fruit and bought the chicken for $4.80.
Wally brought the salad and bought the bread for $4.17.

Mathathon

The girls defeated the boys 80 to –10.

Motorcycle

Luke bought the helmet and got 90¢. Jake bought the tire and got $1.50. Swizzle bought the motorcycle and earned $3.75. Jeremiah bought the goggles and earned 45¢. Malcolm bought the outfit and got 90¢. The "handsome prize" was $7.50.

Notes: The puzzle "key" is the prize money promised by old Mrs. Frizzle. Knowing from clue #4 that 90¢ represents 12%, you divide $.90 by .12 to get $7.50, the "handsome prize." Then, you can determine that 50% of $7.50 is $3.75, that 20% is $1.50, and that 6% is 45¢. From clue #2, you know that Malcolm can have only 90¢, because any other amount plus 60¢ would not total any of the other amounts. Therefore, Jake has $1.50, meaning he bought the tire.

Mountain Climb

Dacon climbed Mirre (7500-foot elevation). Drakon climbed Old Baldy (4500). Macom climbed Goat (8000). Bacon climbed Sleepy (9000). Jake climbed Raleigh (11,000).

Mountain Race

Andy Stiller climbs Mt. Stewart carrying 20 lbs.
Gerald Brown climbs Mt. Morgan carrying 40 lbs.
Dale Dorsey climbs Mt. Waring carrying 50 lbs.
Paul Anderson climbs Mt. McIntire carrying 30 lbs.
Jim McGee climbs Mt. Picard carrying 10 lbs.

Multiplication Jeopardy

Sue Jensen	8 x 15	=	120
June James	9 x 16	=	144
Dale Johnson	5 x 14	=	70
Neil Johns	7 x 18	=	126
Tina Jones	11 x 13	=	143

Ned's Newspaper Route

The Joneses live in the green house and get a *daily only* (clue #4).
The Johnsons live in the blue house and get a Sunday only.
The Smiths live in the grey house and get a Sunday only.
The Browns live in the white house and get both daily and Sunday.
The Simpsons live in the yellow house and also get both papers.

Old House

The Barneses lived 11 years in the red-painted house.
The Carpenters lived 44 years in the green-painted house.
The Lewises lived 5 years in the blue-painted house.
The Parkers lived 2 years in the yellow-painted house.
The Smiths lived 22 years in the brown-painted house.
The Warners lived 4 years in the white-painted house.

Play Ball

Teddie has a white soccer ball that weighs 16 oz.
Teresa has an orange golf ball that weighs 1.5 oz.
Toddy has a yellow Ping-Pong ball that weighs .8 oz.
Tanya has a green tennis ball that weighs 2 oz.
Tom has a brown basketball that weighs 22 oz.
Tillie has a red football that weighs 15 oz.

Pocket Change

Alex started with $4 and ended with 40¢. Scott started with $3 and ended with 95¢. Dan started with $2 and ended with 10¢. Jim started with $1 and ended with 70¢. Duane started with $2 and ended with $1.65.

Potato Chips

Elmo Glitzwhizzle ate 18 bags. Gazelda Kettledrummel ate 6 bags. Amos Grugenminer ate 12 bags. Gerald Crackenberry ate 9 bags. Sally Witteyspooner ate 3 bags. Hubert Jones ate 24 bags!

Queen Rachel's Bridge Toll

Chiquita wears black shoes and pays 18¢ bridge toll.
Cindy wears blue shoes and pays 36¢ bridge toll.
Kurt wears red shoes and pays 14¢ bridge toll.
Taber wears white shoes and pays 38¢ bridge toll.
Caleb wears green shoes and pays 24¢ bridge toll.

Skateboard Contest

Jimmy Cooper rode 8 blocks, from Elm St. Sally Mander rode 3, from Main St. Lenny Linden rode 11, from Chestnut Ave. Roger Chapman rode 7, from Acorn Dr. Kenny Lyle rode 1, from 11th St.

Temperature

The lowest temperature is at the 10:30 a.m. reading. The drop in temperature then is due to all the open doors as the students take their morning break.

Vegetable Soup Contest

	Corn	Peas	Carrots	Asparagus	Beans	Spent
Benny	2	1	4	5	3	$6.43
Lily	1	5	3	4	2	$6.09
T-Bone	5	3	2	1	4	$7.75
Slim	3	4	1	2	5	$7.42 (winner)
Joshua	4	2	5	3	1	$6.66

128

129
6 x 6 = 9 boards
4 x 4 = 25 boards
2 x 2 = 49 boards
83 total

130

131

132

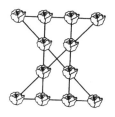

133

134

135

136 Reflections and rotations also correct.

ONE
TWO
+ TEN
THIRTEEN

137

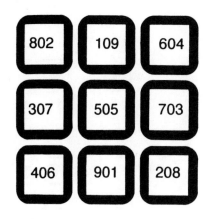

138

140 From the dark star, proceed to 7, 3, 12, 6, 10, 2, 5, 8, 1, 9, 11, 4, white star. Reverse order also correct.

139 Eliminate W, K, and E. Substitute the Roman numerals V, X, and L.

$$
\begin{array}{r}
V \\
I \\
C \\
X \\
L \\
D \\
\hline
666
\end{array}
\qquad
\begin{array}{r}
5 \\
1 \\
100 \\
10 \\
50 \\
500 \\
\hline
666
\end{array}
$$

141 SIX equals VI.

142 One of several possible solutions.

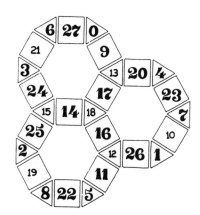

143 Keys needed: 1, 3, 5.

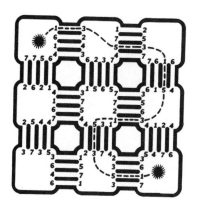

245

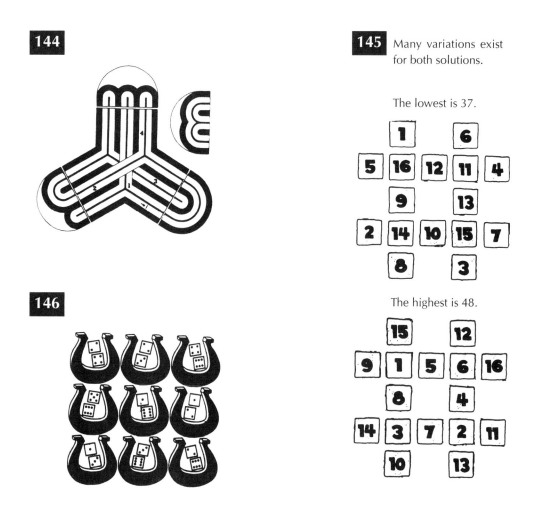

144

146

145 Many variations exist for both solutions.

The lowest is 37.

The highest is 48.

Sox Unseen
Sam has to take out 3 sox; then he's bound to get two of the same color.

Gloves Galore!
This is trickier than the sox, because some gloves fit on the right hand and some on the left. You *might* pick out all 12 left hand gloves, one right after the other, but then the next must make a pair; so you need to take 13 gloves to make sure.

Birthday Hugs
Each girl kisses 3 others; so it looks like 4 x 3 = 12 kisses, but that would be counting Jenny kissing Janey as one kiss, and Janey kissing Jenny as another, counting each kiss twice.
Actually, there are six kisses altogether.

Gold Star answer: Jabberwocky *by Lewis Carroll.*

Sticky Shakes
Same trick as with the kisses. Either you can say each of the 7 shakes with six; so the total is a half of 7 x 6, or 21 shakes. Or you can say John shakes with 6; Jack shakes with 5 others (don't count John again); Jake shakes with 4 others, and so on. The total number of handshakes is 6 + 5 + 4 + 3 + 2 + 1 = 21.

The Wolf, the Goat, and the Cabbage
Take the goat across. Go back; take the wolf across, and bring the goat back. Take the cabbage across. Go back for the goat. Then the goat is never alone with either the wolf or the cabbage.

Floating Family

The two kids row across. One brings the boat back. Then Mom rows across, and the other kid brings the boat back. Both kids row across. One brings the boat back. Then Dad rows across, and the second kid takes the boat back to collect her brother.

Slippery Slopes

Ten days. After 9 days and 9 nights, she is at 9000 feet. On the 10th day she climbs 3000 feet to the summit!

The Long and the Short of the Grass

They mowed the grass on 9 Saturdays, earning 9 x $2 = $18, and missed 6 Saturdays, losing 6 x $3 = $18.

Sugar Cubes

1. The first trick is to count the zeros! To find out how big the big cube is you need to find the cube root of a million. A million has six zeros—1,000,000—so its cube root must have one third of six—two zeros—100.

   The cube root of a million is a hundred. So the big cube is 100 cubes long, 100 wide, and 100 high. Each cube is half an inch; so 100 cubes is 50 inches, or just over 4 feet long. You would not fit this under a table, but it would go easily in a garage.

2. This time you are making a square; so you need the square root of a million. A million has six zeros; its square root must have half six; that is, three zeros—1000. The square root of a million is a thousand. So the big square on the ground is 1000 half inches long and 1000 half inches wide. 1000 half inches is 500 inches; dividing by 12 will give you 41 feet 8 inches. You could fit this square on a tennis court.

3. The pile is a million cubes high; a million half inches, or 500,000 inches. Divide by 12 for 41,666 feet 8 inches. This is higher than Mount Everest. You could make one pile as high as Mount Everest and one as high as Mount Adams, and still have a few cubes left over!

Crackers!

This is surprisingly easy; the trick is to add a plain cracker. Then Marty has a choice of 2—mayo or plain. Marty and Jake have a choice of 4; when Hank arrives they have a choice of 8, since the number of choices doubles with each new person. So when Hank comes there will be 16 choices—or 15 spreads. When Charlie is there they'll have 32 choices—31 spreads. And Fred will bring the total to 64 choices—63 spreads!

Crate Expectations

There are many different patterns that work, but here is an easy one to remember. Now try ten bottles!

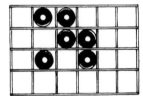

Take It Away!

If you are left with 3, you must lose, because you can't take all three, but if you take 1 your opponent will take 2, and if you take 2 your opponent will take 1. So the first rule for winning is, to *try to leave your opponent with three items!* You can also win if you leave 6, because after leaving 6 you can always leave 3 next turn. And you can win if you leave 9. Can you spot the pattern?

Oddwins

This Oddwins game is so tricky that even math professors haven't been able to find a way to always win. So here's your chance. See if you can master it—then let *us* know!

Witches' Brew

The pan holds 3 pints; fill it and then fill the jug from it. The jug holds 1 pint; so that leaves exactly 2 pints in the pan. Pour it into the cauldron and carry on cooking!

Witches' Stew

Fill the pitcher to the brim. Use it to fill the pot, which leaves just 2 pints in the pitcher. Empty the pot back into the bucket. Pour the 2 pints from the pitcher into the pot. Fill the pitcher again. Now carefully top off the pot from the pitcher. This will take exactly 1 pint, because there are 2 pints in it already. That leaves exactly 4 pints in the pitcher—pour them into the cauldron!

Cookie Jars

Joe has no cookies; so this puzzle is easy. If Ken gave him one, he'd have a total of one; so if they have the same number, Ken must also have one left. Therefore Ken must have two to begin with.

Fleabags

Captain has two fleas; Champ has four.

Frisky Frogs

Freda steps, Fred hops over her, Frank steps, Freda hops, Francine hops, Fergie steps, Fred hops, Frank hops, Frambo hops, Freda steps, Francine hops, Fergie hops, Frank steps, Frambo hops, Fergie steps—and they are all across, in 15 moves.

Leaping Lizards

Try using these guide rules; 1. Don't move a boy next to another boy—or a girl next to another girl—until you reach the other side; 2. Step if you can, hop if you can't step; 3. Once you have moved a girl, keep moving girls till you have to stop; then move boys till you have to stop. The quickest has 23 leaps.

Wiener Triangles

You can make 5 triangles, including the big one round the outside.

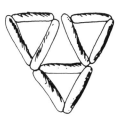

The Power of Seven

After 4 have been killed, and there are 20 left, the commander must put 2 in each corner tower, and 3 along each side wall.

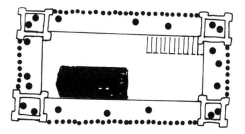

The Power of Seven continues

Yes, they can survive the final attack. Four defenders go in one corner tower, three in all the others. 15 men make 7 on each side!

Old MacDonald

All the 12 wings must have belonged to turkeys, because pigs don't usually have any; so he must have had 6 turkeys (with 2 wings each). The 6 turkeys must have had 12 legs; leaving 12 legs for the pigs, and since each pig has four legs, that makes 3 pigs. So Old MacDonald had 3 pigs and 6 turkeys.

Old Mrs. MacDonald

Mrs. MacDonald counted 12 heads, so she must have had 12 animals. If they had all been chickens she would have had 24 legs; if they had all been cows she would have had 48 legs. The difference between these two is 24, or 2 legs more than 24 for each cow. She counted 34 legs. That is 10 more than 24; so she must have had 5 cows.

Check; 5 cows = 5 heads; 7 chickens = 7 heads;
total 5 + 7 = 12 heads.
And 5 cows = 20 legs; 7 chickens = 14 legs;
total 20 + 14 = 34 legs.

Tennis Tournament

In a knockout tournament, every player has to lose one match—except the winner, who loses none. So the total number of matches is one less than the number of players. If 27 enter, there will be 26 matches.

Stamp Stumper

There are eight sets, however you wish to divide them.

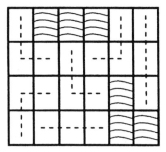

Broken Dishes

You'd have six dishes.

Cut the Pizza

Two cuts will make no more than four pieces. A third cut will make no more than seven pieces. So, in order to make eight pieces from three cuts, you need to think three-dimensionally and stack the four quater-pieces on top of one another.

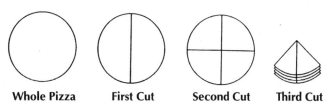

Whole Pizza   **First Cut**   **Second Cut**   **Third Cut**

Fractured Fractions

Since all the numbers are multiples of 4, you can solve the problem by first finding three-fourths of the number and then finding two-thirds of that answer.

For the numger 12, for example: $^3/_4$ of 12 is 9; $^2/_3$ of 9 is 6.

The answer will always be half the original number.

Divide the Time

When you add all the numbers on the face of the clock you get a sum of 78. Since two intersecting lines always make four sections, and since 78 cannot be divided evenly into four sections, the lines you draw must not intersect. Instead, you must draw two parallel lines that divide the clockface into three sections.

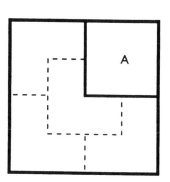

$$11 + 12 + 1 + 2 = 26$$
$$10 + 9 + 3 + 4 = 26$$
$$8 + 7 + 6 + 5 = 26$$

Parcels of Land

Divide the original sqare into fourths. One-fourth (square A) was willed to the landowner's wife. Since there were three squares left to be subdivided among the four sons, removing one-fourth of each remaining square leads to the arrangement at right.

Four Lines in a Square

You can draw a maxium of eleven sections in the square using only four straight lines. To do this, each line must intersect all the other lines.

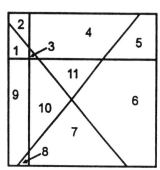

Count the Blocks

The number of blocks are: (A) 35, (B) 49, and (C) 54.

Sides, Edges & Corners

Block A touches nine other blocks, block B touches four other blocks, and block C touches 13 other blocks.

Crayon Constructions

1. How do you determine how many squares of the same size you can construct with 24 crayons?

To find out how many squares, divide 24 by one of its multiples 2, 4, 6, or 8, and then divide the result (quotient) by 4 for the total number of squares. For example:

$$24 \div 2 = 12$$
$$12 \div 4 = 3$$

Or, three squares with two crayons to a side.

$$24 \div 3 = 8$$
$$8 \div 4 = 2$$

Or, two squares with three crayons to a side.

2A. Two squares with three crayons to a side give you one smaller square.

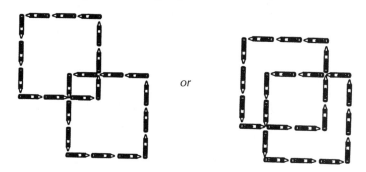

or

2B.

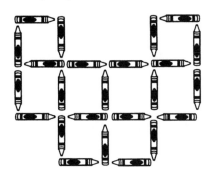

2C.

2D. One larger square.

Two larger squares.

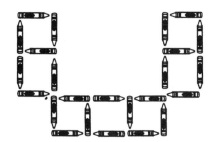

Five larger squares.

In all cases, the correct answer depends on having the minimum number of crayons on the perimeter. The most economical area is the one with the smallest perimeter.

Box the Dots
Here's how you can box the dots.

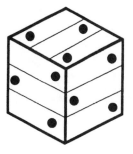

Tree-Chopping Contest

In first place was E; second place, C; third place, A; fourth place, B; fifth place, F; and last place, D.

Filled Glasses

A common-sense solution is in order here: pour the cranberry juice in glass #5 into glass #2 and return empty glass #5 to its original position.

Rare-Coin Thief

Zero. The coin is counterfeit because the term B.C. ("Before Christ") makes no sense on an ancient coin. How could the minter know that Christ would be born 260 years *after* he minted the coin?

Fast Fishin'

Five minutes. Each fisherman takes five minutes to catch a fish no matter how many fishermen are fishing. The time element remains constant and does not influence the outcome of this problem.

Apricot Jam

Count the pits.

The Lumberjack's Brother

The lumberjack was female.

Difficulties in figuring this one out have to do with making a false connection between gender and an appropriate job. This leads to the mistaken assumption that all lumberjacks must be men.

Chasing Shadows

1. The sun rises in the east, so the 7 A.M. to 11 A.M. morning shadows would be to the left of the tree, not to the right.
2. At 12 noon there would be no shadow since the sun is directly overhead.
3. The sun sets in the west, so the late afternoon and evening shadows would be to the right of the tree, not to the left.
4. The shadows should not all be the same length, since they shorten as the day approaches 12 noon, then lengthen again in the late afternoon and evening.

216

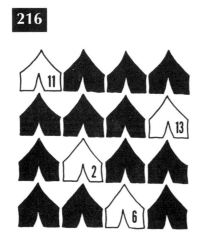

217

Down 3   Up 4   Down 1

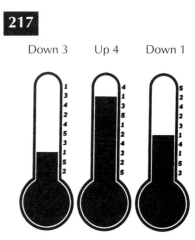

218 This puzzle is solved by turning over, or "capsizing" the 9/8 hat. Now, 8/6 + 10/6 = 3.

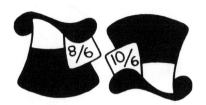

219

220

221

222

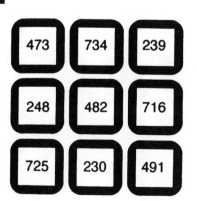

223

253

224 Cut four threads.

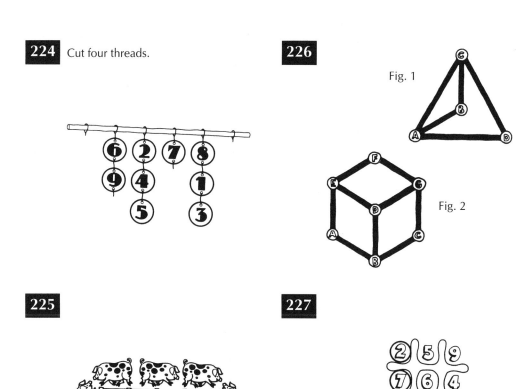

226

Fig. 1

Fig. 2

225

227

228 Each square totals twenty.

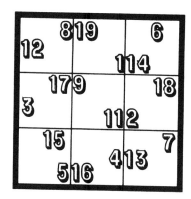

Index

Contents

10 9 8 7 6 5 4 3 2 1

Published by Sterling Publishing Company, Inc
387 Park Avenue South, New York, N.Y. 10016
Material in this collection was adapted from
Simple Chemistry Experiments with Everyday Materials © 1994 by Louis V. Loeschnig
Simple Earth Science Experiments with Everyday Materials © 1996 by Louis V. Loeschnig
Simple Experiments in Time © 1997 by Louis V. Loeschnig
Simple Kitchen Experiments © 1993 by Louis V. Loeschnig
Simple Nature Experiments with Everyday Materials © 1995 by Louis V. Loeschnig
Simple Science Experiments with Everyday Materials © 1989 by Louis V. Loeschnig
Simple Space & Flight Experiments © 1998 by Louis V. Loeschnig

Distributed in Canada by Sterling Publishing
c/o Canadian Manda Group, One Atlantic Avenue, Suite 105
Toronto, Ontario, Canada M6K 3E7
Distributed in Australia by Capricorn Link (Australia) Pty Ltd
P.O. Box 6651, Baulkham Hills, Business Centre, NSW 2153, Australia
Distributed in Great Britain and Europe by Chris Lloyd
463 Ashley Road, Parkstone, Poole, Dorset, BH14 0AX, United Kingdom

Sterling ISBN 0-8069-9467-3

GIANT BOOK OF SCIENCE FUN

BY LOUIS V. LOESCHNIG

Sterling Publishing Co., Inc. New York

Before You Begin

Ordinary materials can be used in extraordinary ways. And that's exactly what you do in the experiments in this book: you taste electricity with a lemon, make a water trombone with a straw, use a spot of butter to tell which light bulb is brighter, and more and more.

We chose these experiments because they are fun, easy to do, and because they explain interesting scientific principles. They get you thinking about science in a different way. They also *work*—we were amazed at how many experiments in science books *don't*. They're safe, too. You won't be dealing with dangerous materials.

If you're missing some of the ingredients, try using substitutes for them. For example, you could use a paper clip or a marble as a weight, instead of a nail or stone. Use your imagination—and experiment!

It's a good idea to set aside a special corner or shelf for the odds and ends you'll be using. A shoebox makes a good storage bin. You might want to keep a notebook to jot down what you do and what happens.

Don't be discouraged if an experiment doesn't seem to work. Read over the instructions and try it again. You'll probably spot the problem right away. Often you learn more from "failing" than you do when everything goes right.

The simpler experiments are at the beginning of the book, but you can start anywhere without reading what comes before.

Have fun—and amaze your friends—with these ordinary things that aren't so ordinary!

CHAPTER ONE

SIMPLE SCIENCE EXPERIMENTS

MAKING A PAPER STRAW

Cut out a strip of paper 2" x 10" (5 cm x 25 cm). Holding the paper at one corner, start rolling it diagonally in a narrow cylinder shape until it is all rolled up. Then fasten the sides with tape.

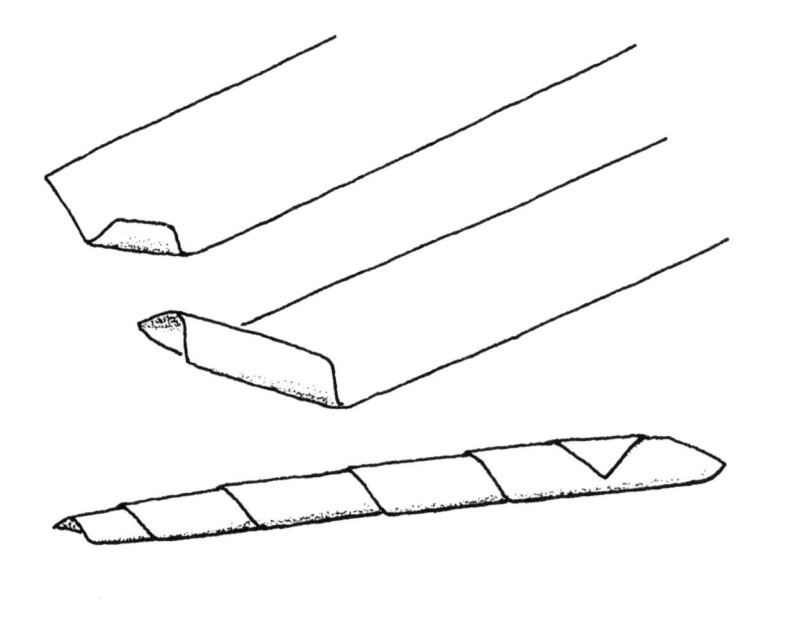

How Does a Straw Work?

Do you think you use a straw to pull liquid up into your mouth? Not so!

You need:

a drinking straw   a jar (or empty glass)
a glass of water

What to do:
Suck a little water into a straw. Then hold your finger across the top of the straw and take the straw out of the liquid. Place the straw over the jar. Then remove your finger from the top of the straw.

What happens:
While your finger covers the top of the straw, the liquid remains in the straw. When you remove your finger, the water flows out.

Why:
Your finger on top of the straw lessens the pressure of the air from above the straw. The greater pressure of air under the straw holds the liquid inside it.

When you suck through a straw, you are not actually pulling the liquid up. What you are really doing is removing some of the air inside the straw. This makes the pressure inside the straw lower than the pressure outside. The greater pressure of the outside air then pushes the liquid in the glass up through the straw and into your mouth.

A pipette, a tube scientists use to measure and transfer a liquid from one container to another, works the same way.

Straw Oboe

You can make music with a straw. The first wind instruments were probably hollow reeds picked and played by shepherds in the field.

You need:
a straw
scissors

What to do:
Pinch flat ½″ to ¾″ (12–19 mm) of a straw at one end. Cut off little triangles from the corners to form reeds. Put the straw far enough into your mouth so that your lips don't touch the corners. Don't pucker your lips, but blow hard. Cut 3 small slits along the length of the straw an inch or so apart. Separate the slits so that they form small round holes. Cover one of them and blow. Then cover two, then three, blowing each time.

What happens:
Each time you blow, you hear a different sound. You can play simple tunes by covering and uncovering the holes.

Why:
As in a real oboe, the two wedges—called reeds—opening and closing at high speed first allow air to flow into the straw and then stop the flow. Vibrating air creates the sound. As you cover and uncover the holes, you regulate the length of the air column and that determines the pitch. The shorter the air column, the faster it vibrates and the higher the note.

Make a Water Trombone

With a soda bottle, some water, and a straw, you can make a slide trombone.

You need:
a soda bottle
a straw
water

What to do:
Pour water into the bottle until it is about ¾ full. Put the straw in the bottle. Blow across the top of the straw. Then either lower the bottle or lift the straw and continue to blow.

What happens:
As you lower the bottle, the sound gets lower in pitch.

Why:
You are lengthening the column of air in the straw. This is how a slide trombone works.

Shaping Up

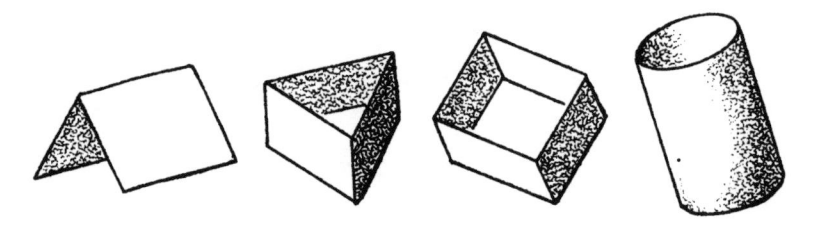

Which of these shapes do you think is the strongest? No matter what materials you are working with, you can make a structure stronger by simply changing its shape.

You need:

4 sheets of writing paper   transparent tape
a can   books

What to do:

Fold the sheets of paper into various shapes, such as those shown in the illustrations.

1. Fold a sheet in half and stand it on its edges.

2. Fold a sheet in thirds and tape the ends together.

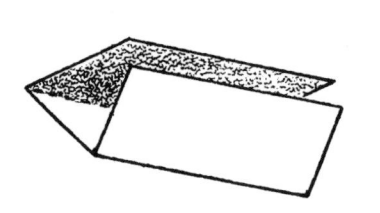 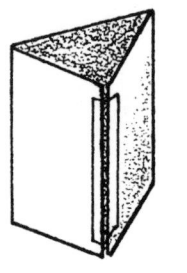

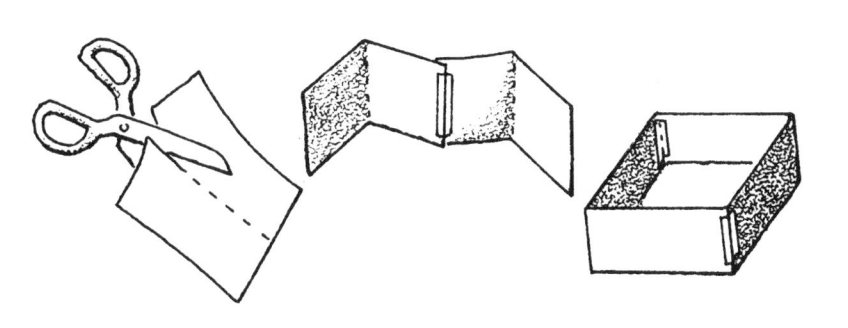

3. Fold a sheet in half lengthwise, cut on the fold, and tape the two halves together at the top and bottom. Then fold the attached halves in half again from top to bottom. Spread the sheets to form the cube.

4. Roll a sheet of paper around a can, secure the paper with tape, and remove the can.

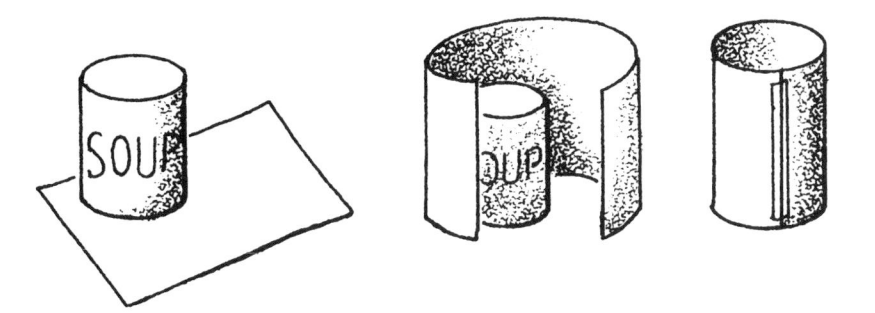

Set a light book on top of each shape. Some will collapse immediately. Keep piling books on the others until they collapse.

What happens:
The round paper pillar holds a surprising number of books.

Why:
A hollow tube is the strongest because the weight is distributed evenly over it.

Corrugated Paper

What makes a corrugated box strong?

You need:

3 sheets of typing paper   1 jar or glass
a can

What to do:

Make a crease about ¼-inch (6 mm) from the edge of one sheet of paper, fold it down, and press down on the fold. Using the first fold as a guide, fold a second crease back. Alternate folding back and forth until the entire sheet is pleated, as in the illustration.

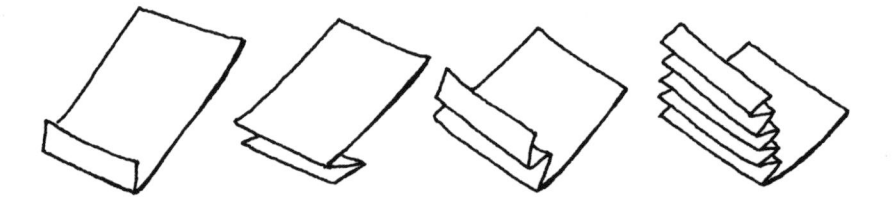

Roll the second sheet of paper around a can and tape the ends together. Remove the can. Do the same thing with the third. Line up the two circles of paper 4″ (10 cm) from one another on a table. Then place the pleated sheet on them. Rest the jar on top of the pleated sheet.

What happens:

The pleated paper holds the jar.

Why:

You have added strength by using corrugated paper, which you created by folding the sheet back and forth. An engineer devised this way of making paper stiffer—and stronger.

Powerful Paper

Just how strong can paper get?

You need:

a corrugated carton a quart-sized fruit juice can
scissors (1 litre)
a small board rubber bands or tape
  (a cutting board will do)

What to do:

Cut a strip about 4″ x 12″ (10 x 30 cm) from a corrugated box. Wrap the strip around a large can and secure it with rubber bands or masking tape. Then remove the can.

Place a small board on top of the cardboard circle. Stand on it.

What happens:

The cardboard circle will hold your weight.

Why:

That strength comes from the combination of circular shape and corrugated paper.

Tough Newspaper

Your strongest blow cannot
budge this fearless newspaper!

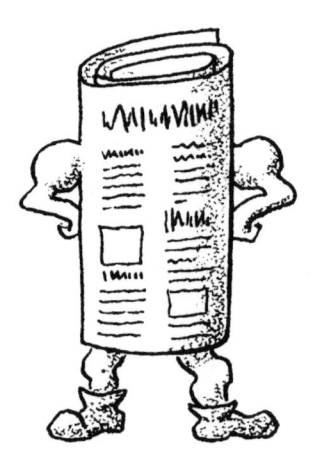

You need:

a newspaper   a wooden ruler or
a table   piece of scrap wood

What to do:

Place a ruler on a table so that an inch or two (3–5 cm) projects over
the edge. Spread a double sheet of newspaper over the ruler so that the
paper lies flat along the table edge.

Strike the projecting edge of the ruler as hard as you can.

What happens:

The newspaper doesn't budge.

Why:

It is air pressure on the paper that prevents it from moving. Air pushes
down with almost 15 pounds of pressure on every square inch of surface (1 kg per square centimeter). For an average sheet of newspaper,
the total resistance is about two tons.

Invisible Shield

If you've ever been caught in the rain on your way home and tried to keep dry by putting a newspaper over your head, you know that water doesn't treat paper very well. But in the following experiment, the paper seems to be protected by an invisible shield.

You need:

a sheet of newspaper
a pot of water
a glass or jar

What to do:

Crumple the sheet of newspaper and stuff it into the empty glass or jar tightly enough so that it doesn't fall out when you turn the glass upside down. Holding the glass bottom up, sink it deep into a pot filled with water. Hold it there. After a minute or so, pull the glass out of the water and remove the paper.

What happens:

The paper is dry.

Why:

Water cannot get into the glass because the "empty" glass is already filled with air. And the air cannot get out because it is lighter than water.

Charming a Paper Snake

It's easier than you think to charm a snake.

You need:

thin cardboard or heavy paper   a pencil
scissors   string
a lamp

What to do:

Draw a spiral snake (as in the illustration) on thin cardboard or any slightly heavy paper, such as oaktag or wrapping paper or even a large index card.

   Cut out the spiral snake and tie a string to its "tail."

   Suspend the snake over a lighted bulb or a heated radiator.

What happens:

The snake dances.

Why:

Hot air is less dense than cold air and therefore it rises. The moving air spins the spiral snake.

   To make a stand for your snake: With a pin, attach the head to the eraser end of a pencil, letting it curl around the pencil. Stand the pencil in the center hole of a spool of thread.

Dancing Dolls

Never thought you'd see paper dolls dance?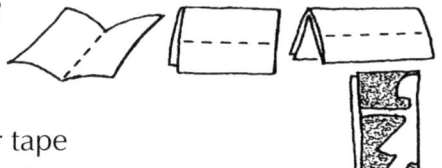

You need:

a piece of stiff paper
  such as oaktag
a large sheet of cardboard
scissors

paste or tape
2 paper clips
a magnet
a pencil

What to do:

Fold the stiff paper from top to bottom twice. Draw the right half of a doll along the exposed top fold, extending the doll's arm and leg to the bottom of the exposed fold, as in the illustration.

Cut along the lines you drew without opening up the folded paper. Form a circle of dolls by pasting the two ends of the group together. Attach the paper clips so that the dolls stand on them.

Balance the large cardboard so that a portion of the cardboard hangs over a table edge. Stand the circle of paper dolls on top of the cardboard so that one of the clips is on the overhanging portion.

Move your magnet underneath the cardboard—first to the right and then to the left.

What happens:

The paper dolls dance.

Why:

The paper clips are made of steel. Therefore, the magnet attracts them—even through cardboard.

Invisible Ink

You can use a lemon to write a secret message.

You need:

the juice of half a lemon

a cotton swab (or a toothpick
  wrapped in absorbent cotton
  or a dried-up pen)

a lamp

paper

What to do:

Dissolve the lemon juice in water and dip the swab into it. Then use the swab to write a message on ordinary white paper. When it dries, the writing will be invisible. When you want to read the message, heat the paper by holding it near a light bulb.

What happens:

The words appear on the page in black.

Why:

The juices of lemons and other fruits contain compounds of carbon. The compounds are nearly colorless when you dissolve them in water. But, when you heat them, the carbon compounds break down and produce carbon, which is black.

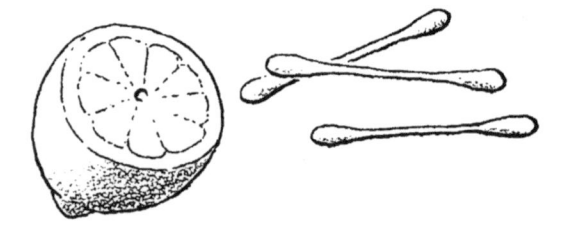

Lemon Cleaning Fluid

Write an invisible message with flour and water and make it appear with iodine. Then use lemon to make it disappear again.

You need:

a few drops of lemon juice
1 tablespoon flour (15 ml)
2 oz. of water (60 ml)

cotton swabs
a paper towel
a few drops of iodine

What to do:

Mix 2 ounces of water with a tablespoon of flour. Write your message on the paper towel with a swab. When the message dries, it will be invisible.

When you are ready to read it, use a swab to apply a few drops of iodine. Your message will appear in blue-black.

Next, dab on a few drops of lemon.

What happens:

Your message disappears.

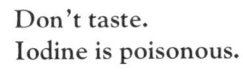

**Don't taste.
Iodine is poisonous.**

Why:

The iodine reacts with the flour, a starch, to form a new compound that appears as blue-black.

When you apply the lemon juice, the ascorbic acid (Vitamin C) of the lemon combines with the iodine to make a new colorless compound. So, if you spill iodine on anything, you can use lemon juice to remove it. It also removes ink, mildew, and rust stains—from paper and cloth.

Blowing Up a Balloon with a Lemon

Put chemistry to work for you!

You need:
juice of 1 lemon or 2 oz. of
  vinegar (60 ml)
a balloon
an empty soda bottle
1 oz. water (30 ml)
1 teaspoon of baking soda (5 ml)

What to do:
Stretch the balloon to make the rubber easier to inflate. Dissolve the teaspoon of baking soda in an ounce of water in the clean, empty soda bottle. Then stir in the juice of a lemon or two ounces of vinegar. Quickly fit the stretched balloon over the mouth of the bottle.

What happens:
The balloon inflates.

Why:
When you mix the base (the baking soda) and the acid (the lemon or vinegar), you create carbon dioxide, a gas that rises into the balloon and blows it up.

Lemon Rocket

Combine lemon juice with baking soda, and you can launch a rocket!

You need:

2 oz. lemon juice or vinegar (60 ml)

water

1 teaspoon baking soda (5 ml)

a square of paper toweling

2 paper towel strips, 1″ x 10″ (2.5 cm x 25 cm)

empty soda bottle with cork to fit

tacks or tape

What to do:

Fit a cork to a soda bottle, trimming it or padding it with paper toweling, if necessary. Tack the 2 paper towel streamers to the cork. Put the cork aside: it will be your rocket.

Pour a mixture of water and lemon juice into the soda bottle until it is half filled. Wrap the baking soda in a little square of paper toweling.

Go outside where your rocket has plenty of space to travel. Then launch it—by dropping the paper towel with the baking soda into the soda bottle and inserting the cork loosely.

What happens:

The cork will eventually shoot up.

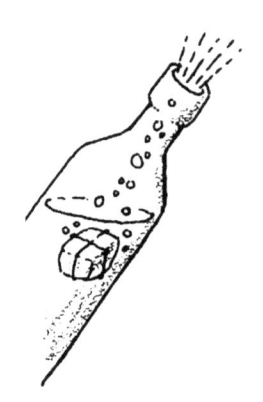

Why:

As the water and lemon juice soak through the paper towel, the baking soda reacts to produce carbon dioxide. As more gas forms, pressure builds up inside the bottle and sends the cork flying.

Shock Them All!

Want to shock your friends? You can do it by repeating an experiment first done by the Italian physicist Alessandro Volta 200 years ago.

You need:
lemon juice
9 1″ x 1″ strips of paper towel (2.5 cm x 2.5 cm)
5 pennies or other copper coins
5 dimes (or any other coin that is not copper)

What to do:
Soak the paper towel strips in the lemon juice. Make a pile of coins, alternating dimes and pennies. Separate each one with a lemon-soaked strip of paper towel.

   Moisten one finger tip on each hand and hold the pile between your fingers.

What happens:
You get a small shock or tingle.

Why:
You have made a wet cell, the forerunner of the battery we buy at the hardware store. The lemon juice, an acid solution, conducts the electricity created by the separated metals of the two coins.

   What we call a battery is actually two or more dry cells. In each dry cell, 2 metals (a zinc metal container and a carbon rod) are separated by blotting paper soaked in a strong acid.

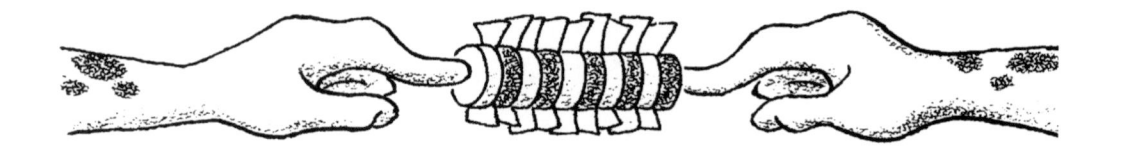

Make a Plastic Toy

Perhaps you have made toys out of paper but here you'll create your own plastic—and mold it into a toy.

You need:

1 cup of milk (240 ml)   5 tablespoons of vinegar (75 ml)
a small pan

What to do:
Warm the milk in a saucepan. Stir in the vinegar.

What happens:
The liquid becomes a rubbery blob. Wash off the blob and shape it as you wish. In a few hours, the material will harden.

Why:
When the vinegar and milk interact, the milk separates into 2 parts: a liquid and a solid made of fat, minerals and protein casein. Casein is made up of very long molecules that bend like rubber but eventually harden.

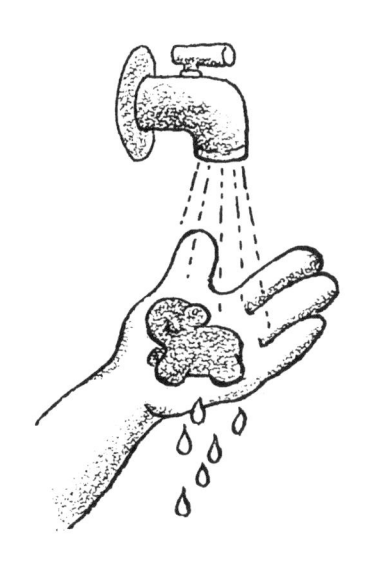

Plastics were originally made from milk and plants. But, increasingly over the past 50 years, they have been produced from petroleum. Unlike earlier types, plastics made from petroleum do not decompose. That is why scientists are now so concerned about finding ways to recycle today's plastics.

Magnifying Glass

A magnifying glass made out of water? Impossible?

You need:

butter or cooking oil

a paper clip
  or piece of wire hanger

water

a telephone directory or
  newspaper or postage stamp

What to do:

Straighten a paper clip or snip off a 4-inch (10 cm) piece of wire hanger by bending the wire back and forth a number of times. Form a small loop at one end of the wire and rub a little butter, margarine or cooking oil on it. Dip the loop into a glass of water and lift it out. You now have a lens— a sort of frame that holds a layer of water

    Use the lens to read the small print in a telephone directory, the classified ads in a newspaper, or the fine details of a postage stamp.

What happens:

The print is magnified.

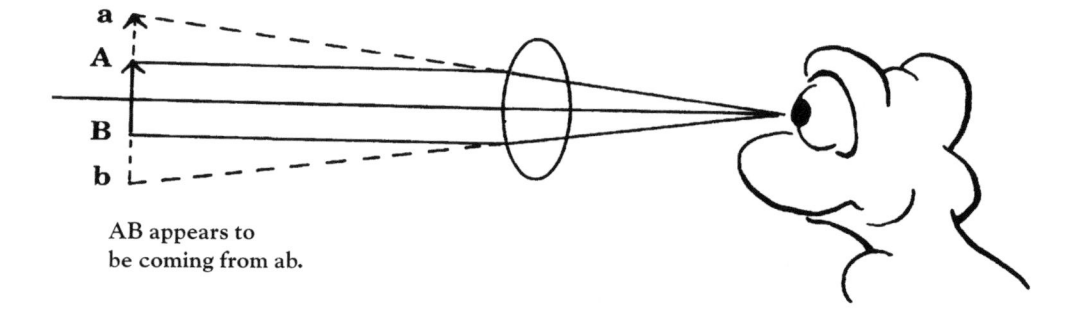

AB appears to
be coming from ab.

Why:

The water lens, just like a glass or plastic lens, has a definite shape. It bends light rays as they pass through it. First, it bends light as the light enters. Then it bends it again as the light leaves. The angle at which the water bends the light depends upon the shape of the lens.

Reflected light spreads out from the object you are looking at, hits the lens, and is bent back to your eye. Your eye sees the light as though it came on a straight line from the object—and the object seems to be much larger than it actually is.

HOW MUCH BIGGER?

You can find out just how much larger a lens makes an object by using a piece of graph paper. You can also use an ordinary typing sheet, but you need to draw graph lines on it like this:

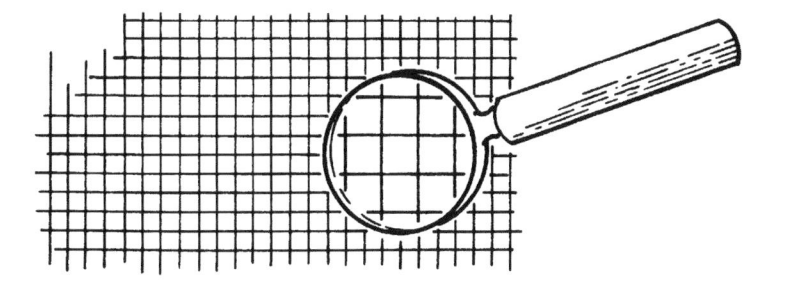

Look through your magnifying glass at the lined paper. Count the number of lines you see through the "lens" compared to the number you see outside of it.

If there are 4 lines outside compared to one inside, the lens magnifies 4 times.

Cut String Without Touching It

Can you cut a string without laying a hand on it—when it is inside a covered glass jar? See how easy it is when you "concentrate"!

You need:

a string   a jar with a top
tape   a magnifying glass

What to do:
Suspend the string from the inside of the jar lid with tape and insert it into the jar. Screw on the jar lid.

   With the magnifying glass, focus the rays of the sun on the string for a few minutes.

What happens:
The string breaks in two.

Why:
The magnifying glass concentrates the heat of the sun on one spot on the string. The heat becomes intense enough to burn right through the string.

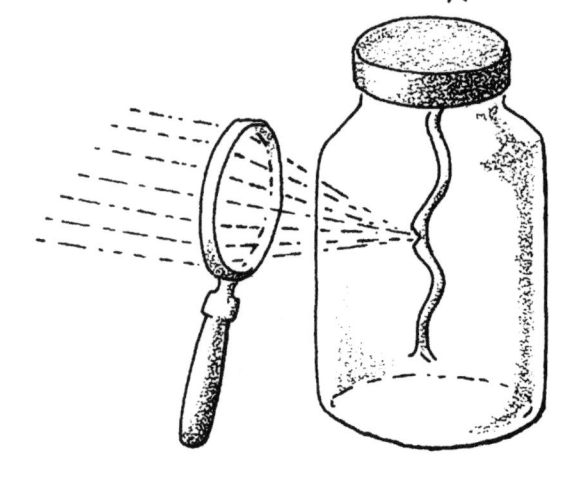

Rescue an Ice Cube

A great "icebreaker" for a party! Challenge your guests to use a string to rescue an ice cube from a glass of water without getting their hands wet. Tell them they may use anything on the party table except the dishes or utensils. After they fail, show them how to do it.

You need:

a 6" string (15 cm)   a glass of water
  or sewing thread   salt
an ice cube

What to do:
Float the ice cube in the glass of water. Hang one end of the string over the edge of the glass. Place the other end of it on the ice cube. Then sprinkle a little salt on the ice cube and let it stand for 5 or 10 minutes.

What happens:
The string freezes onto the ice cube. Then you pull on the string and lift the ice cube out of the water.

Why:
When the salt strikes the ice, it lowers the freezing point of water to a little below 32°F (0°C) and causes the surface of the ice cube to melt a little. As the ice refreezes, it traps the string.

Lazy Bones

You might expect the thin threads that support the stick in this experiment to break, but instead . . .

You need:

2 long pieces of thread   a wooden hanger
a thin wooden stick   a metal-edged wooden ruler

What to do:

Tie a piece of thread to each end of the stick. Then tie the other end of each thread to the hanger so that the stick is suspended underneath. Use clove hitch knots if you like. (See box on p. 31.) Strike the stick with the metal edge of the ruler.

What happens:

The threads do not break! If you strike hard enough, the piece of wood breaks!

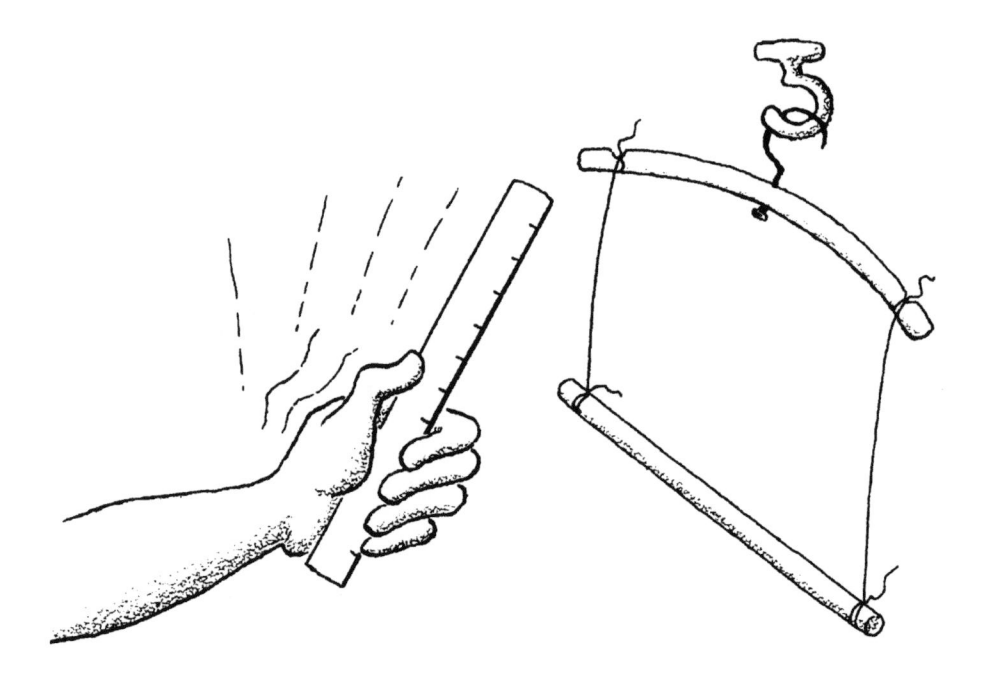

Why:

You are applying force not to the thread but to the stick. The stick resists moving—so much that it would rather break than move. It's the law of inertia again: bodies at rest tend to stay at rest.

MAKING A CLOVE HITCH KNOT

The clove hitch allows you to join a rope to something else, such as a stick or a hanger.

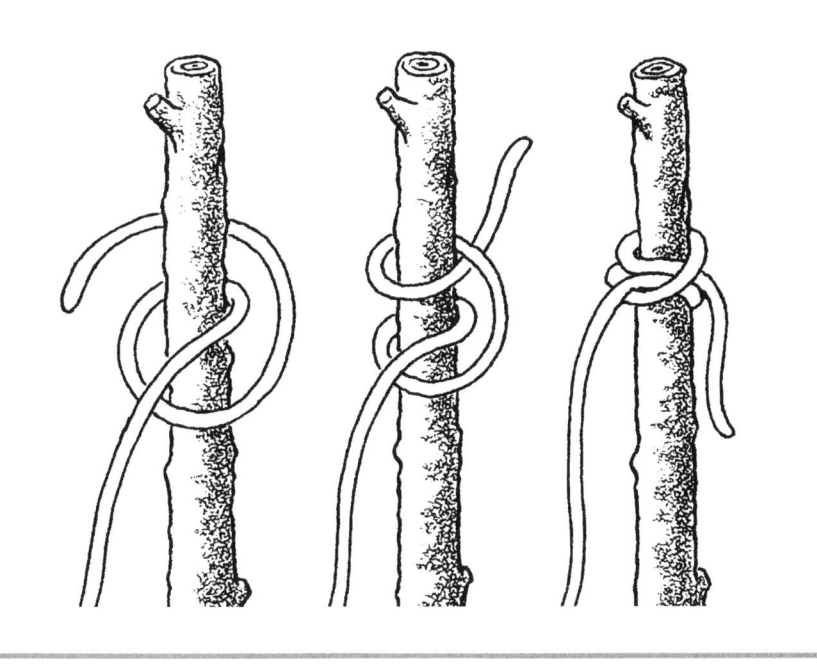

Soapy Shipwreck

What does soap do to water that makes washing easier? Watch!

You need:

teaspoon of liquid soap
  (either dishwashing or
  laundry detergent)

pin or needle
cup of water (250 ml)
tweezer or hairpin

What to do:

Float a pin on a cup of water. It's easier if you lower the pin with a pair of tweezers or a hairpin or even a fork. Then carefully add liquid soap drop by drop.

What happens:

As you add soap, the pin sinks.

Why:

To start with, the pin isn't actually floating. It is resting on the water's invisible elastic skin.

Water molecules are strongly attracted to one another and stick close together, especially on the surface of the water. This creates tension—enough tension to support an object you'd think would sink. Surface tension also prevents water from surrounding the particles of dirt, soot, and dust on your skin or clothes.

When dissolved in water, soap separates the water molecules, reducing the surface tension. That's why the pin sinks—and why soapy water washes dirt away.

Soap Power

Can you use soap to power a boat? Well, maybe, a very small one—in a basin or in the bathtub.

You need:

a pinch of detergent

an index card

scissors

a pot of water

What to do:

From an index card, cut out a boat approximately 2" x 1" (5 cm x 2.5 cm), with a small slot for the "engine" in the rear, as in the illustration. Then float the boat in a pot of water.

Pour a little detergent into the "engine" slot.

What happens:

Your boat travels through the water.

Why:

The soap breaks the water's elastic "skin", the surface tension (see page 32), behind the boat. The boat sails forward—and will stop only when the soap reduces the surface tension of all the water in your "lake."

Picky Toothpicks

Make a circle of toothpicks come and go at will.

You need:

a piece of soap   a cube of sugar
a bowl of water   6 toothpicks or matches

What to do:

Arrange the toothpicks in a circle in a bowl of water. Place a cube of sugar in the center of the circle.

Change the water and arrange the toothpicks in a circle again. This time place a piece of soap in the center.

What happens:

When you place sugar in the center, the toothpicks are drawn to it. When you place soap in the center, the toothpicks are repelled.

Why:

The sugar sucks up water, creating a current that carries the toothpicks with it toward the center. The soap, on the other hand, gives off an oily film that spreads outward. It weakens the surface tension (page 32), and the film carries the toothpicks away with it.

Polluting the Duck Pond

Is anything wrong with washing your clothes with detergent in a lake or pond? Take a look!

You need:

liquid detergent   a plastic bag
wax paper   a large pan or bowl of water
felt–tipped pen (optional)

What to do:

Stuff a plastic bag with bits of plastic or wax paper. Close it with its regular fastener or staple it closed. If you wish, draw a duck on the bag with a felt-tipped pen. Float your "duck" in the pan or bowl. Then add a little detergent.

What happens:

The duck sinks.

Why:

The wax paper and plastic are water-repellent—just the way a live duck is. A duck's feathers are oily. This oil repels water and helps a duck to float. But a detergent enables water to stick to greasy materials. Detergent may be fine for washing dishes and clothes, but it is deadly for the duck.

Handmade Bubbles

Bubbles are globs of air or gas inside a hollow liquid ball. Soap bubbles are globs of air enclosed in a film of soapy water. You can make bubbles by blowing through a pipe or a ring dipped in soapsuds. You can do it with just your hand, too.

You need:

2 tablespoons dishwashing
  liquid (30 ml)

a cup of warm water

What to do:

Gently stir the dishwashing liquid into the warm water. Curl your fingers and dip your hand in the soapy mixture. Blow into your curled hand.

What happens:

Bubbles form.

Why:

When you blow into the mixture of water and detergent on your wet hand, you add the air that forms the center of the bubble.

BUBBLE STAND

To make a "stand" for your bubbles, all you need to do is place a plastic cup or container upside down.

Or you can place a pencil in the hole of a wooden spool of thread and wind a wire loop about it, as in the illustration at the right. Transfer a bubble from a bubble blower to the stand by simply shaking it off gently. You can then observe the bubble—and make others.

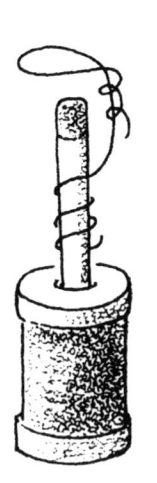

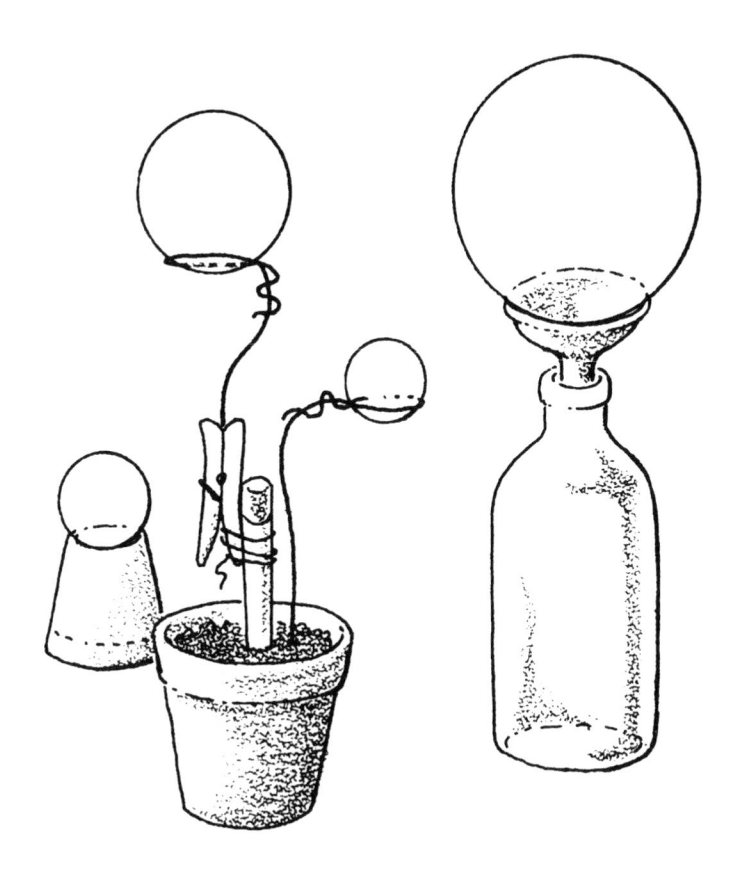

Rainbow in a Bubble

A rainbow in a bubble? Yes!

You need:

a bubble blower,   bubble mix
  such as a wire ring   a refrigerator
a tablespoon of sugar (15 ml) a bubble stand

What to do:

Add a tablespoon of sugar to the bubble mix. Place the solution in the refrigerator for a few minutes. This will make the bubbles last longer.

  Dip the bubble blower into the mix. When you have a film of soap on the ring, blow gently. Attach your bubble to the bubble stand by shaking the bubble blower over the stand.

What happens:

After a few minutes,
you see different colors.

Why:

When light hits a bubble, most of it passes through it because the bubble is transparent. But as the air in it evaporates and the bubble gets even thinner, some of the rays that make up white light don't pass through. Instead, they are reflected back from either the inside or the outside. That's why you see various colors of the spectrum. The colors change and disappear, because the bubble's thickness is not the same all over and is constantly changing.

Bubble in a Bubble in a Bubble

Use your bubble stand to put a bubble in your bubble's bubble.

You need:

a plastic cup or
  other bubble stand
bubble mix

a bubble ring or
  other bubble blower
a straw

What to do:
Wet the top of a plastic cup or the wire loop of a bubble stand. Blow a large soap bubble with the wire ring and attach it to the bubble stand. Wet a plastic straw in the bubble mix and put it through the large bubble. Blow a smaller bubble inside the large one. Then carefully push the straw through your smaller bubble, and blow an even smaller one.

What happens:
You get a bubble in a bubble in a bubble.

Why:
Anything wet can penetrate the bubble without breaking it. The wet surface coming into contact with the soapy film becomes part of it. Don't touch the wet wall with your smaller bubble or you won't get a separate bubble.

Putting a Bubble to Work

We can make an ordinary soap bubble do work for us!

You need:

an empty thread spool   bubble mix
a 3-inch square of paper (7.5 cm)   a long needle
a ½-inch cork (12 mm)

What to do:

Stick a needle through the cork, point up.
Place the cork on a level surface such as a
table or desk.

Fold the paper diagonally twice. Unfold it. Balance the center of the paper square (where the creases meet) on the point
of the needle, as in the drawing.

Dip the spool in the bubble mix and blow a bubble on one
end. Hold the other end toward the paper.

What happens:

The paper moves.

Why:

Air escaping from the bubble moves the paper.

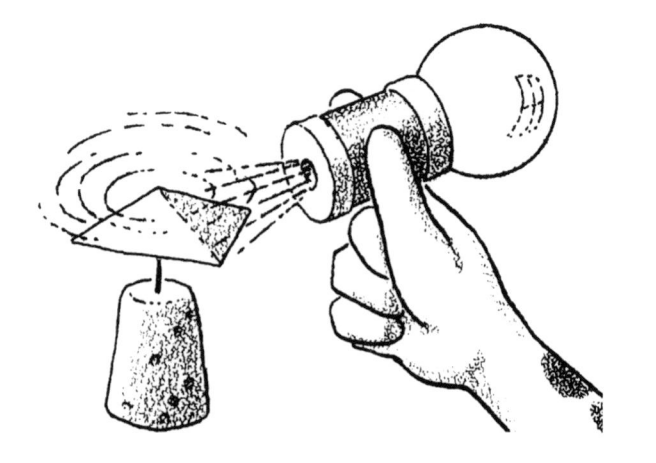

CHAPTER TWO
SIMPLE KITCHEN
EXPERIMENTS

FOOD FOR THOUGHT

What makes us hungry? Why do salted potato chips make us thirsty? How does the temperature of food affect its taste? What does salt do in the pot—and in our bodies? Is it better to use honey than sugar? And more . . .

ABOUT HUNGER AND FOOD

Why do we cook? First of all, to make food digestible and safe. But we also cook for other reasons. We cook to make food tasty so that we will enjoy eating as we satisfy our hunger. But what makes us feel hungry?

Chemicals in the body—in our blood, our digestive hormones and our nervous system—all give us signals, sensations such as stomach movements. When these signals reach the brain, it recognizes them as a need for food.

Our sense of hunger and satisfaction is also influenced by other things. Sometimes we want and eat food when we don't need it. Maybe we eat because it's our favorite food, or because we are upset about something and think food will make us feel better. Or maybe we eat just because everybody else is eating. Sometimes, too, we refuse food even though we need it—perhaps because we are sick or worried or afraid we'll gain weight. Sometimes, we don't eat enough because we don't like the taste or smell or looks of a particular food.

Mapping Your Tongue

Several hundred tiny bumps on the surface and under the tongue help us experience various tastes.

You need:

water
2 tsp salt
2 tsp sugar
aspirin
2 tsp lemon juice

4 small cups or glasses
4 cotton swabs or toothpicks
 with paper towels
paper towels
paper and pencil

What to do:

Place two ounces of water in each cup

To #1, add two teaspoons of salt. To #2 add two teaspoons of sugar. Break up an aspirin in a spoon and add it to #3. To #4, add two teaspoons of lemon juice.

Wipe off your tongue with the paper towel or a tissue to get rid of saliva. Dip the cotton swab into #1 (the salty solution). Shake off any drops of liquid and touch the swab to the middle, edges, and back of your tongue. Where was the sensation of saltiness strongest? On which part of your tongue? Write down each answer as you test.

Then rinse your mouth with cold water. Dry your tongue and repeat the process with the three other solutions.

What happens:

You probably sense saltiness and sweetness best at the tip of your tongue. Many people taste bitterness most at the back of the tongue and sourness at the sides.

Why:

The sensation of taste arises from the activity of clusters of cells (the *epitheliads*) that are embedded in the small bumps (the *papillae*) on the tongue's upper surface.

The taste buds in these areas contain nerve endings that respond strongly to each particular taste, and they send their messages on to the brain.

Tasting Through Your Nose

The smell of a food is as important as its taste! In fact, its smell actually influences how it tastes! If you doubt it, try this experiment.

You need:

a small peeled potato   a small peeled apple
2 spoons   a grater

What to do:

Grate part of a peeled potato and put it on a spoon. Grate an equal amount of a peeled apple and put it on a second spoon.

Close your eyes and mix up the spoons so that you're not sure which is which.

Hold your nose and taste each of the foods.

What happens:

You will have trouble telling which is which!

Why:

The nose shares the airway (the *pharynx*) with the mouth. Therefore, we smell and taste food at the same time.

Only salty, sweet, bitter and sour are pure tastes. Other "tastes" are combinations of taste and odor. Without the help of your nose, you may not be able to tell what you are eating.

Which Boils Faster—Salted or Plain Water?

What effect does salt have when you boil water?

You need:

2 small pots half full of   2 T salt
  cold water

What to do:
Add two tablespoons of salt to one of the pots of cold water. Don't add anything to the other pot. Heat both pots on the stove. Which one starts to boil first?

What happens:
The pot *without* the salt boils first!

Why:
The point at which a substance changes from a liquid to a gas is called the boiling point.

   The more salt in water, the higher the temperature must be for the water to boil. Salt molecules turn to gas at much higher temperatures than water molecules.

   So we add salt to cold water if we want our food to cook faster since it will be cooking at a higher temperature. Spaghetti and other pastas, for instance, cook well in vigorously boiling salted water. The difference in temperature between salted and unsalted water can be important when we're cooking sauces and custards that call for exact temperature or timing.

What Pot?

Does it matter what size pot we cook in?

You need:

a tall, narrow pot   a short, wide pot
2 cups of water

What to do:

Pour a cup of water into each pot. Place both pots on the stove over a medium flame.

What happens:

The water in the short pot boils first!

Why:

There is less atmosphere in the shallow pot. That means there is less air pressure keeping the molecules down and they have an easier time escaping into the air. The tall, narrow pot is under greater pressure from the air, its molecules have to work harder to escape into the air—and so its boiling point is about 1° higher.

Salt Versus the Sweet Stuff

If someone pulled the labels off identical containers of sugar and salt, could you tell which was which? There are ways to tell besides tasting them.

You need:

¼ tsp salt   2 small saucepans
¼ tsp sugar

What to do:

Place the salt in one of the pans and the sugar in the other. Heat each for a few minutes over a low flame.

What happens:

Nothing happens to one. That one is salt. The other melts and gets brown. That one is sugar.

Why:

All sugars are simple carbohydrates. They all contain carbon and hydrogen and oxygen. Heating sugar separates its molecules. At about 360°F (189°C), the sugar breaks down into water (the hydrogen and oxygen) and carbon. The carbon makes the sugar turn brown (caramelizes it). Have you ever toasted marshmallows over an open fire? Then you've seen it happen.

Freezing Salt and Sugar

Here's another way to tell whether a substance is salt or sugar!

You need:

1 T salt
2 cups food coloring—
    2 colors
1 T sugar
water
an ice cube tray with
    separators

What to do:

Fill the cups halfway with water and color each one with a few drops of a different food coloring. Dissolve the salt in one cup and the sugar in the other.

   Pour the solutions into opposite ends of an ice cube tray with separators. Put the tray in the freezer for an hour or two.

What happens:

The sugar cubes freeze. The salt cubes remain liquid.

Why:

Plain water turns into ice at 32°F (0°C). Both sugar and salt lower the freezing point of the water. But sugar molecules are heavier then salt molecules. There are more salt molecules than sugar molecules in a tablespoon. So salt lowers the freezing point twice as much as sugar.

How to Feed Celery

Plants feed us, but how do plants get fed?

You need:
a stalk of celery with its leaves
a half glass of water
1 tsp of red food coloring

What to do:
Stand the stalk of celery in a half glass of water colored with a teaspoon of food coloring. Start it off in bright light and let it remain overnight.

What happens:
The leaves turn reddish.

Why:
The celery stalk is the stem of the celery plant. It absorbs water and minerals from the soil through its root hairs by means of osmosis. Osmosis is a process by which some liquids and gases pass through a membrane—a kind of skin. The water passes into nearby cells and is carried up through its center tubes to the plant's stem and leaves.

Storing Carrots

What's the best way to keep carrots, beets and other leafy root vegetables fresh and tasty?

You need:

2 carrots with top leaves
2 carrots with top leaves
  removed

4 plastic bags big enough to store
  the carrots

What to do:
Wrap one of the carrots with leaves in a plastic bag that has air holes punched in it. Wrap one carrot without leaves the same way. Store them both in the crisper of the refrigerator.

Wrap the other carrots in a plain plastic bag without air holes and store them in the crisper too.

Observe the carrots daily for a week.

Taste each one of them.

What happens:
The carrot that tastes and looks the best is the one *without leaves* wrapped in the plastic bag with holes in it.

Why:
When the leaves are not removed from the carrots, the sap continues to flow from the root to the leaf, depriving the part we eat of some of its nutrition and flavor. In addition, the leafy tops wilt long before the sturdy roots and start to rot the carrot.

In the bag with holes in it, the air can circulate. This prevents a bitter-tasting compound (*terpenoid*) from forming.

CARROTS HATE FRUIT!

If you like your carrots sweet, it is better not to store them near apples, pears, melons, peaches or avocadoes. All of these fruits manufacture ethylene gas as they ripen. That gas also helps develop terpenoid.

No Way to Treat a Lettuce

People have been eating lettuce since ancient times. There are many kinds—Bibb, Boston, Iceberg, Romaine, Red-leaf, among others. Most of the time, we eat these leaves raw in salads, though we can cook them in a variety of ways—even into soup.

But lettuce has to be treated right!

You need:

2 lettuce leaves   2 bowls

What to do:

Tear one of the leaves into bite-size pieces and place them in a bowl.

Leave the other leaf whole and place it in a bowl.

Let both stand for an hour or so.

What happens:

The torn lettuce turns limp, while the whole leaf stays crisp.

Why:

The torn leaf exposes greater areas to the air, so more of the vegetable's water evaporates and escapes into the air. Tearing also releases an enzyme that destroys vitamin C. That's another reason why it's better not to tear lettuce until just before you serve it.

Salting lettuce in advance also makes it wilt.

Taking the Starch Out of a Potato!

What is starch? It's what people sometimes add when they wash shirts and
it is an ingredient in many medicines.
But it's also an important food!

Plants make starch from sugar
molecules in order to store food for the winter. Plants also use starch
to feed seedlings or new sprouts. The starch is stored in the seeds of corn
and wheat, in the stem in sorghum (a grain similar to Indian corn), and
in the roots or tuber (underground stem) of yams and potatoes.

How do we know potatoes have starch?

You need:

a potato (peeled)
a strainer or cheesecloth
aluminum foil
a paper towel
½ tsp flour
a grater
a bowl
a drop or 2 of tincture of iodine
½ tsp salt

What to do:

Grate a tablespoon or two of potato into a bowl. Squeeze the potato mush
through cheesecloth or a fine strainer onto a piece a piece of aluminum
foil. Pat the mush dry with a paper towel. Then apply a drop of iodine to it

Place the salt and the flour on the aluminum foil. Apply a drop of iodine to each.

What happens:

The salt takes on the light brown tint of the iodine. The potato and the flour turn blue-black.

Why:

The blue-black color tells us that starch is present. A chemical change takes place as the iodine combines with the starch. Starch is a carbohydrate, made up of carbon, hydrogen and oxygen.

In the supermarket, you may see packages labeled "potato starch." Inside is a white, powdery substance ground from potatoes by machines. Huge screens filter out the potato fiber, and the potato starch is then left to dry in large vats.

Potato starch is used to thicken sauces and gravy and to replace wheat flour in cakes, if you don't want to eat wheat.

Milking a Potato

Plants draw water from the earth by osmosis. And food gets into our cells by osmosis. We talked a little about osmosis on page 51. What is it and what does it have to do with cooking?

You need:

3 large raw potato
  cubes of the same size
3 glasses of water
a ruler
salt

What to do:

Put each cube into a glass of water. To glass #1, add a large handful of salt. To glass #2, add a pinch or two of salt. Leave glass #3 plain.

After an hour, measure the potato cubes.

What happens:

#1 will be smaller than it was; #2 will stay same size; #3 will be a little bigger.

Why:

The more salt you add to the water, the stronger the mixture (the solution) becomes. The stronger the solution, the lower its concentration of water.

Osmosis is the flow of a liquid through a membrane (a thin wall). The liquid will always flow into a stronger solution—one where the concentration of liquid is lower.

In #1, the potato cube shrinks as the water in it moves from the weaker potato juice into the (stronger) heavily salted water. In #2, where the

concentrations are equal, there is no movement. In #3, the potato juice is the stronger solution, so the water moves into its tissues and makes the cubes swell.

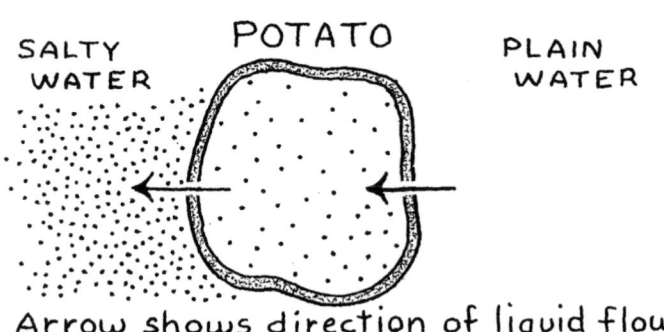

Arrow shows direction of liquid flow

Potato Treats

You need:

2 cooked potatoes, one baked, one boiled
1 tsp butter or 1 T milk
salt and pepper

½ oz (14g) cheese, sour cream or yogurt
chives or scallions

Mash one of the potatoes you've just cooked with a bit of margarine or butter or milk and season it with salt and pepper. Try the other with melted cheese, sour cream or yogurt. Sprinkle chopped chives or scallions on them for an oniony flavor and a bit of color.

If you cleaned the potatoes well, the skins will be nutritious, too. But the skin of the potato from the oven will be crisper and tastier. The slow baking dehydrates and browns it.

Why Do Some Vegetables Smell Bad?

Same nutritious—and delicious—vegetables don't always get to our plates because of their unpleasant odor!

You need:
a small turnip
a pot of water

What to do:
Peel the turnip and cut it in half. Cut one half into cubes. Leave the other half whole.

   Place all the turnip pieces in a pot of boiling water. Test each half with a fork after 15 minutes or so to find out if it is soft. Continue until both halves are firm but tender.

What happens:
The cubed turnip cooks in less than a half hour. The other half needs more time and after a half hour it begins to smell bad.

Why:
Turnips and rutabagas contain hydrogen sulfide, which smells like rotten eggs. When you cook these vegetables, you release this bad-smelling gas. The longer you cook it, the more smelly chemicals are produced and the worse the odor and the stronger the taste.

   Shorter cooking time also means that you save more of the vitamins and minerals.

Keeping of the Green

Green vegetables, such as broccoli, zucchini, spinach, green beans and peas, often come to the dinner table looking drab and unappetizing! Why?

You need:

a few broccoli stalks or
 a small zucchini
pot of boiling water

What to do:

Cut off the stem and separate the broccoli flowers. Place the flowers in a pot of boiling water. After 30 seconds, scoop out half the broccoli. Let the rest continue to cook.

What happens:

During the first 30 seconds, the broccoli turns a deep green. The broccoli left in the water loses color.

Why:

The color intensifies because gases trapped in the spaces between cells suddenly expand and escape. Ordinarily, these air pockets dim the green color of the vegetable. But when heat collapses the air pockets, we can see the pigments much more clearly.

Longer cooking, however, results in a chemical change. The chlorophyll pigment that makes vegetables green reacts to acids. Water is naturally a little acid. When we heat broccoli or zucchini or spinach, its chlorophyll reacts with its own acids and the acids in the cooking water to form a new brown substance (*pheophytin*). That's what makes some cooked broccoli an ugly olive green.

Looking Good but Feeling Rotten!

Restaurants sometimes add baking soda to a vegetable to make it look good or cook faster. Does it work?

You need:

broccoli flowers or
  zucchini strips

a pot of boiling water
1 tsp baking soda

What to do:
Place the broccoli in the boiling water and add the baking soda.

What happens:
The vegetable stays green, but after a short time it turns mushy.

Why:
Baking soda is an alkali, the chemical opposite of an acid. When it is added to the water, it neutralizes some of the acids of the water and the vegetable. Because there are so few acids, the vegetable stays green—but the alkali dissolves its firm cell wall. The vegetable tissue rapidly becomes *too* soft.

Baking soda also destroys the vegetable's vitamins. It's a high price to pay for looking good!

Cold or Hot

We always start cooking green vegetables in boiling water. Why?

You need:
broccoli or spinach
2 pots

What to do:
Place half of the broccoli or spinach in a pot half full of *cold* water. Place the other half in a pot half full of *boiling* water. Cook both until the vegetables are tender.

What happens:
The vegetable in the cold water loses more color than that in the boiling water.

Why:
Plants contain *enzymes*, proteins that cause chemical reactions. They change the plant's color and also destroy its vitamins. The particular enzyme (*chlorophyllase*) involved here is more active between 150° and 170°F (66–77°C) than at other temperatures, so less pigment is lost if the vegetables don't have to be heated through the 150–170°F range. Water boils at 212°F (100°C). If the vegetable is put into boiling water, it avoids the lower range completely.

Keeping a Lid On

How can you preserve a vegetable's color better—cooking it covered or uncovered?

You need:

broccoli or zucchini   2 pots, one with a cover

What to do:

Cut off the stalk and separate the flowers of the broccoli or cut the zucchini into quarters.

Cook half the vegetable in a large quantity of boiling water in a covered pot for five to seven minutes.

Cook the other half in a large quantity of boiling water in a pot without a lid for five to seven minutes.

What happens:

The broccoli in the uncovered pot retains its color. The broccoli in the covered pot does not.

Why:

The color changes less in the uncovered pot because some of the plant's acids escape in steam during the first two minutes of boiling. When the pot is covered, the acids turn back into liquid, condense on the lid and fall down into the water.

The bad news is that, without the lid, you lose more vitamins into the air. And because it takes longer to cook without a lid, the nutrients have more time to be drawn out of the food.

Bite or Bake?

There are hundreds of varieties of apples to choose from. Which do you bite and which do you bake?

You need:

1 Red or Golden Delicious apple   dash of nutmeg (optional)
1 Rome, York Imperial, Stayman,   water
 Winesap or Jonathan apple
2 to 3 T sugar or raisins

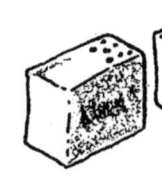 

What to do:
Core both apples and cut away a circle of peel at the top. Place them in a baking dish. Fill the center hole of the apples with sugar or raisins. Sprinkle with nutmeg. Add water to cover the bottom of the dish. Place it in a 400°F (200°C) oven for about an hour or until the apples are tender. Taste each one.

What happens:
The Delicious apple is mushy and shapeless.
    The Rome is firm and tasty.

Why:
The Delicious apple becomes mushy for two reasons. First, it lacks enough fiber (cellulose), the part of the cell wall that keeps it firm, to hold the peel intact.

Second, the Delicious apple doesn't have enough acid to counter-balance the added sugar. The apple that is less sweet remains firmer and retains more fiber. Fiber is indigestible roughage that is good for us because it helps the intestines and bowels to work better to eliminate waste products.

Of course, a raw apple contains the most fiber!

WHY ARE GREEN APPLES SOUR?

What makes unripe apples sour? Malic adid. All apples have it, but as an apple ripens on the tree, the amount of malic acid declines and the apple becomes sweeter. Depending on the soil and climate in which they are grown, some varieties stay more tart than others. Some people prefer apples like Granny Smiths, which stay green, just because they are sour.

Bursting an Apple

Suppose you *want* a mushy apple!

You need:

2 apples	pot with cover
water	¼ cup water
parer (optional)	1 tsp lemon juice or dash of
knife	cinnamon and nutmeg

What to do:

Wash both apples, peel them and cut them in four sections. Cut away the core and slice each quarter into cubes. Cook the pieces in a small amount of water in a covered pot until they are tender. Add the cinnamon and nutmeg—or the lemon juice—and cook a few minutes longer.

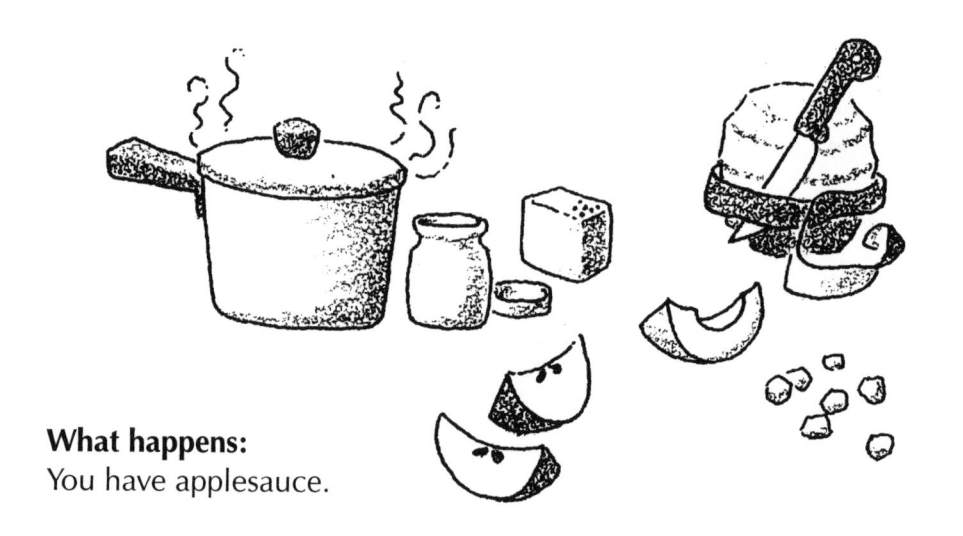

What happens:

You have applesauce.

Why:

With the peel removed, the pectin—the cementing material between cells that stiffens the fruit—dissolves. The water inside the apple's cells swells, bursts the cell walls, and the fruit's flesh softens. An apple turns into applesauce.

Apple in the Cookie Jar

An apple in the breadbox or cookie jar will affect our bread or cake!

You need:

2 cookie jars or tins   2 slices of apple
1 slice of bread   1 slice of cake (or a cookie)

What to do:

Place one apple slice in a cookie jar with the slice of bread. Place the other in the cookie jar with the slice of cake. Don't open the jars for a day or so.

What happens:

The bread gets stale—and the cake stays moist!

Why:

Sugar dissolves in water. It will absorb water from the atmosphere, if given the chance.

   The more sugary food draws water molecules from the other food. The apple has more sugar than the bread, so the bread loses water to the apple. But the cake has more sugar than the apple, so the apple loses water to the cake.

How to Ripen a Fruit

All too often, the fruit we buy is not quite ripe. What do we do with it?

You need:

2 unripe peaches, nectarines,
  or other fruit

a brown paper bag
your refrigerator

What to do:

Place one of the unripe fruits in the crisper of the refrigerator for a day or two.

Place the other in the paper bag and close it securely. Put it somewhere out of the way—on top of the refrigerator, for instance. Let it stand for a day or two.

Taste both.

What happens:

The fruit in the refrigerator softens—but it is not very tasty.

The fruit in the paper bag softens—and sweetens!

Why:

In the paper bag, you are trapping and concentrating the ethylene gas that comes from the fruit naturally. This gas speeds up the ripening process. In the refrigerator, the ethylene gas is shared with the other contents of the crisper.

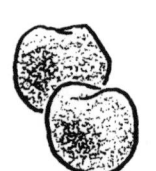 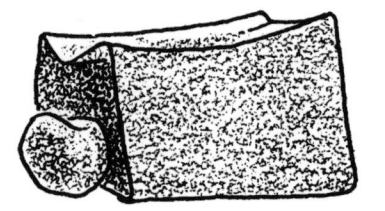

Not in the Refrigerator

Bananas are picked and shipped green, but green bananas are not digestible. You can ripen them in a few days—but is it true that you should never put bananas in the refrigerator?

You need:
2 green bananas

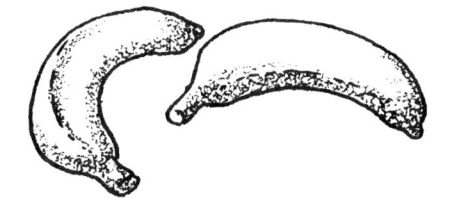

What to do:
Place one banana on the counter and one in the refrigerator.

What happens:
Within a few days the banana on the counter turns yellow and its flesh becomes soft and creamy. The one in the refrigerator blackens and its insides remain hard.

Why:
Bananas release ethylene gas naturally to ripen the fruit. On the counter, the skin's green chlorophyll disappears and reveals yellow pigments (*carotenes* and *flavones*). Also, the starch of the banana changes to sugar and the pectin, which holds the cells of the banana firm, breaks down. And so the flesh softens and is easy to digest.

   In the cold of the refrigerator, the tropical bananas suffer cell damage and the release of browning and other enzymes. The fruit doesn't ripen and the skin blackens instead of turning yellow.

   Once a banana is ripe it is safe to store it in the refrigerator. The skin may darken but the fruit inside will remain tasty for several days.

Powerful Pineapple

Gelatin is a protein that comes from the connective tissue in the hoofs, bones, tendons, ligaments and cartilage of animals. Vegetable gelatin, *agar*, is made from seaweed. Gelatin dissolves in hot water and hardens with cold. We can put all kinds of fruit in it to make terrific desserts—but we're told on the package *not* to add raw pineapple. Why?

You need:

1 envelope of unflavored gelatin
½ cup of cold water
a few bits of raw pineapple (or frozen pineapple juice)

a can of pineapple chunks
1 ½ cups of boiling water

What to do:

Stir gelatin in the cold water and let it stand one or two minutes. Then add the boiling water and stir until all the gelatin is dissolved. Pour into 2 cups or dessert dishes.

To one, add raw pineapple bits or frozen pineapple juice. To the other, add canned pineapple bits or canned juice.

Put both in the refrigerator.

What happens:

The gelatin with the canned pineapple becomes firm. The gelatin with the raw pineapple remains watery.

Why:

Pineapples, like figs and papayas, contain an enzyme that breaks proteins down into small fragments. If you put raw pineapple in gelatin for a dessert or fruit salad, this enzyme digests the gelatin molecules and prevents the gel from becoming solid. It remains liquid.

Cooking stops the enzyme from working. That's why you can add canned pineapple to the gelatin with no bad effects. Since it has been heated, it no longer contains the active enzyme.

What Is Toast?

Toast is defined in the dictionary as a slice of bread browned on both sides by heat. But what causes the bread to brown?

You need:

a toaster, an electric broiler   2 slices of bread
  or an oven

What to do:

Place the pieces of bread in the toaster, in the oven under the broiler. Let one stay in twice as long as the other.

What happens:

One turns golden brown. The one kept in too long turns black.

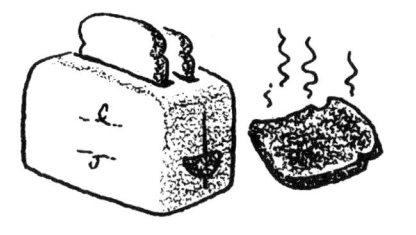

Why:

Too much heat releases the carbon of the starch and sugar. It is this carbon that makes the bread turn black.

Toasting is a chemical process that alters the structure of the surface sugars, starches and the proteins of the bread slice. The sugars become fibre. The amino acids that are the building blocks of the protein break down and lose some of their nutritional value. Toast, therefore, has more fibre and less protein than the bread from which it is made. Some nutritionists believe that when you eat toast instead of bread you are getting color and flavor at the expense of nutrition.

Science for Breakfast

Hot cereal feels good, especially on a cold morning. Does it matter whether you start it in cold or boiling water?

You need:

l½ cup water   ²/3 cup oatmeal
salt (optional)   2 small pots

What to do:

Stir ¹/3 cup of the oatmeal into a pot with ¾ cup of the water. Bring it to a boil, lower the flame, and simmer for five minutes, stirring occasionally. Cover the pot and remove it from the heat. Let the mixture stand.

In a second pot, bring the rest of the water to a boil. Add salt and pour in the other half of the oatmeal. Lower the flame and simmer for five minutes, stirring occasionally. Again, cover, remove from the heat and let the mixture stand for a few minutes.

Taste the first pot of oatmeal. Then taste the second.

What happens:
Both are cooked and taste good. The oatmeal that started in the cold water is creamier than the oatmeal that started in boiling water.

Why:
As you heat the grains, the starch granules absorb water molecules, swell and soften. Then the nutrients inside are released and are more easily absorbed by the body.

When you start cooking the oatmeal in cold water, the granules have a longer time to absorb the water. The activity starts at 140°F (60°C), well below the 212°F (100°C) boiling point. The complex carbohydrates (*amylose* and *amylopectin*) that make up the starch change. They break up some of the bonds between the atoms of the same molecule and form new bonds between atoms of different molecules. The water molecules then get trapped in the starch granules, which become bulky and eventually break, releasing the nutrients inside.

Add milk and raisins or bananas or blueberries to the oatmeal and you have a terrific dish that also furnishes vitamins, minerals and complete protein.

Why Not Eat Flour Raw?

Flour is the finely ground meal of wheat or other cereal grains. But we can't eat it raw.

You need:

1 T of sugar
1 T of flour
2 glasses half full
 of cold water

What to do:

Stir the sugar into one of the glasses of cold water.

Stir the flour into the other glass of cold water.

What happens:

The sugar disappears. The flour does not.

Why:

The sugar dissolves in the water. The grains of flour are too big to dissolve. When you stir the flour and water together, you get a paste in which each grain is hanging suspended in the water.

When you chew your food—but before you swallow it—saliva works to help you digest it. Sugar molecules separate and mix with saliva immediately.

Flour, however, is suspended in the saliva, just as it is in the glass of water. The tough wall of plant cells around each grain of flour prevents the starch molecules from getting out. Nothing can get in unless the wall is broken—neither water needed to soften the starch nor the enzymes that would digest it. Heat breaks that wall. That's why flour needs to be cooked.

CHEMICAL BUBBLES

It wasn't until the middle of the 1800s that people started using chemicals to put air into breads and cakes. Today, instead of yeast, we often use either baking soda or baking powder—sometimes both. It takes much less time to bake with them. Batters, such as those used for pancakes and certain cakes, contain much more liquid than doughs used for breads and other cakes made with yeast. These batters are so thin that slow-acting yeast can't trap enough air to make bubbles. That's why we use the modern chemicals.

About Baking Soda

Baking soda is *sodium bicarbonate*—sometimes called bicarbonate of soda. Some people use it for brushing their teeth, for absorbing refrigerator odors or as an antacid for indigestion!

But we can also use baking soda to puff up bread and cake.

You need:
2 tsp of baking soda
a glass of orange juice
  or lemonade
a glass of water

What to do:
Add 1 teaspoon of baking soda to the glass of water. Add 1 teaspoon of baking soda to the orange juice.

What happens:
Nothing happens in the glass of water.

In the glass with the orange juice, you get bubbles. You have made orange soda!

Why:
When you add an acid (orange juice) to the baking soda, you free the carbon dioxide of the baking soda—the bubbly gas.

Try adding baking soda to buttermilk, sour cream, yogurt, molasses, apple cider. They are all acidic and they will all bubble.

When baking soda is added to dough made with any of these or other acidic liquids, bubbles form and cause the dough to rise.

About Baking Powder

How is baking powder different from baking soda?

You need:

2 glasses of water   ½ tsp baking soda
½ tsp baking powder

What to do:

Add the baking powder to one glass of water. Add the baking soda to the other.

What happens:

The water with the baking powder bubbles. The water with baking soda does not.

Why:

Baking soda is an alkali, the chemical opposite of an acid. When it combines with an acid, it forms carbon dioxide.

Baking powder is a combination of baking soda and an acid. When you add baking powder to water or milk, the alkali and the acid react with one another and produce carbon dioxide—the bubbles.

There are three types of baking powder. Each one contains baking soda. In addition, they each contain an acid—either cream of tartar (tartrate baking powder), monocalcium phosphate (phosphate baking powder) or a combination of calcium acid phosphate and sodium aluminum sulfate (double-acting baking powder). More about these on page 78.

Powder Versus Soda

What happens if we add baking powder to an acid?

You need:

2 half-filled glasses of sour milk   ½ tsp baking powder
  or orange or lemon juice   ½ tsp baking soda

What to do:

Add baking powder to one of the half-filled glasses of sour milk and baking soda to the other glass.

What happens:

The sour milk with the baking powder does not bubble as much as the one with the baking soda.

Why:

When you add baking powder to an acid, you are tampering with the balance of acid and alkali. You are adding more acid than alkali. The result is that you actually reduce the amount of carbon dioxide produced.

Therefore, if you want to bake with sour milk *or* buttermilk instead of regular milk, you could do it by eliminating the extra acid. You would just replace each teaspoon of baking powder in the recipe with ½ teaspoon of baking soda.

Model Muffins

If you want light, fluffy muffins, take care to treat the batter right! See what happens if you don't!

You need:

1 cup (112 g) all-purpose
  unbleached flour
a small egg
3 T sugar
1 tsp baking powder
¼ tsp ground cinnamon
¼ tsp ground nutmeg
2 large bowls
a wooden spoon
¼ cup (60 ml) oil
½ cup (120 ml) milk
a whisk (optional)

1 small bowl
3 muffin pans
oil or margarine for greasing

What to do:
Grease the muffin pans.

Using the smaller bowl, beat the egg with a spoon or a whisk. Then add the milk and oil.

In one of the large bowls, combine the flour, sugar, baking powder, cinnamon and nutmeg. Make a hole in the center of the dry ingredients. Dump the liquid ingredients into the hole. Stir the mixture about 12 to 14 times, just enough to moisten the dry ingredients. The batter should be rough and lumpy.

Pour half of the batter into a second large bowl. Mix that batter until it is smooth.

Spoon a heaping tablespoon of the lumpy batter into one of the muffin cups so that it is ²/₃ full. At the opposite end of the same muffin pan, do the same thing with the smooth batter.

Repeat the process with the two other pans. Now you have three muffin pans, each with one muffin of smooth batter and one of lumpy batter.

Turn on the oven to 400°F (205°C). Don't preheat it; instead immediately put in one muffin pan.

After 10 minutes, put in the second pan.

In about 25 to 30 minutes, when the muffins are a golden brown, remove them from the oven. (Use pot holders!)

Then, put the third muffin pan into the hot oven and turn the heat up to 450°F (230°C). After 25 or 30 minutes, remove this pan from the oven.

Let them all cool and sample each muffin.

What happens:

The muffins from the lumpy batter in the preheated oven—pan #2—look and taste the best.

Why:

For delicious muffins, you don't need to work hard! Overmixing develops the gluten and results in knobs or peaks on the top and long holes or tunnels inside the muffins.

It is also important to preheat the oven before you put the muffins in. If the oven is not hot enough, the muffins will be flat and heavy. That's because the baking soda isn't activated soon enough to cause the batter to rise.

However, if the oven is too hot, the carbon dioxide goes to work too soon, and muffins will be poorly shaped and tough.

CHAPTER THREE
SIMPLE NATURE
EXPERIMENTS

UNDERGROUND

When you walk through a park, over a hill, or down a dusty road, you probably don't give much thought about the ground under your feet. But the ground is an important part of nature. The soil we use to grow our plants and the rocks we use to build our homes and highways are valuable in many ways.

Soil is mostly made up of rock that has been broken up into very small pieces. This sand, created over many years (hundreds of thousands), is the result of weather, erosion, and freezing and thawing. The climate and the slope of the land (hillside or river valley) also affect how fast sandy soil forms in a particular area. Soil also contains air, water, and decayed matter (known as *humus*). Basically, there are three types of soil: clay, sandy, and *loam* (a rich mixture of clay, sand, and humus that is good for growing plants).

There are also three different kinds of rocks. *Igneous* rock, such as granite, is formed from melted minerals, so it is often found near volcanoes. *Sedimentary* rock usually forms underwater, as a result of layers of material, called sediment, pressing down on other layers. Sandstone and limestone are examples of this type of rock. *Metamorphic* rock, such as marble, is formed by the great heat and pressure deep inside the Earth's surface.

The experiments here will help you learn about the soil and rock in your special part of the world.

Soak It Up

Good soil, like that in a garden, always has some water in it. Here's how to find it.

You need:
coffee can with garden soil
sheet of glass or plastic
black construction paper
tape
a sunny window or use of
  heating radiator

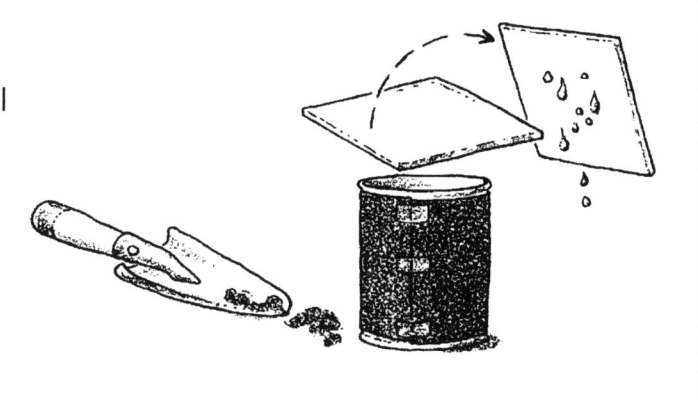

What to do:
Fill the can about one-half full of garden soil. Tape a piece of black construction paper around the can, and place the glass or plastic plate over the top. Put the can in a sunny window or on a warm radiator for a couple of hours.

What happens:
Water droplets begin to form on the underside of the lid. To prove that the water is from the soil, not the air, clean out and dry the can and repeat the experiment, but without putting in any soil. Compare the results.

Why:
All soil contains some water. How much is held by the soil depends on what else is in the soil, the outside temperature, the weather at the time, and the climate in the area—wet or dry. Soil water is necessary for plant and animal growth, but most plants will need more water (from rain, rivers, or lakes) to keep growing.

Nutrients Away

The food, or *nutrients,* in the soil can wash away when there is a lot of rain. Here's how it happens.

You need:

½ cup of dry soil
blue powdered tempera paint
  (from hobby or art store)
a measuring spoon
a measuring cup
a wide-mouthed jar
a funnel
coffee filter
cups or containers
water

What to do:

Add ¼ teaspoon of the blue tempera paint to the ½ cup of soil and mix thoroughly. Set the funnel in the mouth of the jar and put a coffee fil-ter in the funnel. Pour the soil mixture into the filter. Pour ½ cup of water into the funnel. Look at the color of the water running into the jar. Pour the water in the jar into a cup or container and put the funnel over the jar again; repeat this again with another ½ cup of water. Pour off the water, and repeat it another two or three times.

What happens:

At first, the water that flows into the jar will be dark blue in color. Each time more water is poured over the same soil mixture, the color will

get lighter. Eventually, the water will have no more blue in it and run clean into the jar. How many ½ cups of water did it take for that to happen?

Why:

The blue tempera paint you added to the soil represents the nutrients that are naturally in the ground. These nutrients are necessary for plants to grow. However, when there is a lot of rain or water runoff, these nutrients are washed away, leaving a nutrient-poor soil. Excessive rains and water runoff can remove from the soil the valuable food and minerals needed for plant growth. If you look at places in your area where a lot of soil has eroded away, you will see that there are very few plants growing there. Any plants still there are the kind that don't need much food to grow.

Deeper and Deeper

Soil is made up of different layers. Here's how you can look for them.

You need:

a small shovel or trowel   pencil and paper
magnifying glass   small sealable plastic bags
tape measure or ruler   sheets of white paper

What to do:

Find a place where you can dig a hole (be sure to ask permission first). Try to dig about 2 feet (60 cm) or so *straight down*. Notice the colors of the soil layers along the sides of the hole as you dig. Measure the distance from the surface down to the different soil layers and write it down. Place a small sample of each layer's soil in a plastic bag.

At home, put some of each sample on clean white paper. Use a magnifying glass, or a microscope, to examine the samples.

What happens:

Depending on where you live and dig, you may find one or more soil colors in layers as you dig down.

Why:

The soil near the surface is usually a dark, rich color. This layer, called *topsoil,* is the thinnest and it usually contains lots of organic matter (dead and decaying plants, insects, and animals which make up humus). Topsoil is best for growing plants and food crops. The next layer, known as subsoil, is often lighter in color and has a lot of sand and rocks in it. The last layer of soil is called the bedrock. If you dig down far enough to reach it, you will see it is the hardest layer to dig through. This is because there is no organic matter to soften it; bedrock is mostly made up of rocks, pebbles, and stones packed tightly together. (Note: Always remember to fill in any holes you make after you have finished obtaining soil samples.)

Making Bricks

You can make your own bricks using the same technique that the early pioneers did.

You need:

ground clay, or a mix of *organic* (not modelling) clay with soil	straw water a bucket

What to do:

Put some ground clay (or you own "homemade" clay), straw, and enough water to make a doughy mixture in a bucket. Mix it together thoroughly. Place portions of the mixture into moulds (frozen-vegetable packaging or small juice containers are good). Let them sit overnight in a warm place, then gently tear away the sides of the moulds and let the bricks dry in the sun for several days. Use them to build something, like a little tower or house.

From Dust to Dust

When soil is blown from one place to another by the wind, it is known as wind erosion. This is a serious problem in many parts of the world. Is it happening where you live?

You need:

stirring paddles (from paint store) double-sided sticky tape
  or wide pointed sticks felt marker

What to do:

Stick some two-sided tape on one side of several different paddles. Stick the paddle handles into the ground in various places near your home. The paddles should face in different directions—North, South, East, and West (mark the direction on the paddles). At regular intervals, once or twice every week for example, look at the paddles and record the amount of dust, dirt, or soil sticking to the tape.

What happens:

Depending on the amount of wind and the direction it blows where you live, you will see that certain paddles collect more dust and dirt than other paddles do.

Why:

More soil sticks on the paddles where wind erosion is taking place. If there are no barriers, such as trees, plants, and grass, to slow down or stop wind erosion, great quantities of soil can be swept into the air from one location and left somewhere else. One way to prevent wind erosion is to grow trees and plants to cut the wind and cover and protect the ground. This is why wind erosion is much less of a problem in dense forests than it is in the desert, which has sandstorms!

EROSION EXPLOSION

Erosion can move large quantities of soil and seriously affect the lives of plants and people. Some examples of wind or water erosion are: a sand bar in a stream or off a beach, whirling dust devils, a muddy river after a storm, sand drifted against a fence or in a gully or canyon.

Some erosion quite common in and around the home is called wear. It's caused by friction rather than wind or water. Here are some examples of wear erosion to look for:

1. Coins that are smooth from handling
2. Shoes with the heels worn down

3. An old car tire with no tread
4. A countertop with design or finish worn away

Can you list more evidence of erosion in and around your home?

Stem the Tide

Plants are important in many ways, but can they do anything to prevent or slow down soil erosion?

You need:

2 cake pans
soil
grass seed
water
a pitcher
2 books

What to do:

Fill two cake pans with soil. In one pan, plant some grass seed. Water the soil in both pans equally. Place the pan with the grass seed in a sunny location and water gently for several days. When the grass is about 3 inches (1 cm) high, place one end of each pan against a book or block of wood so that they lie at an angle. Fill the pitcher with water and pour it at the top of the first pan. Do the same thing with the pan that has grass growing in it.

What happens:

In the pan without grass, the water flows freely across the surface. Some of the dirt is carried by the fast-running water towards the bottom of the pan. In the other pan, with the grass, less soil is washed away.

Why:

The grass slows down the flow of the water over the surface and that stops much of the soil from being eroded away. You have looked at mountains or hillsides with very few plants and noticed that lots of soil has been washed away, except for rocks too big for the water to move. The use of plants helps keep soil in place and prevents erosion damage.

DID YOU KNOW?

In the United States alone, more than seven billion tons of topsoil is eroded away into streams and rivers every year. Louisiana and Hawaii are the only states that continue to grow in physical size.

About 75 percent of all the rocks on the Earth's surface are sedimentary rocks (rocks formed when small grains and particles of sediment are pressed together under tons of water for long periods of time).

Each year, the world's deserts grow by as much as 16,000 square miles (41,600 sq km).

Drip, Drip, Drip

With this experiment you'll be able to remove salt from saltwater. Let's try it.

You need:

water
table salt
a measuring cup
measuring spoons
a large bowl
a small cup
plastic food wrap
a small stone

What to do:

In the large bowl, mix three teaspoons of salt into two cups of water until it is thoroughly dissolved. Use a spoon to carefully taste a small sample of the saltwater. Set the small cup in the middle of the bowl. Cover the bowl with plastic food wrap and place a small stone in the center of the wrap (directly over the cup) to weigh the plastic down. Carefully, set the wrapped bowl, with stone in place, in the sun for several hours. Look at the wrap after a while and you will notice beads of water forming on the underside of the plastic food wrap and dripping into the small cup. Later on, remove the plastic wrap carefully and taste the water that has collected in the cup.

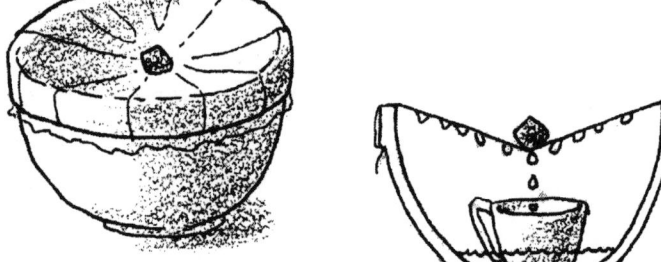

What happens:

The saltwater inside the large bowl evaporates into the air inside the bowl. It then condenses as beads of water on the underside of the plastic wrap. With the plastic covering lower in the center, the beads of water roll down to the lowest point and drip into the small cup. The water in the cup is no longer salty!

Why:

This experiment illustrates the natural process of *solar distillation*. Distillation involves changing a liquid into a gas (evaporation) by heating and then back into a liquid (condensation) by cooling the gas vapor. The sun's energy can evaporate water but not salt (salt molecules are heavier than water molecules), so the salt remains in the bowl. The water can now be used for drinking purposes and the salt can be used for food-seasoning purposes. This entire process, often referred to as *desalination* (removing salt) is used in many countries, such as those in the Middle East to make fresh water from saltwater.

Plant Requirements

Plants have certain needs for their growth and survival, just as we do.

Air To live, plants take two gases from the air. They use carbon dioxide, a natural product of animal life, to make food by a process called photosynthesis, and oxygen as fuel for the energy that helps them breathe.

Water To make their food, plants need water. Minerals in the water help plants to grow and replace damaged cells. Water is taken in through a plant's roots and is carried to the leaves.

Temperature Each plant variety requires a specific temperature range. Over many years, plants have adapted and learned to thrive where other plants could not survive. For example, a cactus or a palm tree could not live at the North Pole, where the cold temperatures would be harmful.

Sunlight Most plants, especially green leafy ones, need sunlight to grow. The light converts a plant's food into usable energy. But certain plants, such as mushrooms, don't like light and grow only in the dark.

Soil Land plants need some type of soil in order to grow. It is usually a combination of organic material (decayed animal or vegetable matter known as humus) and sand or clay that also help hold the plant erect. Plants also get nutrients, or minerals, from the soil.

Hey, What's Inside?

Did you know that inside every seed is a very small plant waiting to grow? When the conditions are right, a new plant can begin life. What does it need?

You need:
dried lima beans (from
  grocery store)
a container of water
a dinner knife
an adult, to use the knife
a magnifying glass

What to do:
Soak several lima bean seeds in a container of water overnight. The next day, choose some of the seeds and place them on a countertop or some paper. Ask an adult to use a knife to pry along the edge of the seed's coat (the hard covering of the seed) and open it up for you. (Knives, especially sharp ones, are *dangerous* and must be handled carefully.) When the two halves of the seed have separated, use your magnifying glass lens to examine the embryo in the seed (it will look like a miniature plant). You may want to look inside other seeds for their embryos, too.

What happens:
You will be able to see the three basic parts of a seed—the seed coat, the food storage area, and the embryo.

Why:

Many plants, such as lima beans, reproduce sexually—that is, a sperm cell from a male plant and an egg cell from a female plant combine in the flower of a plant and a seed begins to form. Inside the seed is a miniature plant called an embryo. There is also some food material in the seed so that a newly forming plant will have a ready food source as it begins its life. Covering the embryo and food source is a seed coat that serves as protection for the seed until the new plant is ready to start. Then, when the conditions are right (moisture and warmth), the seed *germinates,* or begins to grow. The embryo breaks out of the seed, like a chick out of an egg, and starts its life as a new plant.

Help Me Out

Do you know what seeds need to begin growing? Here's how you can find out.

You need:
36 radish seeds
6 small (sealable) plastic bags
3 paper towels
safety scissors
water
bottle of nail polish
felt-tip marker

What to do:
Label each small bag with a number. Cut three paper towels in half. Moisten three of the towel pieces with water. As directed below, place the towels in the bottoms of the bags. Drop six radish seeds into each bag and then finish setting up each bag as follows:

Bag **1**: moist paper towel (water), no light (put in a drawer or closet), room temperature.

Bag **2**: moist paper towel (water), light, room temperature.

Bag **3**: dry paper towel (no water), light, room temperature.

Bag **4**: no paper towel, water (seeds floating), light, room temperature.

Bag **5**: moist paper towel (water), no light, keep in refrigerator or freezer.

Bag **6**: moist paper towel (water), no light, room temperature, seeds covered by nail polish.

Record the date and time you began this activity and check each of the bags twice daily for any changes.

What happens:

The seeds in bag **1** and bag **2** germinate (begin to grow). You may see some small difference in the seeds in bag **4**. The seeds in the other bags do not start growing. What is wrong?

Why:

Seeds need favorable temperature, enough moisture, and oxygen to germinate. Light is not needed for germination (the seeds, after all, usually germinate underground), but light is necessary later for growth. The seeds in bag **6** can't get any air or moisture through the nail polish, so they don't germinate.

Swell Time

In order to begin the growing process, seeds need to take in water. Here's how they do it.

You need:
2 small, sealable, plastic bags
dry seeds
water
container or tray

What to do:
Fill each of the two bags with dry seeds (bean seeds work best). Finish filling one of the bags with as much water as it can hold, then seal both bags and place them outside or on a tray in a sunny location.

What happens:
After several hours, the seeds in the bag with the water begin to swell up. Eventually, the expanding seeds pop the bag open and seeds spill out all over the place.

Why:
To begin the growing process, or sprout, seeds need to take in water. Water is absorbed through the skin of the seed (seed coat), and the seeds begin to expand. Because the bag had been *filled* with the dry seeds and now all the seeds in the bag were absorbing water and expanding, there wasn't enough room in the bag. So, the expanding seeds forced the bag open and spilled out. In nature, seeds take in water and expand in the same way.

Top to Bottom

Plants need both roots and shoots in order to develop properly. To watch the growth of both plant parts at the same time, do this.

You need:
several large seeds
2 small sheets of glass or
   clear plastic
blotting paper
string
a baking pan
water
bricks

What to do:
Trim the blotter to fit the glass or plastic sheets. Wet the blotter well and lay it on top of one. Arrange some seeds on the blotter, placing them at least 2 inches (5 cm) in from the edge. Put the other clear sheet on top. Tie the "seed sandwich" together securely with string and place it on edge in the pan. Support it upright, at an angle of about 45 degrees, with one or more bricks. Pour ½ inch (1 cm) or so of water into the pan. Add more when needed, to keep the blotter wet.

What happens:
In a few days, the seeds will sprout, the shoots going up and the roots going down. Use a marker to make lines on the glass or a thin strip of masking tape to mark the daily or weekly growth of the seeds.

Why:
The seeds sprout because you have provided them with water, light and air. The roots always grow downwards and the actual plant upwards. Depending on the seeds used, you may see tiny leaves form. All seeds in nature demonstrate this same type of growth.

THE NAME GAME

How would you like to spell your name with plants? Here's how.

Fill a large flat cake pan with soil. Smooth it over so that the soil is level and moisten it with water. Using a toothpick or the end of a knife, trace your name into the surface of the soil.

Open a packet of radish seeds and carefully plant the seeds in the grooves you made for the letters of your name. (Be sure to follow the directions for proper planting depth and distance between seeds given on the seed packet.) Cover the seeds with soil and place the pan in a sunny location and water occasionally. After a few days, the radishes will sprout into the shape of your name.

Later, you may want to write your name in plants again, using different varieties of seeds (grass seed and mung bean seeds work especially well).

Water In, Water Out

Plants take in water in order to grow, but they also give off water.

You need:
a small potted plant
a clear plastic bag
water
tape or string

What to do:
Water the plant thoroughly. Place the plastic bag over the green, leafy part of the plant and close it up gently around the stem with tape or string. Place the plant in a sunny location for several hours.

What happens:
Water droplets form on the inside of the bag.

Why:
Plant leaves have tiny openings called *stomata* in them. In most plants, stomata are located on the underside of the leaves. During a plant's food-making process, air is taken in and released through these openings. Water, in the form of water vapor, is also released through the stomata into the atmosphere. You can see that water vapor, as it condenses and forms water droplets, on the inside of the plastic bag.

One of the reasons why a jungle is so humid is because of all the water vapor being released by the many trees and the vegetation in the area. The amount of water a plant loses varies with the weather conditions as well as the size and shape of its leaves.

Follow That Light

Do plants always grow towards the light? Here's a great experiment to prove that they do.

You need:
2 shoe boxes
a healthy plant

What to do:
Cut two corners of cardboard from one of
the shoe boxes. Tape the pieces
inside the other shoe box as shown.
Cut a hole in the top side. Place
a healthy plant (a growing bean plant is fine) in the bottom and place the
lid on the box. Put the closed shoe box in a sunny location. Every other
day or so, remove the lid for a moment and quickly water the plant.

What happens:
The plant grows towards the light source, even bending around the
cardboard pieces to do it.

Why:
All green plant life needs light in order to grow. Through a process
known as *phototropism,* plants grow in whichever direction is towards
the light. In your experiment, the plant grew towards the sunlight, even
though the cardboard pieces were in the way. One of the reasons we
turn our potted houseplants occasionally is so they will be able to get
equal amounts of light on all sides and grow straight. If we did not, the
plants would "lean" in the direction of the light.

Hanging On

The previous experiment showed how plants always grow towards a light source. This experiment will now demonstrate how powerful that process is.

You need:

a small potted plant with
  a strong root system

2 large sponges
string

What to do:
Carefully remove the plant from its pot (try to leave as much soil around the roots as possible). Wet the two sponges, wrap them around the root system, and tie them together with string. Turn the plant upside down (roots upwards) and hang it from the ceiling near a sunny window. Check the plant occasionally, and keep the sponges moistened.

What happens:
After a few days, the stem and top of the plant will turn and begin to grow upwards towards the light.

Why:
The leaves and stems of a plant will grow in the direction of a light source, following the process of phototropism, even if the plant is made to "stand on its head!" Also, a plant's roots will always grow downwards, trying to reach the necessary nutrients in the soil.

Hold That Mould

Would you believe that there are millions of plants growing right in your kitchen?

You need:
3 slices of white bread
3 small sealable plastic bags
water
magnifying glass

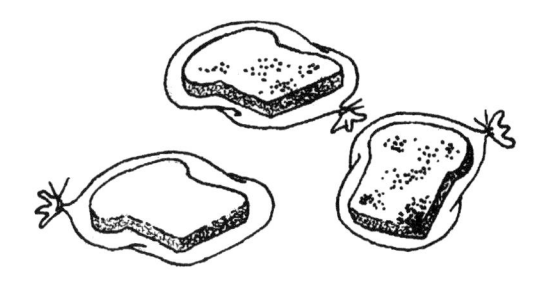

What to do:
Take *two* slices of bread and wet them lightly (don't soak them). Carefully, rub one slice across a kitchen table or countertop (do it gently so you don't tear the bread). Place the slice of bread in a plastic bag and seal it. Then take the second moistened slice and gently rub it over the surface of the kitchen floor. Put it in a second bag and seal it. Now, place the third (dry) slice of bread in the third bag and seal it. Place all three bags in a closet or other dark place for a couple of days.

What happens:
You find mould growing on the surfaces of the two slices of bread that were moistened, rubbed over the kitchen surfaces, and placed in the bags. There *may* be some mould on the "dry" slice, too (some bakeries use preservatives to keep their breads fresh longer). Examine the mouldy plants with the magnifying lens, or under a microscope. Try this experiment with other types of bread (wheat, rye) or rub slices over other surfaces (fence wall, sidewalk, tree trunk).

Why:
Moulds and other microscopic plants are everywhere. In order to grow they need special conditions, such as moisture, warmth, and *darkness* instead of light.

Feathered Friends

Birds are important members of every environment and they are fun to watch. Here's how to attract more birds to your house.

You need:
a clean plastic milk container
scissors (with pointed tips)
an adult
wild birdseed
some strong string

What to do:
Have an adult cut a panel from the side of the milk container, leaving a border around the opening. Tie the string tightly around the top, fill the container with some birdseed, and hang the new feeder in a nearby tree so you can see it from your window. Watch the birds that visit the feeder. What types of birds come to eat? How many, and at what time of day? Record your observations in a journal.

What happens:
The feeder, if kept filled with food they like, attracts all kinds of birds. A book will help to identify the species, or types, of birds that live near you. You may learn to recognize certain individual birds that return often.

Why:
Birds are affected by climate, and by the availability of food. They *adapt,* or get used to, an environment and will stay as long as they have the food, water, and shelter they need in order to live and raise their young. Offering them clean water (bird bath), a birdhouse, and pieces of string and hair during nesting season are ways to encourage birds to stay nearby.

WELL FED

In cold weather birds need to eat fat to maintain their body temperature. Here's how to help.

You need:
fat, lard, or suet (from butcher or
   supermarket)
use of stove and pot
help of an adult
birdseed
a tin can
a nail and hammer
3 feet (90 cm) of string
can-size circle of cardboard

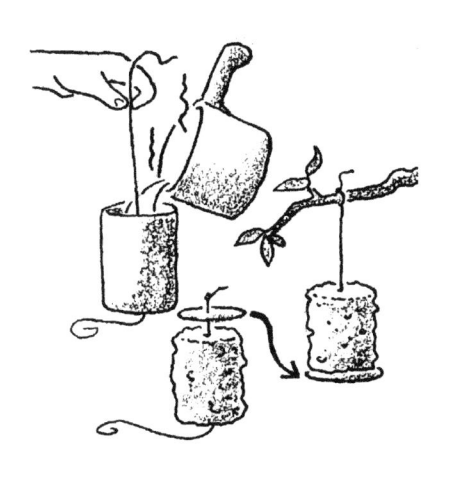

What to do:
Have an adult melt the fat or suet in a heavy pot. Then add birdseed (twice as much seed as fat) to the liquid fat and stir carefully. Let it cool and thicken slightly.

Carefully, using a hammer and nail, punch a small hole in the middle of the can bottom (an adult can help here, too) and the cardboard circle. Thread the string through the hole in the can and out the top. Pour the soft seed mixture into the can (if it is too liquid, you may have to seal the hole with clay or gum). When the fat has hardened, gently remove the can and push the string through the cardboard. Knot the string, then tie your seed feeder to a nearby tree, and watch the birds that visit it. (Experiment with other containers for different-shape feeders.)

Look Ma, No Hands!

Can you imagine how difficult it is to build a nest from things like twigs, grass, and feathers that you may find lying on the ground?

You need:
twigs
dried grasses
yarn
scraps of paper

What to do:
Take a walk around your neighborhood or park and locate several different bird's nests. Look carefully at how the nests are constructed (be careful not to disturb any occupants). Using the materials listed above (and any others you think might help you—but *no glue*!), try to build a bird's nest. Work with just your two hands and make a round nest that has room for two or three eggs.

What happens:
You discover that nest building is not as easy as it may look. Hmmm, those birds must be smart!

Why:
Birds are able to construct their nests with just their feet and beaks (no hands). And most birds seem to have learned the construction process by only seeing—from sitting inside it—what their parents once built!

It's amazing to think that bird's nests are some of the most complicated homes in the animal kingdom—homes that are able to withstand bad weather and protect young birds as they grow and develop. So, the next time anyone calls you a "bird brain," be sure to thank them for the compliment.

Creepy Crawlies

What do snails do? What do snails eat? How do snails travel? Here's how to discover the answers to those questions.

You need

live land snails   damp soil
pieces of lettuce   magnifying glass
black construction paper   cheesecloth
large wide-mouthed jar   string or rubber band

What to do:
Find some land snails from around your home (look in the moist soil of gardens in the early morning hours). Put a 2-inch (5 cm) layer of damp soil in a large clear jar and place the snails in it. Place some cheesecloth over the jar opening and fasten it down securely with string or a rubber band to keep the occupants inside (snails can crawl up glass).

Sprinkle the soil every so often to keep it wet. Keep the jar in a cool shady place. Put in some pieces of lettuce every so often. You will be able to keep and observe the behavior of the snails for several days.

Move one or more of the snails to a sheet of black construction paper to see it better. Place a snail in the middle of the sheet and surround it with bits of food—a slice of apple, a lettuce leaf, a piece of celery, some cereal—and watch what happens.

What happens:
The snails leave trails behind them on the paper as they slowly move towards the kind of food they prefer. Did you turn one over to see how it moves over the paper?

Why:
As snails travel using only one foot that pushes them along, they produce and leave a trail of mucus behind them. This mucus protects them from sharp rocks and other harmful objects they travel over in their environment. (A snail can even travel over a razor blade without hurting itself.) Most snails enjoy eating food that has a lot of moisture, such as fresh leaves and other vegetation. That is why they are considered a pest by home gardeners.

Worm World

Would you be surprised to learn that earthworms are some of the most useful animals to human life? Be prepared to be surprised.

You need:
large wide-mouth (pickle) jar
tin can
gravel or small pebbles
soil
5 or 6 earthworms (from a garden,
  bait shop, pet store, or garden
  supply store)
dark construction paper

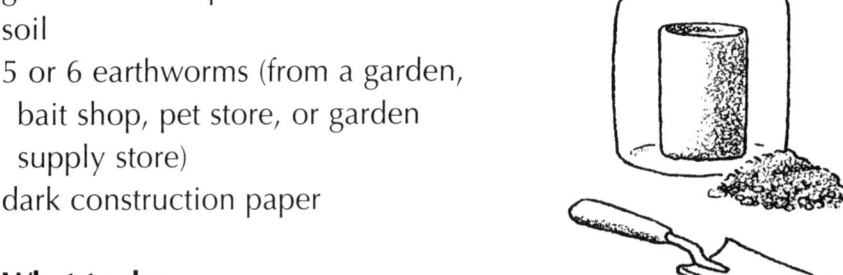

What to do:
Stand the tin can in the middle of the jar. Place a layer of gravel or small pebbles about ½ inch (1.5 cm) deep on the bottom of the jar, between the can and the jar sides. Fill the jar with garden soil up to the height of the tin can. Place the worms on top of the soil.

Wrap the dark construction paper around the outside of the jar to keep out the light. (Note: Check the condition of the soil every so often and moisten it as needed.)

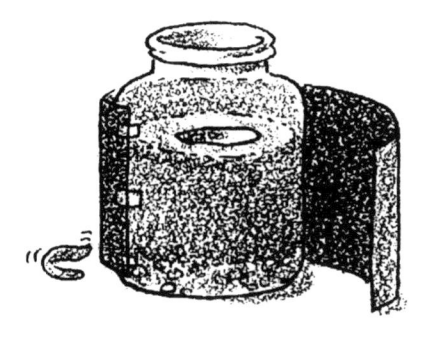

What happens:

The worms will begin burrowing into the soil. After several days, they will have dug a series of tunnels. You will be able to see these tunnels by carefully removing the construction paper from the sides of the jar. (Replace the construction paper after observing their work so the worms will continue to tunnel in the darkness.) You should be able to watch the worms' behavior, without harming them, for three or four weeks, but then you should put them back outside.

Why:

Worms feed by taking soil through their bodies, creating tunnels as they go. These tunnels *aerate* the soil—providing plants with the oxygen they need to grow. If it weren't for earthworms, many varieties of plants would not be able to survive. Farmers consider earthworms some of the best "friends" they have.

Mealworm Magic

Here's an animal you don't think about much, but you can keep in your home for a good while and maybe see some strange things.

You need:

mealworms, from any pet store (they usually come in large or small sizes)

a plastic shoe box (from variety or department store)

bran
flour
bread
apples

What to do:

Fill the plastic shoe box about two-thirds full with a mixture of bran, flour and small pieces of bread. Place 20 to 25 mealworms in the box and put on the cover. Lift the cover every few days, or have an adult drill several small holes in the lid to let some air in. Keep the box in a warm location—between 75 and 80°F (24 and 26°C). Put in a slice of apple and replace it with a fresh piece every few days.

What happens:

That depends on how long you keep and watch your mealworms and just how old they are.

Why:

The mealworm is the larval stage (part of the life cycle) of the darkling beetle. The *larvae,* which are young mealworms, grow for about six months. They then turn into *pupae,* a stage which lasts for about three weeks. Afterwards, the adult beetles emerge from the cocoon. The cycle is then repeated (male and female beetles mate, eggs are laid, the eggs hatch into mealworms, the mealworms turn into pupae, the pupae turn into adult beetles). You can watch each stage of insect growth (egg, larvae, pupae, adult) by looking though the sides of the plastic box or carefully sifting through the bran mixture with your fingers. The bran provides the nourishment these animals need, and the apple slices provide the necessary moisture.

Mealworms are raised primarily to serve as a food source for other animals (lizards and salamanders love them). They are a big part of many environments, living deep within the soil. By adding to the bran mixture and replacing dried-out apple slices, you can keep your "colony" of mealworms for some time. Later, you may want to release them to a new home, a warm and moist area near a rotting log, for example.

Sea Shrimp at the Seashore

Brine shrimp, though tiny, are some of the most amazing animals! Let's grow some.

You need:
brine shrimp eggs (from
  a pet store)
kosher or non-iodized salt
2-quart pot or container
water
teaspoon
medicine dropper
hand lens or
  inexpensive microscope
aged tap water
  (see below)

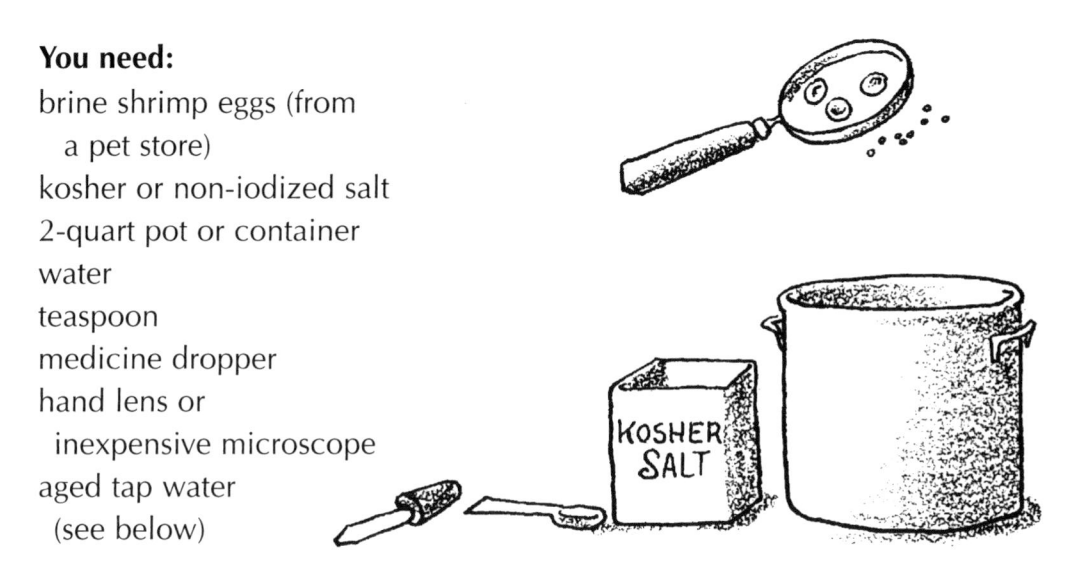

What to do:
Fill the pot with 2 quarts of water and allow it to sit for three days, stirring it occasionally. (Most city water has chlorine in it, which would kill the shrimp. By letting it "age" for a while, the chlorine gas can escape from the water.) Dissolve five teaspoons of non-iodized salt into the water. Add ½ teaspoon of brine shrimp eggs to the saltwater and place the pot in a warm spot. Use the medicine dropper to remove a few eggs from the water, and observe them with your hand lens or microscope. Examine a drop of water every day. You can draw a series of illustrations in your journal to record the growth of your brine shrimp.

What happens:

The brine shrimp eggs begin to hatch in about two days. They will continue to grow in the water until they reach their adult stage. You can watch this growth process over a period of many days.

Why:

The brine shrimp eggs purchased at a pet store are the fertilized eggs of very tiny animals known as brine shrimp. The eggs you buy are dried so that they can be stored for very long periods of time (especially when kept in a dry place). When these eggs are placed in saltwater, however, they "wake up" and begin to grow. Although they are very small, you can watch them grow for many days.

(Note: Brine shrimp eggs are sold as food for aquarium fish.)

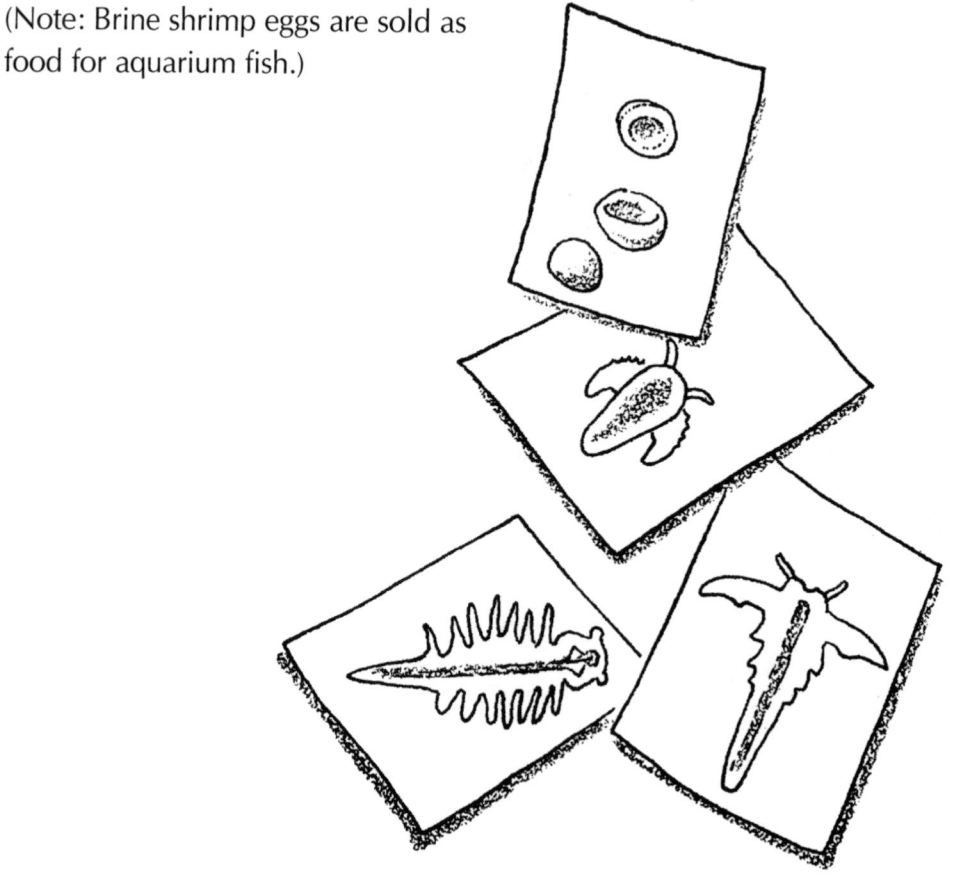

Bag of Bananas

Decomposition, the natural decay of dead organisms, is a continuing process in nature. You can learn about it by doing this experiment in your own home.

You need:
4 plastic (sealable)
  sandwich bags
a banana
a knife
2 packets of yeast
water

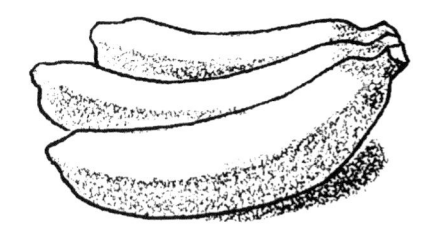

What to do:
Label each one of the four bags: "A," "B," "C," and "D." In Bag "A" put several slices of banana; in Bag "B" put several slices of banana and a packet of yeast; in Bag "C" put several slices of banana and some water; and in Bag "D" put several slices of banana, some water, and a packet of yeast. Seal all the bags and place them on a sunny windowsill for a few days.

What happens:
The banana slices in bag "A" darken slightly. The yeast in bag "B" grows very slowly, but there is some change in the banana slices. The slices in bag "C" show some decay and some mould. The banana slices in bag "D" show the most decay. In that bag, the banana is breaking down. The liquid is bubbling, and carbon-dioxide gas is forming and expanding the bag. The bag may pop open and release a powerful odor into the room.

Why:

When plant and animal life die, they serve as a valuable food source for *micro-organisms*. These micro-organisms feed on the dead materials and break them down. Yeast is made up of millions of such micro-organisms that grow under the right conditions: when moisture, food, and warmth are present. As they grow, the micro-organisms in bag "D" break down the banana slices.

The same process takes place in nature. As a result, micro-organisms can reduce large animals and plants into valuable nutrients for the soil. In other words, when an organism dies it provides what other organisms need in order to live.

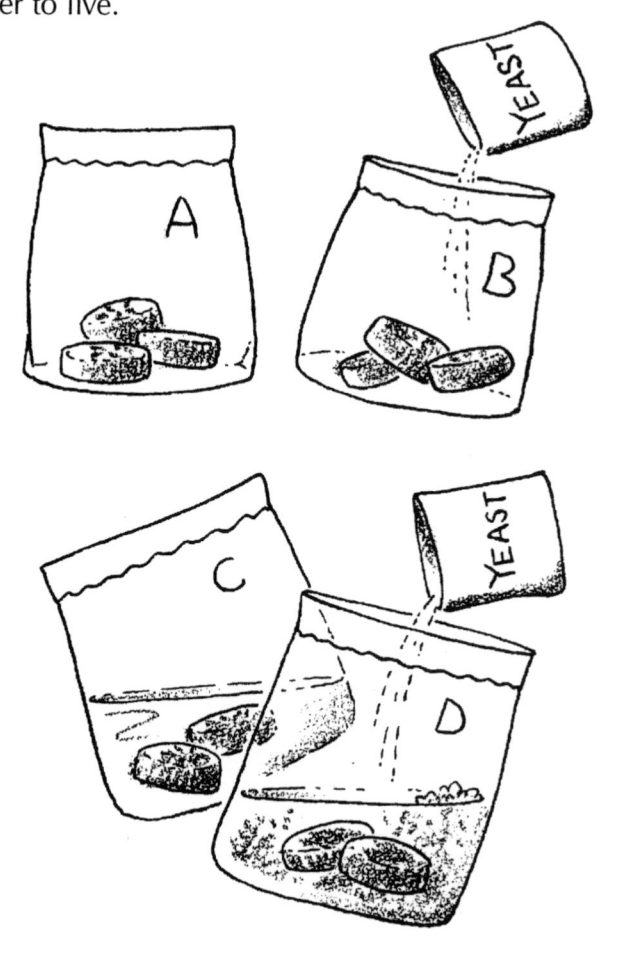

It's Absolutely Degrading!

Do you know what the word "biodegradable" means? Here's how you can find out about this continuing process and how it works.

You need:
a slice of fruit (apple, orange, peach)
a slice of bread
a piece of lettuce
a plastic or styrofoam cup
a piece of aluminum foil
a shovel
water
ice-cream sticks
pencil or felt marker

What to do:
Find a place in your or a friend's yard where you can dig some small holes for this experiment. Dig five holes, each about 8 to 12 inches (20–30 cm) deep. Place the fruit slice in one hole, the bread in another hole, the lettuce in another, the cup in the fourth hole, and the foil in the last hole. Cover each hole with soil and water each one thoroughly. Place a marker stick saying slice, bread, lettuce, cup, or foil (or anything else you are testing for boidegradability) at the location of each hole. After 4–5 weeks, return to the filled holes and dig up what you buried.

What happens:
The fruit, bread, and lettuce have probably "broken down" or disintegrated (in fact, you may find it difficult to even locate these items). The rate at which these items have biodegraded depends on the amount of moisture in the soil and the soil's temperature. The cup and the piece of foil, however, will be whole and easy to locate.

Why:

When organic matter (fruit, bread, lettuce, even dead plants and animals) is left on or in the soil, it starts to "break down." This natural (and constant) biodegrading process caused by micro-organisms releases nutrients into the soil so that other organisms can grow. The cup and the foil are *not* biodegradable, the micro-organisms can't affect them, so they will never decompose. Landfills are filled with lots of non-biodegradable materials that take up valuable space without returning anything to the environment.

Eggs Over Easy

Pollution is a problem all over the world. Let's take a look at one specific pollution problem: oil.

You need:

motor oil (used works best)
water
4 plastic bags (sealable)
masking tape and felt marker

4 hard-boiled eggs
watch or timer

What to do:

Label the four bags "A", "B," "C," or "D." Fill each bag with ½ cup of water and ½ cup of motor oil. Place a hard-boiled egg in each bag. Remove the egg from Bag "A" after 15 minutes; remove the egg from Bag "B" after 30 minutes; remove the egg from Bag "C" after 60 minutes; and remove the egg from Bag "D" after 120 minutes. Each time you remove an egg from a bag, carefully open and peel off the egg shell.

What happens:

The eggs in the oil-polluted water the longest showed the most pollution. The egg in bag "D," for example, had more oil inside its shell than the bag "A" egg.

Why:

When an oil tanker accident spills oil into the water, the oil slick that forms affects all manner of living things. The oil sticks to the bodies and surfaces of birds, plants, fish, and other aquatic creatures and prevents them from doing what they do naturally. (Birds cannot use their wings or fly, fish cannot breathe, and plants cannot carry out the process of photosynthesis.) The longer the oil remains on the organism, the more damaging it is. Many living things die as a result of oil spills.

OIL CHANGE

Repeat the "Eggs Over Easy" experiment on page 121, but this time also put ½ cup of liquid detergent into each bag. Shake each bag gently and allow it to stand for the designated time. Notice what effect the liquid soap has on the pollution of each hard-boiled egg.

For another variation, put the ½ cup of detergent into each bag just before you remove the eggs. While the soap might remove some of the oil pollution from the outside of the eggs, does it have any effect on the eggs themselves?

Not in My Air!

Do you know if there is air pollution in your area, and how much? Here's a way to find out.

You need:
petroleum jelly (such as
  Vaseline®)
3 index cards
masking tape

What to do:
Smear a thin layer of petroleum jelly on one surface of each of the three index cards. Tape two of the cards in different locations outside. For example, one card can be taped to the side of your house and the other hung from the tree branch in your backyard. Or, one card can be taped to a mailbox and the other to a garage door. The third card should be taped someplace *inside* your home. Check the cards every week or so to see how much *particulate matter* (dust, odd bits and pieces of material, pollen, and other small particles that float in the air) have collected on them.

What happens:

After same time (depending on where you live) you will find that the two cards placed outside have collected a good amount of particulate matter (the one placed inside the house may have considerably fewer particles on it). The amount of matter collected on the two outside cards indicates the amount of pollution that is in your air, and that you are probably taking into your lungs as well. (Do this air test several times throughout the seasons, to see if pollution is better, or worse, at some times than at other times.)

Why:

Air pollution is a serious concern in many industrial areas. Factories, trucks and cars, and incinerators are just a few of the causes of air pollution. The polluting particles, often very small, can affect the environment nearby and far away (blown great distances by the wind). The pollutants settle on the ground and on buildings, and sometimes we inhale them into our lungs. Your cards will show you how serious the air pollution is where you live.

CHAPTER FOUR
SIMPLE EARTH
SCIENCE EXPERIMENTS

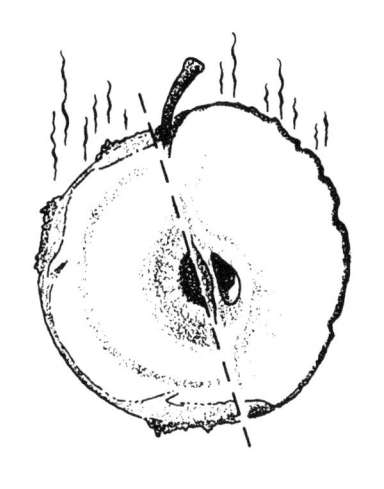

WORLDLY MATTERS

The Earth—a huge ball with an outer crust, inner mantle, and core—travels through space, as do the sun, stars, and other planets. Besides this movement through space, the surfaces of the Earth are also changing constantly. High mountains and deep valleys, both on the land and under the oceans, are all part of the Earth's movement—nothing stays the same. Think of the Earth as an apple sitting in the sun. As the sun warms and dries the apple, its water is lost and the apple shrinks and wrinkles.

While the Earth is not an apple, it undergoes similar changes. The Earth, like the inside of the apple, shrinks or contracts. As the hot interior parts of the Earth cool and shrink, the outside covering is forced to move. The apple's surface makes wrinkly peaks and valleys and, similarly, the Earth's crust forms mountains, valleys, and breaks or cracks called faults.

In this chapter, we'll take a look at some of the forces that affect our Earth, as well as other worldly matters.

Tsunami: It'll Tide You Over

If you receive some money when you're very broke, we say it will "tide you over" or help you out until you get paid. But a *tsunami*, a Japanese term for great ocean waves, will really tide you over . . . tidal wave, that is!

In this activity, you can create conditions that will produce your own tsunami wave, then you'll understand much better how they are formed and the forces and dangers that these giant tidal waves produce. This is a great experiment for a hot summer day because it's likely you will get very wet! So either wear your old clothes, or be very careful.

What to do:

You need:

a deep aluminum or other baking pan	water
	2 blocks of wood

Fill the pan with water and place the blocks of wood in the bottom of the pan so they are completely below the surface of the water. The object of this experiment is to rapidly compress, or squeeze, the water between the blocks. So, take hold of the blocks and quickly bring them together. Do it again, and again. Continue this squeezing action until the blocks can no longer compress the water.

What happens:

The movement of the two blocks coming together rapidly under the water forces swells of water to the surface, where they form waves that splash over the sides of the pan.

Why:

The action of the blocks and the water in this experiment is similar to the conditions in the ocean depths that produce tsunami tidal waves. Great earthquakes and volcanic forces on the ocean floor cause large amounts of ocean water to be compressed, or squeezed together, and pushed to the surface. There, great walls of water are formed and threaten nearby coastal cities. These great tidal waves sometimes reach heights of 50–100 feet (15–30 m). Because they form so suddenly and without warning, they are extremely dangerous and often kill many people.

Photoplay: Say Cheese!

Light energy from the sun is so important that without it there would be *no life on Earth!* Still, we can put this great energy to use right now by making a simple but exciting pinhole camera. It uses light rays from the nearest star—our own sun, Sol—and is one of our brightest ideas. So get ready, set, and smile and say "Cheese!"

You need:

shoebox with lid

black tempera paint (available from craft, hobby, drug, or variety store)

brush

piece of wax or tracing paper cut into a 3 x 5 inch (7 x 12 cm) rectangle

scissors

tape

What to do:

Prepare your camera by painting the insides and the lid of the shoebox with black paint.

Cut a 2 x 4 inch (5 x 10 cm) opening in the middle of one end panel of the shoebox and tape a larger piece of tracing or wax paper over it. You should now have a screen on one side of your pinhole camera.

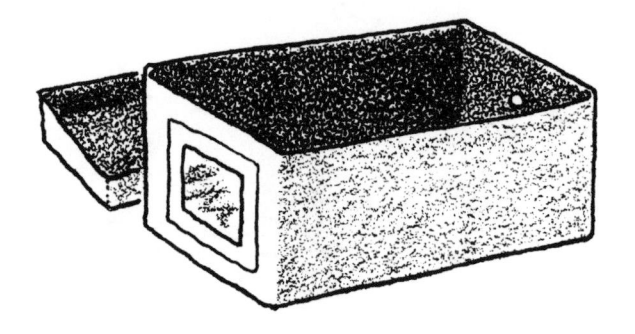

At the other end of the box, again in the middle of the panel, care-fully punch a small ³⁄₈ inch (½ cm) hole in the side with the scissors.

Now you are ready for action. Take your camera outside, find a sunny location, and place something—a friend, toy, or object—in front of it. Point the pinhole side of the camera towards the object, and keep the screen in position in front of you for viewing.

See "Picture Perfect: Watch the Birdie!" for picture-perfect images.

What happens:

When you aim the small opening of the pinhole camera at something, a fuzzy but noticeable, upside-down image of that object appears on the screen.

Why:

The image or picture on the pin-hole camera is reversed because light normally travels only in straight lines. Light rays from the top part of the image are reflected to the bottom part of the screen while rays from the bottom part of the image fall on the top.

129

PICTURE PERFECT: WATCH THE BIRDIE!

To view a perfect picture, or image, through your pinhole camera, place a covering over your head. Wrap it around your head and the screen so that it is completely dark; no light is able to get in. (This may remind you of photographers long ago, with their big cameras on tripods, who had to cover their heads with large dark cloths attached to the cameras in order to take pictures.)

Find something or someone (your subject) in the light while looking through the screen held before your face. A part of a house or a person at sunset is a perfect image. Move the camera away from your face, up or down, closer or farther until the object is in view. Take your time—it may take several trials to adjust your eyes to the dark, get enough light into the box, and find the object, but you will eventually succeed.

I Steam Cone

This is one treat you can't eat, but you and your friends will love. In this great party-trick experiment, you'll build a different type of volcano based on earth science and chemistry—it's definitely something to get all steamed up about! It's simple, easy and you won't need a lot of materials. So, what are you waiting for? Get going and dig in! (Caution! Throw away all chemical solutions and thoroughly wash out all containers when finished.)

You need:

strip of lightweight cardboard, 3 x 8 inches (8 x 20 cm)
small container (spice jar or vitamin bottle)
flat tray or pan
½ tablespoon quick-rising yeast
½ cup hydrogen peroxide
scissors
paper clip or tape
spoon

What to do:

With the cardboard strip, form a cone shape that will fit over the mouth of the small container and fasten it with the paper clip or tape. Cut the end corners off so the cone will stand upright in the tray or pan. Place the small bottle or jar in the tray and get ready for action.

The jar or bottle should be large enough to contain the hydrogen peroxide but fit under the cardboard cone or extend slightly above the cone's mouth. With the cone over the small container, pour in the hydrogen peroxide followed by the quick-rising yeast. Stir the mixture thoroughly. (If easier, you may place the cone over the bottle *after* stirring, but you must be quick!) Continue to stir the mixture, for best results, until the experiment is finished.

What happens:

The mixture of hydrogen peroxide and yeast causes foam, steam, and a hissing noise to come from the cardboard "volcano."

Why:

The ingredients placed in the container under the cone produced a chemical reaction, or change. It is called exothermic because, in addition to foaming, steaming, and hissing, heat is given off. If you touch the rim and sides of the container, or the stirring spoon especially if it is metal, you can feel this warmth.

In a real volcano, hot melted rock called magma, deep within the Earth, erupts or shoots through fissures or cracks. This moving rock, known as lava, sometimes flows from openings in the volcano's sides, or explosively shoots or blows out steam, smoke, ash, and rocks. Although your model volcano is small and simple, it does give you a good idea how a real volcano erupts.

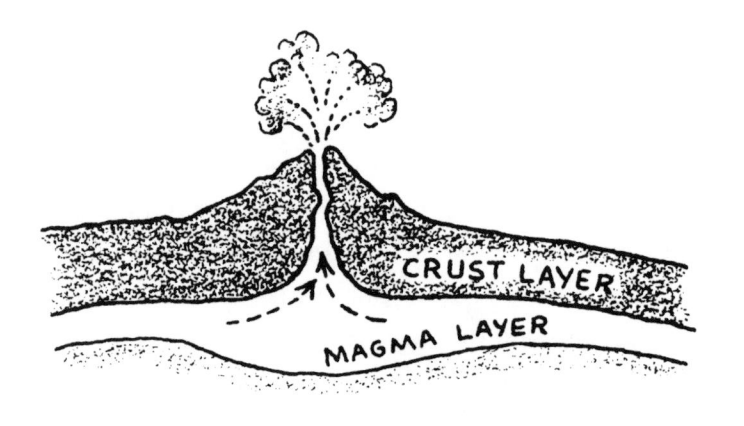

An Earth-Shattering Experience

Limestone caves are hollowed out by rainwater that is slightly acid and, over thousands of years, has gradually, eventually, and greatly dissolved away the soft rock.

You need:

a piece of chalk   small jar
½ cup vinegar

What to do:

Place the piece of chalk in the jar with the vinegar for five minutes.

What happens:

The chalk instantly dissolves in the vinegar solution, or acetic acid.

Why:

School chalk is a form of limestone, or calcium carbonate. It is made up of small bits of seashells and the mineral calcite and is similar to the soft rock caves of limestone. These caves have been formed by the rock that has been dissolved by the acids in rainwater, similar to the chalk that is dissolved by the vinegar (acetic acid). England's famed White Cliffs of Dover are made up of great sheets of chalk, a form of calcium carbonate.

Shell Shock

Replace the chalk with a few seashells, another form of calcium carbonate and limestone, and see how fast or completely they dissolve.

You need:
some seashells
2 small jars
½ cup vinegar
½ cup water
newspaper
spoon

What to do:
Place some seashells in a jar with the vinegar, and a few in a jar with the water (as the control, for comparison). Let the shells sit in the solutions for three to four days.

Remove the shells from the jars, place them on newspaper on a counter or worktable, and carefully try to break them with the spoon.

What happens:
The shells from the jar of water remain the same, while the shells placed in the vinegar should break and crumble quite easily. They will also be covered with a white chalky substance (calcium carbonate).

Why:
The shells in the water are the experiment's control, to be compared against those in the other jar that were affected by the vinegar. Again, there is acid in rainwater as there is acid in vinegar. Acid will dissolve calcium carbonate whether it is in the form of cave rock, chalk, or shells. In some areas of the world, the rain is as acid as vinegar.

Glacier Melt

You can learn a lot about glaciers by making a model of one. It's best to do this outside. Adult help may be needed.

You need:

a small cup or yogurt container
sand
small rocks or pebbles
water
freezer

piece of board, to
  make incline or slant
hammer and nail
a thick rubber band
watch

What to do:

Place a one-inch (2.5cm) layer of sand and gravel in the cup, followed by a few inches of water. Place it in the freezer. When frozen solid, repeat the process, adding sand, gravel, and water, then freezing. The cup should be filled to the top.

Next, carefully hammer a nail partway into the middle of one end of the board. Place that end against something immovable to form an incline or slant. Now you are ready.

Remove your model glacier from the freezer. Warm the sides of the container under warm tap water just enough to get your model glacier to slide out when tapped. With the rock/sand-side down, place the glacier at the top of the incline and fasten the rubber band around its middle and around the nail. How long will it take your glacier to melt, move, and leave rock and sand deposits? Time it.

What happens:

Depending on the weather, melting should begin immediately, even on cooler days. Rock and sand deposits will fall off in clumps, some will

slide down the board, while other separate bits and pieces will form along the board surface in strange patterns, much like moraine or glacial matter.

Why:

Glaciers are large masses of ice that move down mountainsides and valleys cutting further gouges out of the rock and soil. Deposits from glacier movements can be found in such places as the Arctic, Antarctica, Alaska, and Greenland.

These giant masses of ice would not move at all if it weren't for the great pressures they also exert. The force of these pressures causes periods of heating, and melting. The ice refreezes, but just enough thawing occurs to cause the slipping movement.

As glaciers move, they break off and pick up tons of rock and soil and deposit it someplace else. The unusual rock formations or deposits left behind are called moraine. Like the real thing, our miniature-glacier experiment shows us how and why those rock and sand deposits are so unusual and often unevenly placed.

Track Star

Our sun, a star, is a giant ball of hydrogen gas many million of miles away. Yet it is possible to learn something about the sun from tracking, or following, the wavelengths of light coming from it. This can be done in a simple way.

You need:

glass tumbler half-filled
  with water

sheet of paper
sunny outdoor location

What to do:

Find a place outside in full sunlight for your experiment. Place the sheet of paper on a table or lay it on the ground where the experiment is to be done.

Now, hold the glass with the water firmly between the thumb and a finger over the sheet of paper. The glass should be held about three to four inches (7–10 cm) above the paper. Do not hold the glass in the usual way, around the glass. It's important that you hold the glass so that your hand does not block the sides of the glass.

Be careful not to drop or break the glass or you can cut yourself.

Move the glass up and down and slant it slightly, focusing the light on the paper until a clear colorful pattern is noticed.

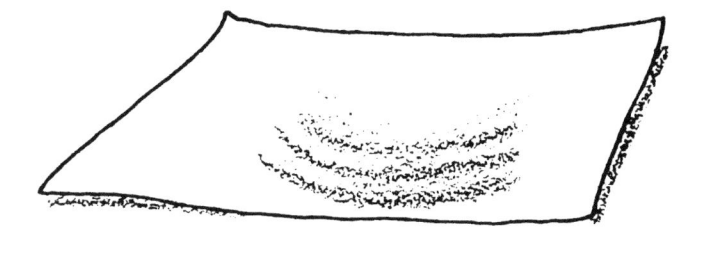

What happens:

The glass of water acts as a prism and casts a rainbow on the paper.

Why:

A glass of water is able to act as a prism, or something that can change the direction of light so the bands of color in it can be seen and studied. White light is really a combination of many colors.

When a wavelength of light is split and changed by the glass of water, color occurs. Light from the sun shows many colors. Astronomers can tell what elements or gases make up a star by studying the bands or spectrums of the light it gives off.

GLASSIFY

Do different types of glass make better prisms for casting rainbow patterns on paper?

Do the same experiment as above, but instead use a different-size glass, then one with a different shape. What about colored glass? Will glasses made of colored glass refract, or split, light into colors, too? Will a full glass of water work better than half a glass?

Do a variety of experiments and write down your observations and results. When you're finished, you'll know just what glass works best.

Highly Focused

The seasons of the year depend on the tilt of the Earth and the concentration of sunlight at different times of the year in the northern and southern hemispheres. This simple experiment explains it all.

You need:

watch or clock

flashlight or electric lantern

thermometer

can or other support
 for thermometer

paper and pencil

What to do:

Record the temperature on the thermometer. Run the thermometer under warm or cool water to get the temperature where you want it, so that it is easy for you to record and calculate.

Prop the thermometer, glass side outward, against the lighted end of the flashlight. Leave it in that position, timing it with a clock or watch, for three minutes. Record the final temperature.

After the first reading against the flashlight, hold the thermometer under cool water until the temperature returns to what it was at the beginning of the first trial.

Now, lean the thermometer against a support to hold it upright and shine the flashlight on it from a set distance away, say one foot or 30 centimeters. Again, record the reading after three minutes.

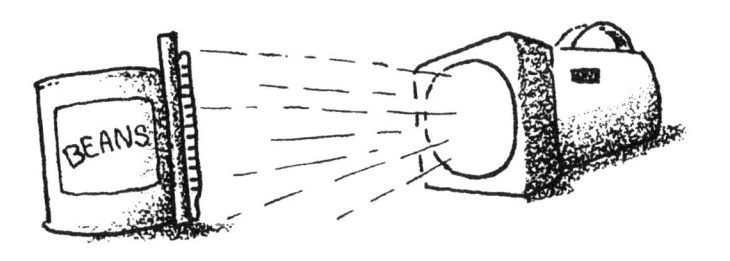

What happens:

The thermometer leaning against the flashlight and in direct contact with the light, so it was more concentrated or had greater strength, registered a few degrees warmer. No noticeable change was seen when the light was shined on the thermometer from a short distance.

Why:

The concentration of light on various parts of the Earth, at any one time of year, is similar to the concentration of light in our experiment.

The greater an area covered by light, the less the temperature. In our experiment, the thermometer that was farther away from the light was not affected by it as much, if at all.

The northern hemisphere, or upper half of the Earth, which is tilted away from the sun in December receives a greater spread of light, while the southern hemisphere, or lower half of the Earth, is tilted towards the sun at that time and receives stronger, more concentrated light. This explains why, in December, it is winter in New York City and summer in Sydney, Australia.

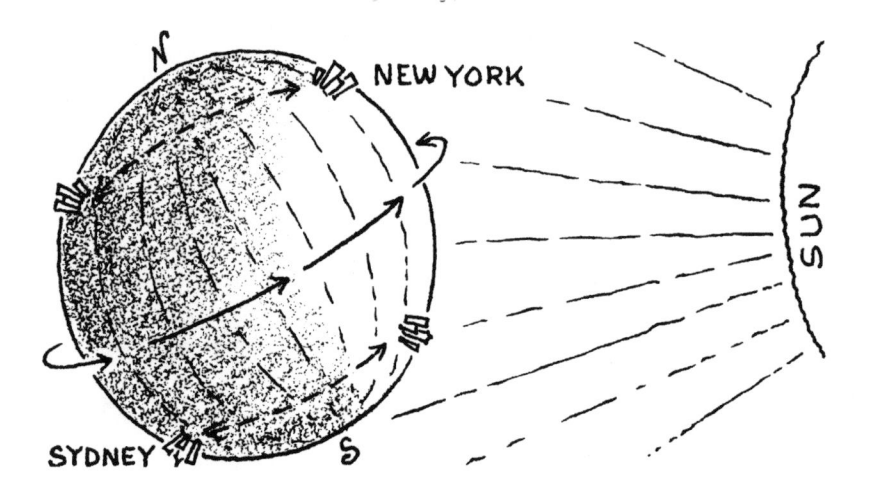

SOIL, BY ANY OTHER NAME, IS STILL DIRT

Scientists have identified four different kinds of soil according to how it feels (texture) and what it contains. The types of soil are sand, silt, loam, and clay.

Sand in made up of broken shells and worn-down bits of rock and minerals such as quartz and basalt, a volcanic-like rock. Although all good soils need sand, too much of it can cause too much water to drain away from plant roots, leaving them to dry and shrivel up. Sand is found in deserts, on beaches, and along river bottoms. Larger grains are called gravel.

Silt, on the other hand, is a very fine-grained, sandy soil. Its parts are smaller than sand but larger than particles of clay.

Clay is a fine soil and it is much needed in all soils. Without it, soils fall apart and fertilizers are washed away. Too much clay in any soil, however, will cause problems with water drainage and eventually produce rotted roots in plants.

The best type of soil for most plants is loam. Loam is a mixture of clay, sand, and silt with enough humus (broken-down plant and animal matter) to make it rich and fertile.

SAND SILT CLAY + = LOAM

Earthshaking Discovery: It's Sedimentary!

The sediment, or different types of soil particles, and how they float and settle, are bound to be unusual and interesting. Just shake up these soil-shakers and watch out.

You need:

jar(s) with lids (depending on how many soil samples you wish to test)

½ cup each soil sample from different locations and depths (topsoil or upper soil vs. subsoil or deeper soil)

water
magnifying hand lens
paper and pencil

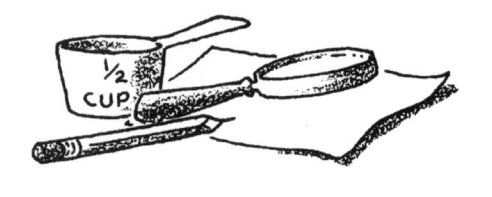

What to do:

Fill the jar with the dirt and add water. The jar should be about three-fourths filled. Screw the lid on the jar tightly and shake well. Repeat the procedure with any other soil samples to be tested.

Be patient and wait about two hours for the soil to settle. (You could sit and watch, but you don't have to.) Then, with the hand lens, observe what happened to the soil samples. Draw a picture of the settled sediment in each jar.

What happens:
The soil in the jar(s) settles into bands or layers depending on the content of the soil.

Why:
In sandy mixtures, heavier, rock-like particles settle first, followed by light-colored silty, sand-like grains.

In most loamy gardening topsoils, the heavier, gravel mix settles to the bottom, while the dark-colored, lighter-in-weight humus floats to the top of the jar. As you can see, this is a good test for determining good, loamy, rich soils.

What now:
Collect soil samples while out of state during long car trips and vacations and discover how much humus and kinds of soil are in each sample. If you're careful, you can keep your dirty secret and still find out what kind of dirty state you're in.

Air Condition

What if you can't *see* what condition the soil is in?

You need
a small jar
½ cup dirt
a cup of boiled and cooled water
magnifying hand lens

What to do:
Place the soil sample in the jar. Pour the cooled, boiled water slowly onto the soil and watch closely.

What happens:
Air bubbles appear and circle the top surface of the soil.

Why:
All dry soil contains air trapped in and around the particles. The bubbles that rise from the soil's surface are formed by air forced from the soil by the water.

Water also normally contains its own air, which is why, for this experiment, it is necessary to use boiled and cooled water. During the boiling, the heated air in the water is boiled away. This experiment, then, reveals that it is air from the soil that causes the bubbles, and not air in the water.

Sand Trap

Quicksand is a thick body of sand grains mixed with water that appears as a dry hard surface. It may look solid, as if it can be walked on, so it can be unexpectedly dangerous because it really cannot support much weight. People have been known to be swallowed up in quicksand.

In this experiment you'll make a type of quicksand goop that will magically and suprisingly support your hand one minute but not the next.

You need:
large bowl
sheet of newspaper
1¼ cup cornstarch
1 cup water
2 tablespoons ground coffee
spoon

What to do:
On newspaper, because this can be messy, place the cornstarch and water in the bowl and mix with the spoon until the ingredients look like paste. The cornstarch mixture naturally will be hard to stir and will stick to the bottom of the bowl. This is to be expected. Next, lightly and evenly sprinkle the ground coffee on the top of the mixture to give it a dry and even look.

Now the fun begins. Make a fist and lightly pound on the surface. Notice what happens and how it feels. Next, lightly push your fingers downward into the mixture.

What happens:
When you used your fist to hit the surface of the mixture, it appeared to hit the surface only and seemed to be mysteriously and magically stopped from going any further. But when you placed your fingers or hand in the mixture, they easily and readily slid into the bottom of the bowl.

Why:
The molecules of quicksand goop behave much like the real thing. Unlike water molecules, the goop's molecules are larger, swell and hook together, and seem to act more like a solid than a liquid. In addition, the coffee grains give the mixture a deceptively smooth and dry look, much like the real sand.

A Down-to-Earth Water Filter

Have you ever wondered how water is cleaned before it reaches your home? How about making a simple water filtration system that will answer many questions. You can get lots of down-to-earth information as you test it.

Remember, though, that however good a job you think you have done, the water from this experiment should *never* be drunk. The experiment will give you a good idea how water filters work, but it is still not a real water treatment plant, and just a few drops of "bad" water can make you very sick.

It will be best to perform this activity outside since it can be messy. Too, the dirt you need to use should be easy to find nearby.

You need:

a medium-size flowerpot (or waxed carton with holes punched in the bottom)
coffee filter, thin cloth, or paper towel
2-litre soda bottle with cap
2 shallow trays or containers

gravel/small stones
sand
funnel
dirt
water

Note: Clean sand and gravel are available in small bags in garden or variety stores.

What to do:

Place the piece of filter or towelling in the bottom of the pot or carton. Fill the bottom of it with gravel or small stones, to a depth of about 2 inches (4 cm). Pour sand into the container until it is about three-quarters full.

Using a funnel, place about one cup of dirt into the 2-litre soda bottle and fill it with water. Screw the cap on and shake the bottle thoroughly.

Pour some of the muddy water into one of the shallow containers. This will be the control or test container, to compare the filtered water against the original sample. Place your filter system in the other container and pour some muddy water into the top of it. Watch the water as it filters through and compare it to the control sample. Be patient, the first samples will not be as clear as later ones. Repeat this procedure several times until the water comes through fairly clear. Continue to compare these samples with the water in the control pan.

Sand-Casting

The sea wears away coastal shorelines and rebuilds new sand formations. In this simple experiment, we'll see how the Earth is constantly being worn away, eroded, and how the process of erosion steadily changes the different shapes and formations on the Earth's surface.

You need:
aluminum baking pan or flat container
sand or very fine soil
water

What to do:
Pile the sand at one end of the tin and firmly pat it down. For the purposes of the experiment, this will represent the sandy beach or shore. Pour some water into the middle of the pan until part of the shore is slightly covered. At first gently, then increasingly faster, slide the pan back and forth until small waves are formed that roll up and onto the shore so that the sand shifts or moves.

What happens:
The action of the waves in the container gradually changes the shape of the shore, moving the sand down the beach and into the water.

Why:
All the seas of the Earth are always changing the land they meet. Some wear away or carve out great rocky areas of land while others take away great sections of sand, depositing it elsewhere. This gradual but persistent action of water against land is called erosion.

Bubble Blowers

Find some porous rock (rocks that are lightweight, with holes or spaces in them) and place them in a pan filled with water for a rocky bubble-blower show.

You need:

porous rock or broken pieces of brick or pottery

shallow tray or tin
magnifying hand lens

What to do:
Place the rocks in the tin and cover them with water. Observe what happens using the hand lens.

What happens:
Streams of bubbles flow from the rocks. The more porous the rock, the more bubbles you will see. Depending on the weight of the rocks and the force of the air escaping from them, the rocks might move slightly, rock back and forth, or bounce and rattle against the pan.

Why:
Oxygen is present, even in the rocks. Air bubbles flow from the spaces in the minerals making up the rocks and rise to the water's surface.

Rapid Transit

City subways or monorail train are often called rapid transit. Now watch how rapidly a ball will transit or move out of a tumbler, and learn about an important Earth force.

You need:
plastic tumbler
a small sphere (ball of clay,
  toy ball, marble)

What to do:
Place the sphere or ball in the tumbler and rapidly slide the glass, open end forward, across a tabletop or hard-surfaced floor. Stop the movement suddenly and observe what happens to the ball inside.

What happens:
The ball shoots out of the end of the stopped tumbler and keeps on rolling straight until something in its way stops it or changes its direction.

Why:
Sir Isaac Newton, an English physicist, discovered several natural laws of gravity and motion. One such law is called inertia. This means that something that is at rest will stay at rest, not moving, until another force works on it or moves it—and it will continue to stay in motion until, again, something works on it to stop it!

The ball in the moving tumbler stayed in it as long as it was moving. The inertia of this force was not overcome until the movement was suddenly stopped. The sudden stop was the force that overcame the inertia of the ball in the moving cup and sent the ball rolling—until a counter-force stopped it.

Weight Lifter

Weight is simply the pull of the force of gravity on you and on other objects. This experiment will demonstrate how this works. To avoid the mess of spills (gravity again), it's a good idea to do this activity outdoors.

You need:
waxed carton bottom
a thick rubber band
heavy string or twine
ruler
sharp pencil or nail
paper clip
a helper
bags or cups of substances to weigh (stones,
  gravel, beans, rice, dirt, sand, marshmallows)

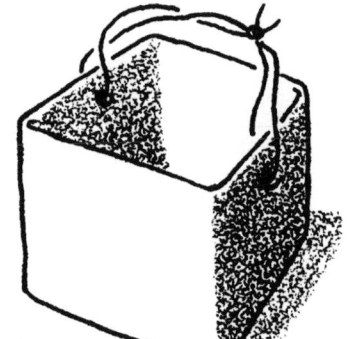

What to do:
With the pencil or nail, poke a hole through one side of the carton about an inch (2 cm) down from the top and another hole directly across from the first, on the other side of the carton. Thread the ends of the string or twine through the holes and tie them securely to form a handle. Attach the paper clip to the top of the string handle and the rubber band to the other end of the clip.

Have your helper hold your homemade spring scale so that the top of the carton basket is even with the top of the ruler. From the substances available, select one and pour some of the gravel, stones, rice, dried beans, or whatever you wish to weigh into the carton. Do this slowly and gradually as you fill the carton.

Hold the top of the ruler to the top of the cup and calibrate, or measure, how many inches or centimeters the gradually filled cup passes as it drops past the ruler.

What happens:
Your homemade spring scale, filled with different amounts of weight, measures the force of gravitational pull on the material in the basket. The carton basket is pulled down past the ruler's measurements according to the amount of force gravity exerts on it.

Why:
The Earth pulls everything toward its center. The more pull gravity is able to exert on an object, based on its denseness or mass, the heavier that object is. As the basket is filled, and the rubber band stretches, the amount of force measured by the spring scale grows.

Don't Needle Me!

Make a magnetic compass that doesn't look like the usual one. It has no case and you won't have to needle it.

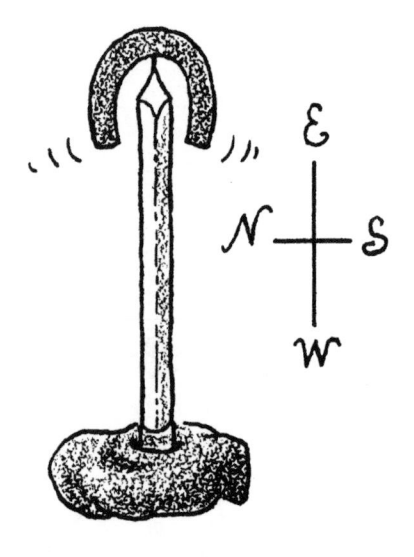

You need:
a very sharp pencil
U-shaped magnet
a large piece of modeling clay
  (to make a stand)
pencil

What to do:
Roll the piece of clay into a ball and flatten it to make a sturdy stand; then push the eraser end of the pencil into the clay stand. Carefully balance the U-shaped magnet on the pencil lead.

What happens:
The magnet gradually positions itself into a north-south direction.

Why:
The Earth is a magnetic ball with north and south magnetic poles. The U-shaped magnet positioned itself in a north-south direction because magnetic metals and liquids buried within the Earth's core have turned it into a giant magnet that naturally attracts all compasses and magnets. These great magnetic forces are concentrated at its north and south magnetic poles, which, incidentally, are not exactly the same as the north and south poles we normally speak of, but they are in the same area.

Needlework on the *Santa María*

Christopher Columbus and other early mariners, or sailors, probably used a wondrous device to help them travel the seas out of sight of land—a magnetized needle floating in a bowl of water.

Modern seafarers now have access to several devices to help them navigate the oceans, even a system of space satellites surrounding the Earth. But let's take a close look at that earlier version of the modern compass and see what a simple sewing needle can do, other than keep you in stitches.

You need:

sewing needle
bar magnet
bowl filled with water

small piece of wax paper
scissors

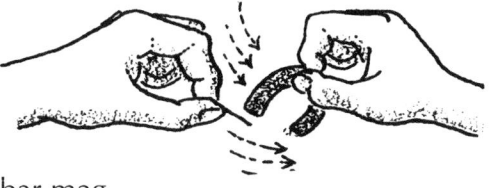

What to do:

Magnetize a sewing needle by rubbing one end of it fifty times with the north end of the bar magnet. Do the same thing with the other end by rubbing it with the south end of the magnet. Be certain to stroke the needle with the magnet in one direction, from the center to the end, and lift the magnet away from the needle each time you go to repeat the stroke.

Cut a small circle about one inch (2 cm) in diameter out of the wax paper. Place the bowl of water on a table or kitchen counter. Stick the needle (be careful) into the wax-paper circle, as you would a needle into cloth. Float the wax paper with the needle on top on the surface in the middle of the water. Try to move it around on the surface. Observe what happens.

What happens:
The needle, when the movement stops, points north and south, no matter how many times you move it around.

Why:
Your floating compass needle is reacting to the Earth's invisible magnetic pull, caused by its giant bar-magnet core.

DON'T GET STUCK: CONTROL YOUR NEEDLE!

How do you know if all needles, when movement stops, position themselves in a north-south position? To find out, set up a control compass or one that lets you know if other things are causing results.

Do the same experiment in the same way but now substitute a non-magnetized needle for the magnetized one.

Move the compass to the middle of the water and again move the needle around. Wait patiently for the needle to stop moving. Do several trials or experiments and compare the control compass with the magnetized needle.

What's Your Point?

Magnetized straight pins with like poles repel each other, while unlike poles attract. True?

You need:

2 straight pins   cotton thread
2 paper clips   a heavy book
a magnet with north and south
  poles marked

What to do:

Magnetize a straight pin. Lay the pin on a hard
surface and rub one end of it with the north side of the magnet. Rub from the center to the end, one way only, and lift the magnet between rubs. Do this about forty or fifty times. Repeat the rubbing action on the other end of the pin using the south end of the magnet. Magnetize the second pin the same way.

    Write down which end (point or head) is north or south. Tie a thread to the center of each pin and attach paper clips to the other end. Dangle the two balancing pins about two inches (4 cm) apart, one on each thread, from the end of the table. Place the paper-clipped ends of the threads on the table and weight them down with the book. Now, try pushing the pins together.

What happens:

Some ends move away from each other, while the other ends jump at each other and bump.

Why:

Like magnetic poles repel or push away from each other while unlike poles attract or pull together.

HOUSEWARMING

A greenhouse is a closed glass house used to grow plants, where heat from the sun is trapped inside and moisture cannot escape.

Scientists see the Earth today as becoming a type of greenhouse. By burning coal, oil, and other such products known as fossil fuels, by over-using and abusing the use of our cars, and by heating and cooling our homes with electricity or gas, carbon dioxide and other harmful gases are being pushed into the atmosphere. These gases act as a dome, or lid, over the Earth's atmosphere, trapping the solar heat and preventing it from escaping into outer space. (See "Fossil Fuelish.")

When trees are cleared from large land areas, such as the tropical rain forests, tons more carbon dioxide gas remains in the atmosphere, instead of being converted into breathable oxygen. It's like putting the Earth into a big glass cooker, where heat from the sun is trapped and the air inside gets *hotter* and *stuffier*.

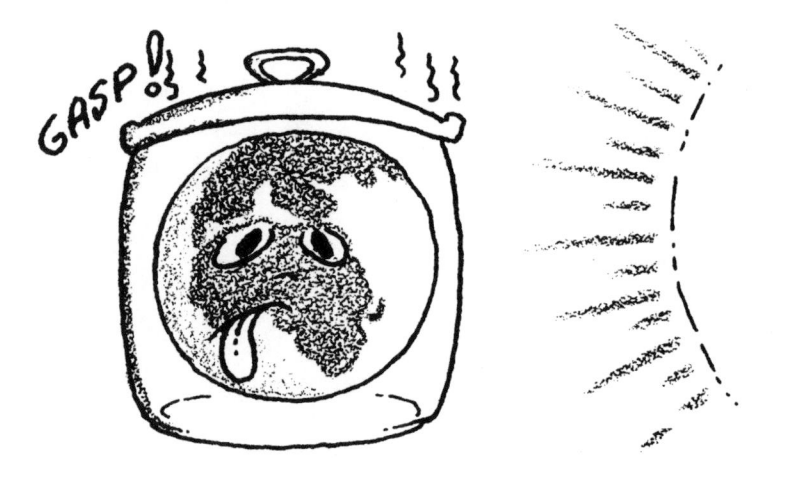

What Green House?

You may or may not find a greenhouse, or even a green house, on your block, but learning about the greenhouse effect and what it means to you and everything on Earth is very important today.

You need:
a glass container with cap or lid   sunny outdoor location
1 teaspoon water

What to do:
Place the teaspoon of water in the glass jar or bottle. Replace the lid or cap and tighten it well so that no air can escape. Leave the container outside in a sunny location for about an hour.

What happens:
Droplets of water form and cling to the sides of the container.

Why:
The sun's heat warms up the jar's atmosphere and the movement of the water molecules in it speeds up. The water then evaporates into the air, but the moisture has nowhere to go, so it gathers into droplets, or condenses, on the cool glass sides. The lid on the jar acts as a greenhouse and produces the greenhouse effect. This is similar to the carbon dioxide gas that is produced by our own personal energy use and by the use of fossil fuels by industry which acts like a lid over the earth and prevents heat that is building up from escaping into space.

Oh, Ozone!

Make a model of the ozone layer, a thin layer of gas in the Earth's upper atmosphere that protects us from the sun's damaging ultraviolet rays.

Learn about CFCs, those chemicals that make life so much easier and better but yet do so much damage (they destroy ozone molecules). Then, watch as your ozone-layer model produces holes, gradually tears apart, and finally disappears!

You need
1 short water or soda bottle
1 stick of chewing gum
very hot tap water
magnifying hand lens

What to do:
Chew the stick of gum thoroughly. When it is soft, take it out of your mouth. Flatten it into a small disk between your fingers because you need a thin flat cap to seal the top of the bottle.

Now, fill the bottle *right to the top* with very hot tap water. Take the flat piece of gum and place it over the top of the bottle to seal it. Try to avoid making any holes, and make sure that the gum cap touches the water slightly. Observe what happens closely with the magnifying hand lens.

What happens:
The gum cap, as it touches the hot water, loses its elasticity, or stretchability, and holes begin to form. Eventually the gum cap breaks apart.

Why:

The bottle represents the Earth in our ozone model while the gum cap represents the ozone layer. The hot water touching the gum cap stands for the CFCs (chlorofluorocarbons), or chemicals that can damage ozone molecules.

CFCs are found in coolants for air conditioners and refrigerators and in the foam-plastic packaging used by some fast-food restaurants. These chemicals are released into the atmosphere as chlorine gas, which eventually destroys ozone.

So, cool it! But do cut down on air conditioner use, and do remind restaurant and business owners that they should act responsibly—that CFCs are harmful and that other types of food packaging are available.

STICK TO IT!

How can you reduce the amount of CFCs in Earth's atmosphere? Of course, you can't do it all alone, but you can do your part. Buy fewer products with CFCs in them, use less air conditioning, and remind others of our responsibilities to Mother Nature. Working together is the way to help save our Earth.

Now, do the same ozone experiment, but instead of filling the bottle to the top with hot water, stop when it is only half full, or less. Does the gum cap still show signs of wearing away? Is there a difference? Now you can see how releasing fewer CFCs into the air, or none, can make a big difference to our ozone layer.

CHAPTER FIVE
SIMPLE TIME
EXPERIMENTS

TALKING ABOUT TIME

We use the word "time" to refer to *when* something happens (date) or *how long* an event lasts (interval).

People have measured time by the Sun, Moon, and stars, by the use of oil and candles and by water and sand, with weights and pendulums, with batteries and electric power stations, and in this century with the atoms of a metal called *cesium*.

In prehistoric times, people needed to know only the seasons and night and day. Now physicists, studying particles of the atom, measure a picosecond, a trillionth of a second. And other scientists—paleontologists, geologists, archeologists, biologists—use "radioactive clocks" and "molecular clocks" to measure billions of years.

Astronomers, physicists, engineers, statisticians—as well as blacksmiths and locksmiths—were all involved in the development of the measuring stick for time, "the clock." Horologists (clock-makers) based their inventions on the scientific theories of Newton, Descartes, Galileo, Bohr, and Einstein, among others.

But it was natural phenomena—the spinning of the Earth on its axis and the rotation of the Earth around the Sun—that provided the first means of measuring time.

How Long Is a Minute?

Do you know exactly how much time it takes before a minute has gone by? Have fun with your friends by seeing who can come closest to "timing" a minute!

You need:

a watch with a second hand   one or more friends
                                    pencil and paper

What to do:
Take turns. A friend holds the watch and gives a signal. You then put your hands on your lips and keep quiet until you think one minute is up—and then shout "Time!" Your friend will record your time. Then you take over the timing while your friend keeps quiet for what *seems* like a minute and you record the time.
   Compare times.

What happens:
You will find that a minute can be quite a long time!

Why:
Time drags when you're concentrating on time passing. But try timing a minute when you are reading or drawing or playing a game and see how short a minute can seem.

About Calendars

Calendars are orderly plans that fit days into months and months into years.

As far back as 3000 BC, Babylonians—who lived in what is now part of Iraq—and Egyptians devised lunar calendars. They were made up of 354 days with months based on the cycles of the Moon. The Athenians had a similar calendar.

Later, because the life-saving floods came every 365 days, the Egyptians changed to a solar year, with a calendar of 12 months, each with 30 days. This left five extra days at the end of the year during which the people celebrated the birthdays of important gods.

The Romans originally had a lunar year of 355 days, but by the time of Julius Caesar, the Roman calendar was three months ahead of the Sun's year. In 45 BC, Caesar reformed the calendar, bringing it closer to the one we use today. He added almost three months to the year 46 BC and, like the Egyptians, devised a solar calendar of 365 days. He added an extra day every fourth year, our leap year. This calendar, called the Julian calendar, was used throughout the Middle Ages.

It wasn't until 500 years after his death that time was related to the birth of Christ. Many non-Christian societies use CE (Common Era) instead of AD (Anno Domini, the Year of Our Lord) and BCE (Before the Common Era) instead of BC (Before Christ). The Muslim Hijri calendar starts counting from AH (Anno Hegirae), the Year of the Emigration—the journey of Mohammed from Mecca to Medina.

Because the year was still too long by about 11 minutes, the Julian calendar was more than a week off by the 16th century Eventually, Easter would coincide with the previous Christmas! So, in 1582 Pope Gregory XIII wiped out 10 days (October 5 became October 15), and decreed that no century year, such as 1700, should be a leap year

unless it was divisible by 400. That meant that three leap years would be omitted every four centuries. Also, the calendar year was to begin on January 1 instead of March 21. September through December were to keep their original names—meaning the 7th, 8th, 9th, and 10th months of the year—even though they were now the 9th to 12th months of a year that began in January. This Gregorian calendar is the one we use today.

The Chinese calendar, devised about 2700 BC, reckoned time with numbered months and years named for 12 different animals. It's still

used for setting the dates of the festivals of the Harvest Moon and of the New Year (which is celebrated between January 20th and February 19th on the Gregorian calendar).

The Orthodox Eastern Church still uses the Julian calendar, so Greeks and Russian Catholics celebrate a number of days after other Christians.

Moon Time

To know when to plant their seeds, and to fix the dates of religious holidays, many ancient peoples devised calendars based on the Moon. One of the first words for Moon meant "the measure of time." The word *"month"* comes from the Moon—*moonth*. You can use a lamp and an ordinary ball to see what causes the various phases of the Moon.

You need:

electric lamp
a white tennis ball
pencil and paper

What to do:
Place the lighted lamp on a table in a darkened room. Hold the ball in your hand at arm's length with your back to the light. Raise the ball high enough to allow the light to strike the ball. Note the part of the ball lighted by the lamp. This represents the full moon. Turn around slowly from right to left keeping the ball in front of you and above your head. Observe the change in shape of the lighted part of the ball as you make one complete turn. Stop at each one-eighth turn and draw the shape of the ball (the Moon) that is lit up.

What happens:
You will observe the various phases of the Moon from the full moon to the half moon to a crescent sliver to the new moon when no part is lit.

Why:
Every day the Moon rises and sets about 50 minutes later than the day before, taking about four weeks to go around Earth. During that time the Moon waxes from new moon to full moon and then wanes to new

moon again. The same half of the Moon always faces Earth as the Moon goes around it. Half of the Moon is lighted by the Sun and half is in darkness. Actually you see a little more than half because Earth's gravity causes the Moon to librate—to vibrate—as it rotates. At new moon the half facing Earth is dark because the Moon is between Earth and the Sun. Of course, you often see the Moon in its various phases in the night sky. But you can also see the crescent moon and the half moon during the day because they rise before nightfall.

DIFFERENT DRUMMERS

Some societies set up their calendars to start with the year of their rulers, with the founding of a city, or with an important event in their religion. The Greeks measured time by referring to the Olympiads, the first of which was held in 776 BC.

Even now, the Hopi Indians express time in their language by what happens "when the corn matures" or "when a sheep grows up." The Trobriand Islanders, near New Guinea, date events by saying they occurred "during the childhood of X" or "in the year of the marriage of Y."

String Calendar

The string calendar comes from Sumatra, an Indonesian island in the Indian Ocean. You can make one for yourself by threading string through each of 30 holes in a sheet of heavy paper as a way of recording the passing of days in a lunar month. Pencil and paper or a bought calendar may be easier ways to keep track of the days of the month, but your own string calendar can amuse your friends.

You need:
sheet of heavy paper
paper punch or scissors
long piece of heavy thread or string

What to do:
Fold your paper lengthwise in half and then in half again. Punch 7 evenly spaced holes in each of the first three-quarters of the page. In the last quarter punch 10 holes, as in the illustration. On the first of the month, knot your string and thread it through the first hole. The next day, thread the string through the second hole.

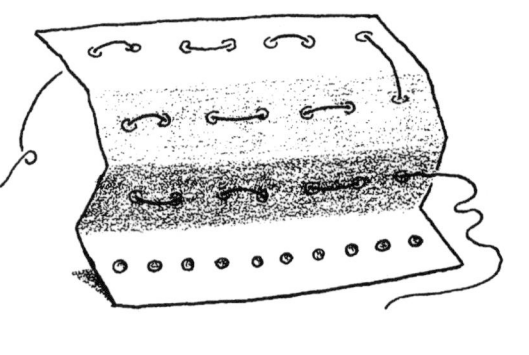

Do the same every day of the month. When you want to know what day of the month it is, just count the number of holes you've covered.

Hand Dial

A sixteenth century German woodcut shows a unique portable dial that requires no special equipment. If you know the latitude of your area (see p. 177), you can tell the time without a watch or sundial. Actually, you can be a human timepiece.

You need:

small stick or pencil
your two hands
sunny day

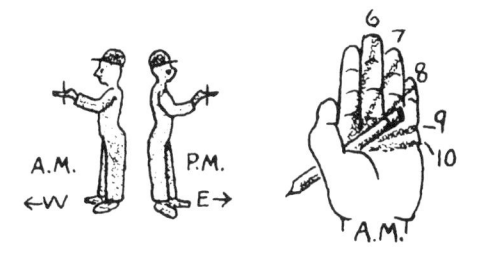

What to do:

Look up the latitude of your area in an atlas or on a globe. Using your left hand in the morning and your right hand in the afternoon, hold the stick with your thumb. Tilt the stick at an angle approximately equal to the angle of latitude of your area, as in the illustration below. Hold your left hand straight up toward the west. Hold your right hand straight up toward the east.

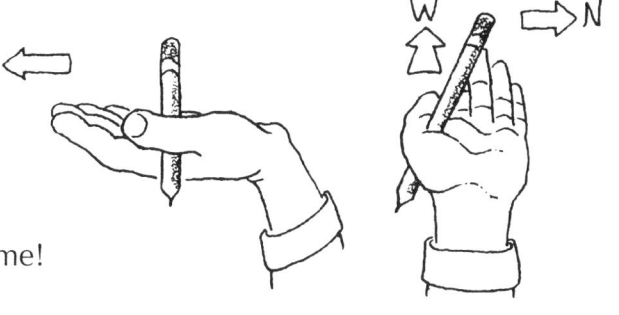

What happens:
The shadow on your
hands indicates the time!

Why:
You have made the pencil into a gnomon and angled it parallel to Earth's axis, as in the experiment on page 177. But remember, your hand sundial may not agree with your clock. See page 179.

Where Does My Shadow Go?

Our ancestors told the time by the shadows made by the Sun. But why do we sometimes see a shadow and at other times "there's none of him at all?"

You need:

flashlight or a lamp   darkened room

What to do:

In a darkened room, place the lighted lamp or flashlight about five feet (1½ m) from the wall. You can hang up a sheet if the wall is a dark color. Stand behind the lamp. Do you cast a shadow? Now stand between the lamp and the wall. Then move closer to the wall.

What happens:

You don't cast a shadow when you stand behind the light. You cast a big shadow when you are near the light and far from the wall. As you move farther from the light, the shadow becomes smaller.

Why:

You cast a shadow by blocking the rays of light. As you move away from the source of light, your shadow becomes smaller because you cut off fewer rays of light. Any object that won't permit light to shine through creates a shadow, an area of lessened light.

Why Am I Sometimes Very Tall?

This simple experiment shows *how* the length of a shadow changes when the source of light changes position.

You need:

2 pencils   spool of thread
sheet of paper   flashlight

What to do:
Stand one of the pencils in the center of the spool over the sheet of paper. Darken the room and hold the flashlight at different angles above the pencil. Record the length of each shadow.

What happens:
When the flashlight is high and right above the pencil, the shadow is short. When the light is low and at a slant, the shadow is long.

Why:
When the light is low and at a slant, the shadow is long because few rays of light pass through. This shows us why the shadows at the North Pole are longer than those at the equator. The Sun hits Earth directly at the equator and indirectly at the Poles.

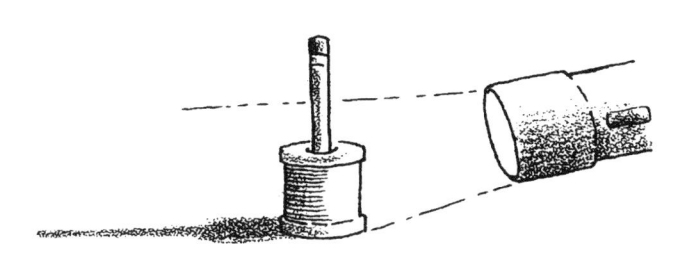

Shadow Watch

At what time of day is the shadow the shortest? You can find out by watching the shadow cast by the Sun—in the same way our distant ancestors did!

You need:
tree or lamppost
chalk or stones
pencil and paper
clock
tape measure

What to do:
Identify a nearby tree or a lamppost that is in sunlight much of the day.

Using either small stones or chalk, mark off the shadow it casts right after you get up in the morning. Measure the shadow's length. Then do the same thing at noon or, if your area is on Daylight Savings Time (Summer Time), an hour later. Finally, mark the shadow cast late in the afternoon toward sunset and measure it.

What happens:
The shadow is shortest at noon. The shadows cast in the early morning and late afternoon are both much longer.

Why:
The Sun is highest in the sky at noon and therefore casts the shortest shadow. However, your clock and the Sun may have a difference of opinion about when it is noon.

Shadow Timepiece

The earliest timetelling device, a crude forerunner of the more accurate sundial, was the Egyptian shadow clock. It dates from between the 10th and 8th centuries BC and was made of stone. You can make your own from materials you have around the house.

You need:

2 empty milk cartons   index card
glue or tape   marker or crayon
scissors

What to do:

Place one of the milk cartons on its side. Glue or tape an index card or a piece of cardboard one inch (2½ cm) from the top of the short flat end of the carton. Hold the second carton perpendicular to the first and attach it to the free end of the index card, as in the illustration. In the morning, go outdoors and place the shadow clock level with the upper carton pointing east. In the afternoon, turn the time-teller around so that it points west. Check with your clock every hour and mark where the shadow falls.

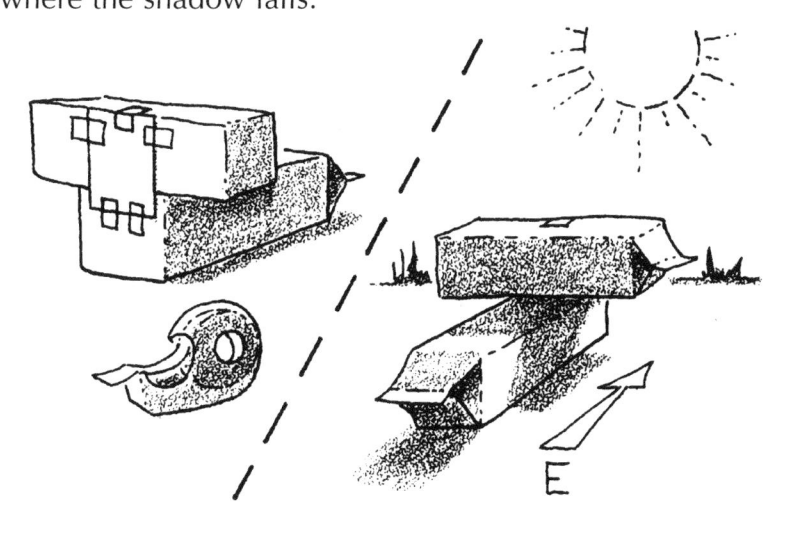

What happens:

The shadow shortens as it gets to be lunch time and lengthens again toward dinner time. And the distances from one hour to the next differ! The shadows are farther apart from one another early and late in the day and closer during the middle of the day.

Why:

Only at the equator will the spaces allotted to hours be exactly equal because the sunlight hits Earth directly. Unlike the day and the year, which are dictated by the revolution of Earth on its axis and around the Sun, the hour is a division devised by people. The day runs from midnight to midnight but it could be divided—and has been—into 20 parts or six parts or three parts instead of 24 hours. Early Egyptians didn't talk about two or three o'clock. They agreed to meet when the shadow was, for instance, four steps long.

What's the Angle?

In about the first century, it was discovered that a slanting object cast a shadow that kept more accurate time than an object that stood straight up. This was especially true if the object, known as the *gnomon*, slanted at the same angle as the latitude of the place where it was being used. In that case, its direction was the same at any hour of the day, regardless of the season of the year.

The term *gnomon* comes from the Greek word which means "know," so named because it "knew" the time.

You need:
2 pieces of heavy card-
  board approx. 6″ x 8″
  (15 x 20 cm)
4″ (10 cm) stick or pencil
protractor
atlas
scissors
paste

watch
marker or pencil

What to do:
In an atlas, look up the latitude of your town—that's its distance north or south of the equator. Subtract it from 90° (for example, 90° − 50° = 40°). From one of the pieces of cardboard, cut two wedge shapes with that angle; see illustration A.

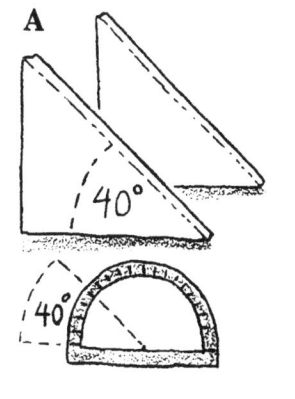

On a second cardboard, draw a line parallel to and 1″ (2.5 cm) away from the long edge, as in illustration B.

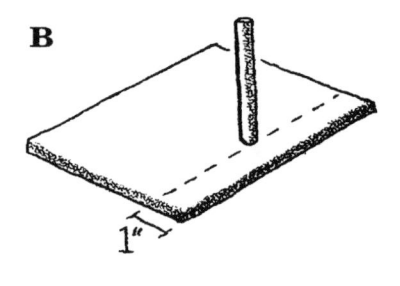

Paste the 4″ (10 cm) stick at right angles to the cardboard through the center of the line. With the protractor, divide the space above the line into 12 angles of 15° each. Label the middle line 12 and the bottom lines 6. Then fill in the other numbers, as in illustration C.

Paste the cardboards to the wedges so that the boards touch at one edge and the hour lines of the upper board point away from the free edge. See illustration D.

Set the sundial level. Place the edge where the two boards meet so that they run east and west. A simple way of orienting the sundial is to set it up at noon and indicate where the shadow falls. Check the sundial each hour, marking the spot where the shadow falls with a marker or pencil.

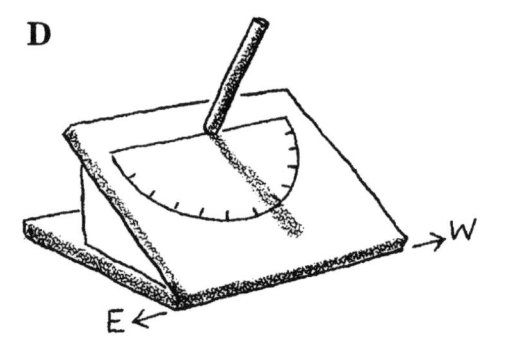

What happens:

The shadow of the stick will point to the time.

Why:

You have set up the sundial so that the gnomon is in the same direction as Earth's axis and the upper board is parallel to the ground at the North Pole.

But it will not always agree with your clock.

WHY THE DIFFERENCE?

L.A.T., local apparent time, is time measured by the actual movement of Earth and the Sun. It differs from season to season and from place to place. It is the time measured by the sundial.

L.M.T., local mean time, measures the average speed at which the Sun rotates and Earth spins in its orbit. Our clocks and watches show local mean time.

Candle Timekeeper

Religious candles are reminders of the candle timekeepers of old, which date back to the 9th century.

You need:

2 white candles (not the tapered kind)
4 or 5 2-inch (5 cm) lengths of heavy thread
2 candle holders

2 plates
4 or 5 bolts or paper clips
ruler
clock

What to do:

Attach a bolt or clip to one end of each 2-inch length of heavy thread.

Even out the candles by cutting or burning off the tips. Measure the candles. Jot down the results. Then insert one of the candles in a holder and place it on a plate. (Work near a sink—with adult supervision if that is the rule in your house.) Light the candle in the holder and let it burn for ten minutes. Then blow out the flame. Measure the candle again and figure out how much of the candle burned in 10 minutes. Loop one of the lengths of string around the second candle at the 10-minute mark and secure it with a knot. Mark off the rest of the first candle in 10-minute segments. Measure it each time and wrap a length of string, with a bolt or clip attached, at the proper spot on the second candle.

Depending on the size of your candle, you may be able to use more or less than four lengths of string. Insert the second candle in a candle holder, place it on a plate, and light the wick. Check your watch every time you hear the clang of the bolt or clip.

What happens:

Every ten minutes, you will be alerted by an "alarm" as the thread burns off and the clip or bolt hits the plate.

BY A NOSE!

Add to eyes, ears, and touch the sense of smell in the service of time-telling! In the early 1300's the Chinese developed an incense clock. They placed aromatic powders into grooves carved into a hardwood disk and lit it. It burned for 12 or so hours. Each hour was recognized by its particular scent.

Having It Both Ways

A more accurate water clock has water flowing in and out of containers at the same time.

You need:

yardstick   glass bowl
masking tape   or a pot
2 heavy paper cups
punch or nail
water source
marker
watch

What to do:
Punch a small hole in the bottom of the paper cups.
Hold the yardstick up and tape the cups to it, as in the illustration. Tape the yardstick to the side of a large pot or bowl with the cups facing inward so that they are over the pot.

Cover the hole in the top cup with a piece of tape. Fill the cup with water. Then place it under a slow-running faucet as you uncover the hole.

Every five minutes, use tape or a marker to indicate the water line in the bottom cup and the one in the bowl or pot.

What happens:
The water flows out at a regular rate and the marks are equally distant from one another.

Why:
Because the amount of water that flows in comes from a cup that is always kept full, the water pressure remains the same and therefore the water flows out at the same rate.

Hourglass Timekeepers

Hourglass timers were once engaged in serious jobs. They timed sermons, speeches, court presentations. Four-hour models were used aboard ship to measure watches right up to the late 18th century, when accurate ship chronometers were invented. Now, the most common task of the hourglass is to time boiled eggs.

You need:
2 small clear jars (baby food or jelly size)
heavy paper or cardboard
masking tape
salt or sand
nail or punch
scissors
clock or watch

What to do:
Cut a circle out of a piece of heavy paper or cardboard to fit the mouth of the jars. Punch a small hole in the center of the circle with a nail or a paper punch. Place a few ounces of sand or salt in one of the jars and cover it with the disk. Tape the second jar to the first, mouth to mouth. Make sure they are taped securely. Then turn the jars upside down and time how long it takes for the top jar to empty.

Now make the hole larger and change the amount of sand. Time these.

What happens:

By making the hole larger or smaller—or changing the amount of sand or salt—you can change the time it takes to empty the top jar.

Why:

Gravity is what forces the sand to drop at a steady rate. The advantages of the hourglass over the water clock? It is portable—no sloshing water—and weather does not affect it. You can use it over and over and time longer periods—if you just keep track of how many times you turn it over. This "minute glass" should be fun and you may even find it useful.

A KNOTTY PROBLEM

For many years, it was the practice at sea to throw overboard a thin rope weighted at one end with a piece of wood and knotted at regular intervals. A seaman would hold the rope as it was dragged through the water and feel how many knots passed through his hands during the time it took for a timed sandglass to empty. In this way, he estimated the speed or "knots" at which the ship was moving. Nautical speed is still measured in knots.

Invent Your Own Clock

Timetellers have ranged from natural phenomena to manmade devices, from primitive to sophisticated, from simple to complex. The writer Albert Camus tells of an old man who thought a watch a silly gadget and an unnecessary expense. He devised his own "clock" designed to indicate the only times he was interested in. He worked out the times for meals with two saucepans, one of which was always filled with peas when he woke in the morning. He filled the other, pea by pea, at a constant, carefully regulated speed. Every 15 pots of peas it was feeding time!

Fifth graders from the Fieldston School in Riverdale, New York, invented their own timers—one made a fizzy alarm clock using vinegar dripping into baking soda, another timed how long it took heat to blow up a balloon.

Can you devise a "clock" from items around the house or activities you do often?

Star Map

Draw a star map of the constellations that circle around the Pole Star and use it to note the changes in the sky from hour to hour.

You need:
circle of cardboard or plastic
flashlight
red cellophane and tape (optional)

What to do:
Copy this illustration onto your circle of cardboard or plastic.

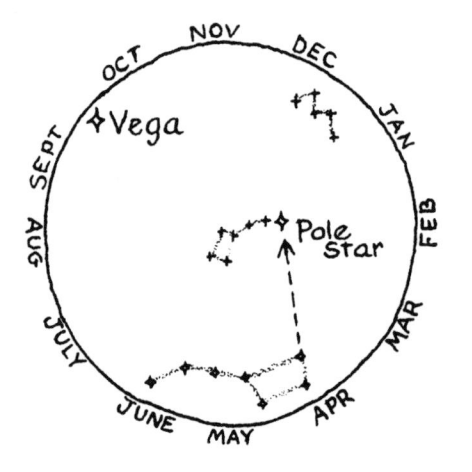

Tape the cellophane over your flashlight.

(1) At 9 o'clock on a dry moonless night, take your star map and the flash outdoors. (The red covering will prevent it from being too bright for you to see the stars.) Rotate the chart so that the month in which you are observing is on the top. Hold the chart above your head and look for the same pattern in the sky.

(2) On another night, go out at 7 o'clock or at 10 o'clock and match the star map with the sky.

What happens:

At 7 o'clock you have to turn the chart one month clockwise to match the sky. At 10 o'clock you have to turn it a half-month counterclockwise.

Why:

The Pole Star remains at approximately the same place in the sky—far, far away but directly above Earth's North Pole. This is because Earth's axis points to it throughout the year.

But all the other stars and constellations seem to wander around the Pole Star once a day, *moving counterclockwise.* As Earth rotates, it looks as if the entire sky is rotating, though the stars do not change position relative to each other. Since one turn of Earth takes only 23 hours and 56 minutes, a star seems to rise and set about four minutes earlier than the day before. This add ups to 2 hours (30 x 4 = 120 minutes) in a month and, of course, one hour in half a month.

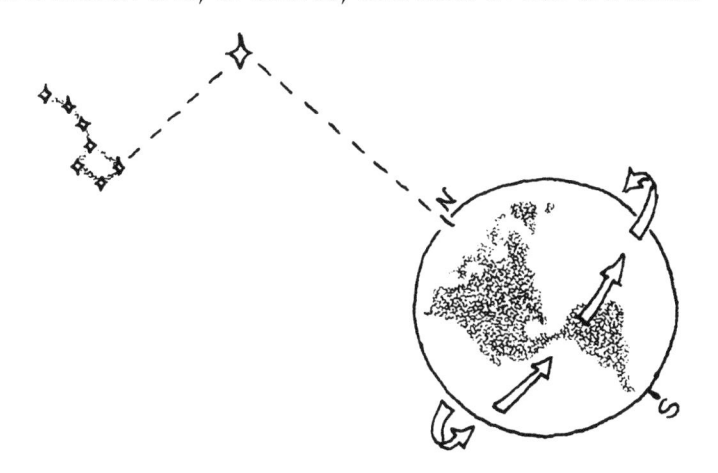

Star Time

Stars tell us the time and direction on land, on sea, and in the air. You can have fun estimating the time by observing certain stars.

You need:

3 pieces of cardboard	punch or nail
marker	fastener
compass (optional)	flashlight
ruler	sheet of paper
scissors	paste or glue
tape	

What to do:

Mark out circles on two of the pieces of cardboard. Make one circle about 8″ (20 cm) in diameter. Make the other 1″ (2.5 cm) smaller with four 3″ (7.5 cm) triangles sticking out as in C. Cut out the two disks.

On the larger cardboard disk draw two ¼″ circles around the outer rim. Mark the outer circle with the months of the year. Mark the inner circle with the days of the month.

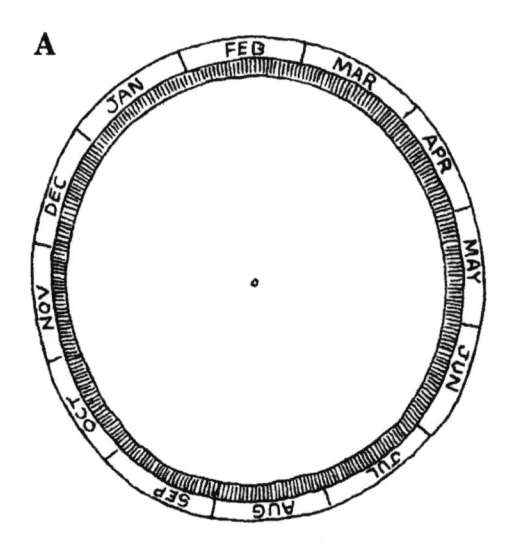

A

From the sheet of paper, cut out an oval 3¾″ (9.5 cm) deep and 4″ (10 cm) wide. Copy the sky map in illustration B.

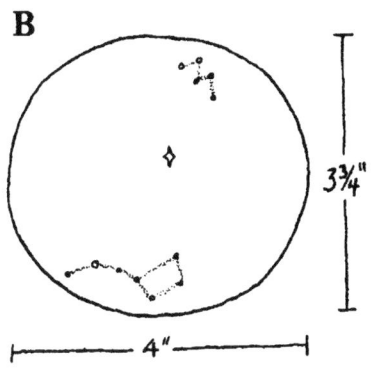

B

3¾″

4″

Hold the larger disk so that September is on top. Paste the sky map to the inner circle above the days of March.

On the smaller disk, 1″ from the bottom, mark out an oval, also 3¾″ deep and 4″ wide. Cut the oval section out.

Around the edge of the smaller disk draw a clock face like the one in illustration C. Notice that the numbers, like the stars, go in the opposite direction from an ordinary clock and cover 24 hours instead of 12.

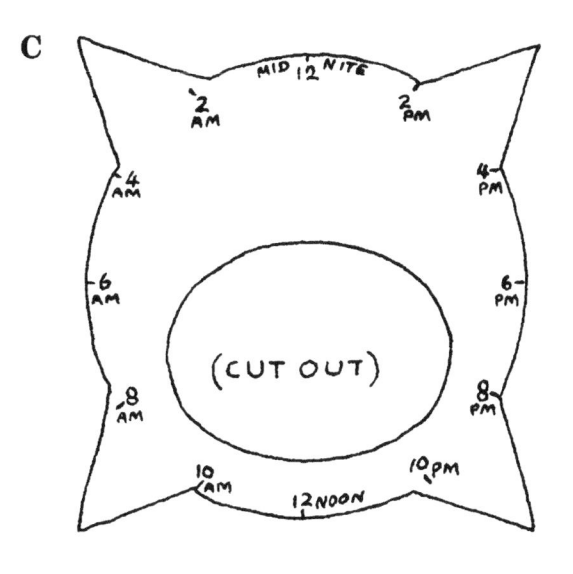

C

MID 12 NITE

2 AM

2 PM

4 AM

4 PM

6 AM

6 PM

(CUT OUT)

8 AM

8 PM

10 AM

10 PM

12 NOON

Place the smaller disk on top of the larger disk so that you can see the map through the "window" of the smaller disk.

Tape the tips of the triangles of the smaller disk to the corners of the third cardboard. Punch a hole through the center of all three cardboards. Fit the fastener through the three center holes.

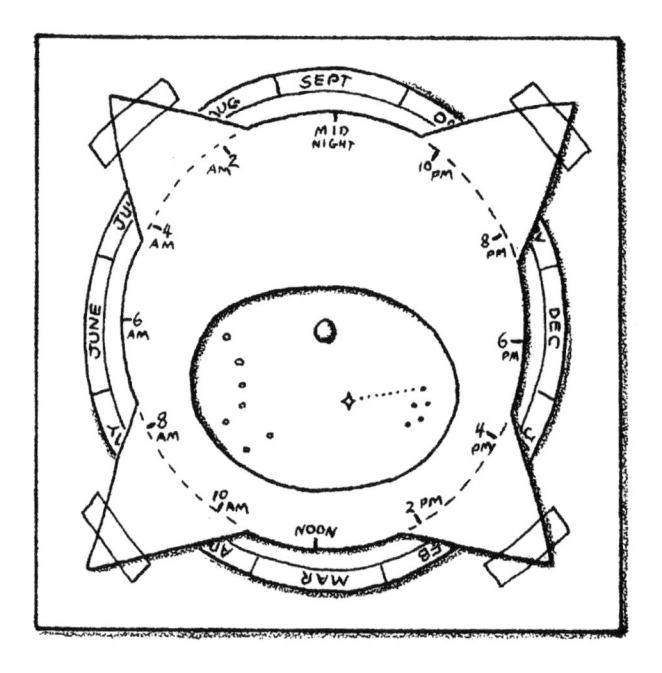

On a clear, preferably moonless, night, pick a spot where street lights, houses and trees don't obstruct your view.

Face north and look for the Big Dipper and Cassiopeia. Two pointer stars of the Big Dipper point to a fairly bright star, the Pole Star (Polaris)—also known as the North Star—which is halfway between the Big Dipper and Cassiopeia. At a latitude of 40° (New York, Denver, Salt Lake City), it is almost halfway up in the sky. The farther north

(London's latitude is 50°) you are, the higher up the Pole Star will be; the farther south (New Orleans is 30°), the lower it will be.

Rotate your Star Timeteller until it looks like the sky.

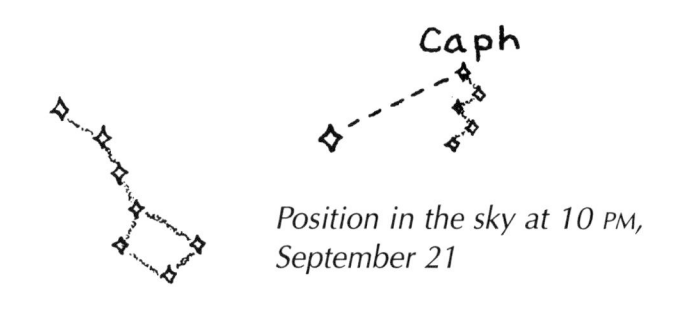

Position in the sky at 10 PM, September 21

Draw an imaginary line from Polaris to Caph, one of the bright stars of Cassiopeia.

For each week after September 21 subtract ½ hour; for each week earlier add ½ hour. If you are on Daylight Savings Time, add an hour.

What happens:
The imaginary line acts as the star clock's hour hand. With a little simple arithmetic, you can find the approximate time.

Why:
You add and subtract depending on when you observe the stars because the solar day is longer than the star day. The star clock runs too fast. As we have seen, it gains four minutes every day. In a week it gains about a half hour (7 x 4 = 28 minutes); in a month it gains about 2 hours (30 x 4 = 120 minutes). Since Earth is rotating counterclockwise, it will be earlier when you observe *after* September 21, so you subtract. And it will be later *before* September 21, so you add.

Grandfather Clocks

In 1656 Christian Huygens van Zulicham, a Dutch scientist, invented the first pendulum clock. Based on the principle established by Galileo's experiments in 1583, the new clock was driven by a single weight—the bob—suspended on a long rope.

You need:
4 lengths of string or heavy thread:
   10″ (25 cm), 20″ (50 cm), 39″ (97.5 cm), 48″ (120 cm)
metal washers or coins or pebbles
clothes hanger or ceiling hook
watch with a second hand

What to do:
Tie a weight to the longest string and suspend it from a clothes hanger or a ceiling hook so that it hangs freely. Pull the string slightly to one side and let it swing. Count the number of swings it makes in 60 seconds. Then pull the string farther over to one side and let it swing again, counting the number of swings in 60 seconds. Add additional washers or coins or heavy pebbles and try swinging the string. Again count the number of swings made in 60 seconds. Jot down your results.

   Do the same thing with strings of different, lengths—10 inches, 20 inches, and finally 39 inches. In each case, note how many times the weight moves back and forth in 60 seconds and jot down the results.

What happens:
When the string is 39 inches long, the weight moves back and forth 60 times in one minute.

Why:
A pendulum takes the same length of time to make every swing no matter how far it travels or how heavy the weight at the end of it. But the longer the pendulum, the longer the time it takes to complete its swing; the shorter the pendulum the more quickly it travels back and forth. Since it takes one second for a length of string measuring 39 inches to swing back and forth, time can be measured with accuracy.

Because they were housed in tall wooden cases designed to hide the unattractive weights, pendulum clocks were known as tall clocks.

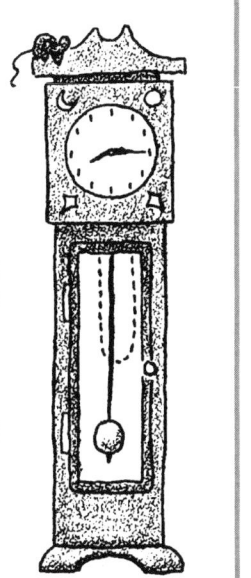

SECONDS

When pendulum clocks became more accurate, first minute hands and eventually second hands were added to clock faces. English physicist Robert Hooke was the first one to use the word *"second"* for one-sixtieth of a minute. Since there are 60 minutes in an hour, Hooke divided a minute into 60 parts, too. He called each part a *second* because he was dividing by 60 a *second* time.

International Date Line

Do you know what the International Date Line is all about? Let's take a trip around the world and find out.

You need:

sheet of paper   scissors
pencil   2 coins or pebbles
tape

What to do:

Fold the paper in thirds lengthwise, as in A. Then fold in half three times, as in B (1, 2, 3).

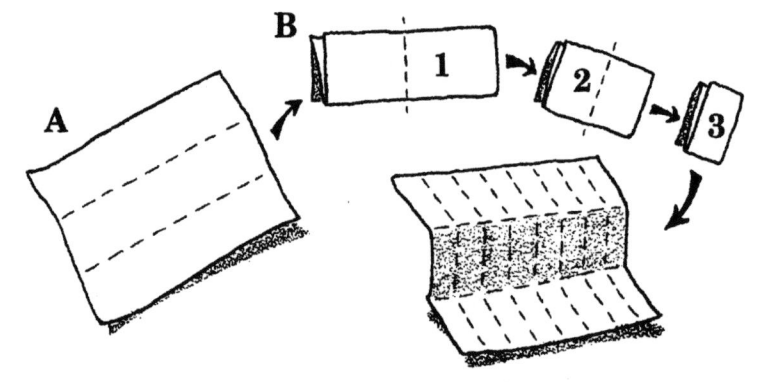

MIDNIGHT	1 A.M.	2 A.M.	3 A.M.	4 A.M.	5 A.M.	6 A.M.	7 A.M.
WELLINGTON, FIJI, WAKE IS.	SAMOA	HAWAII, ALEUTIANS	ANCHORAGE, YUKON	LOS ANGELES, VICTORIA	DENVER	CHICAGO, WINNIPEG	NEW YORK, TORONTO
−12	−11	−10	−9	−8	−7	−6	−5
8 A.M.	9 A.M.	10 A.M.	11 A.M.	NOON	1 P.M.	2 P.M.	3 P.M.
PUERTO RICO, HALIFAX	BUENOS AIRES	MID-ATLANTIC	CAPE VERDE	LONDON	BERLIN	ATHENS	MOSCOW
−4	−3	−2	−1	0	+1	+2	+3
4 P.M.	5 P.M.	6 P.M.	7 P.M.	8 P.M.	9 P.M.	10 P.M.	11 P.M.
ABU DHABI, MUSCAT	KARACHI, BOMBAY	TASHKENT, CALCUTTA	JAKARTA, BANGKOK	BEIJING	TOKYO	SYDNEY	SOLOMON ISLANDS
+4	+5	+6	+7	+8	+9	+10	+11

Number the strips and fill in the times and the names of the locales, as in illustration C.

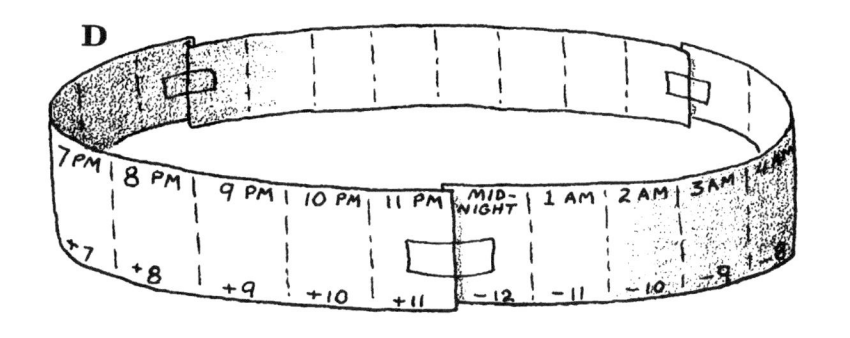

Then cut along the dotted lines. Tape the strips to one another, matching the numbers so that 5 follows 4 and –5 follows –4. Tape the ends (+12 and –12) to one another. Each of the numbers represents a time zone one hour later or one hour earlier than Greenwich Mean Time in London.

Let us assume it is noon on Tuesday and our two coins are going on a trip around the globe. They both start in London, but one travels east to Berlin and one goes west towards New York. Their planes meet one another on a remote Pacific island, west of Eniwetok (a coral island in the Marshalls) and east of Fiji.

The one traveling eastward sets its clock ahead for each 15° of longitude to gain 12 hours. The one traveling westward sets its clock back one hour for each 15° so that it loses 12 hours.

What happens:
The two clocks differ by 24 hours in one calendar day.

The problem was solved by international agreement. At the International Date Line—at 180° of longitude, located in the Pacific

Ocean—travelers are required to change the date. The one traveling east moves the calendar back a day; the one traveling west moves ahead a day.

The 180° meridian runs mostly through the open Pacific. But the date line zigzags to avoid a time change in populated areas—in the north to take the eastern tip of Siberia into the Siberian time system, to include a number of islands in the Hawaii—Aleutian time zone, and, farther south, to tie British-owned islands into the New Zealand time system.

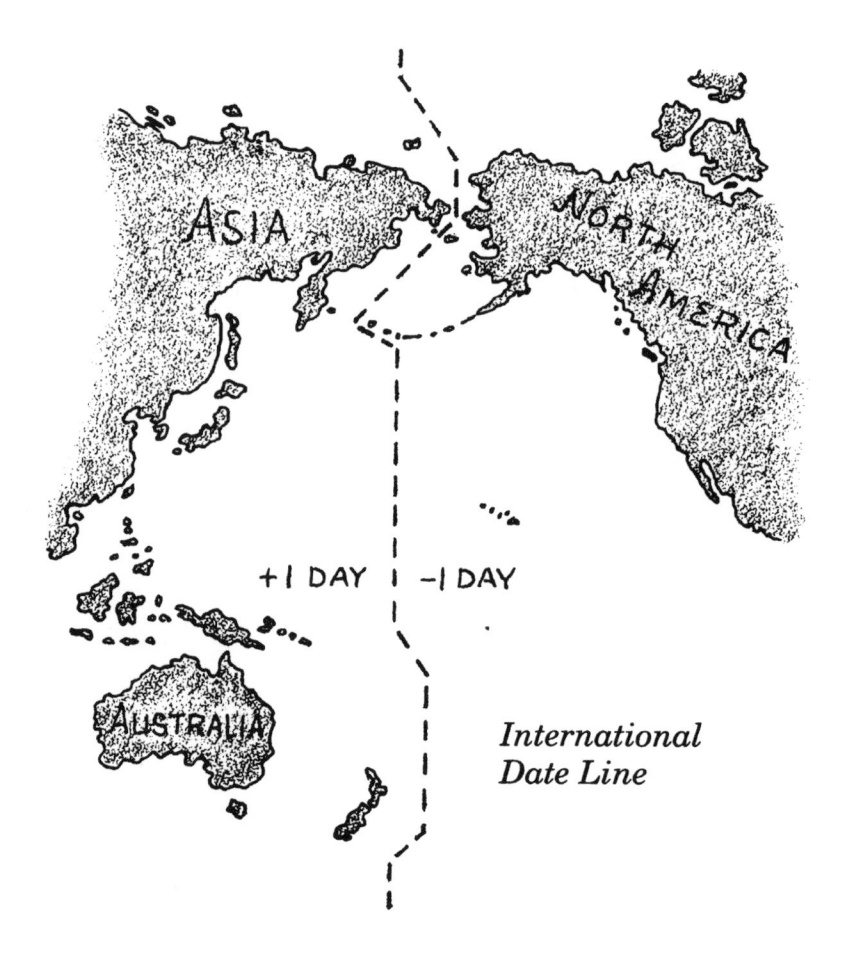

+I DAY   −I DAY

International Date Line

DAYLIGHT SAVINGS TIME

Daylight Savings Time, also known as Summer Time, is a system of putting clocks ahead an hour in the late spring and summer in order to extend daylight hours during the time people are awake. It was first suggested—perhaps as a joke—by Benjamin Franklin in 1784, but not until the 20th century was the idea put into effect. During World War I, Germany, the United States, Great Britain and Australia all adopted summer daylight savings time to conserve fuel by decreasing the use of artificial light. During World War II both the United States and Great Britain used it year-round—advancing clocks one hour during the winter and two during the summer.

Summer time observance was formally adopted as U.S. government policy in 1966, but even now it is not used in Indiana and Arizona. All of Canada observes Daylight Savings Time during the summer, but only some parts of Australia move clocks forward during their summer months starting the last Sunday in October.

AM AND PM

Meridians are imaginary lines that run along Earth's surface from the North to the South Pole. When the Sun is over one of these meridians, for those on that meridian it is noon. East of that meridian it is post meridian, PM (after noon). West of that meridian it is ante meridian, AM (before noon).

CHAPTER SIX
SIMPLE CHEMISTRY
EXPERIMENTS

WHAT'S THE MATTER?

AIR, H$_2$0, AND OTHER THINGS

Everything in this world takes up space and has weight: you, and even air, as this chapter will show!

The three states of matter are solid, liquid, and gas. This refers to how a thing feels, how hard it is, or how it moves or looks, even if it's invisible, like air. A table is a solid object, water is a liquid, and air is a gas, and these three things are made up of small parts called molecules and even smaller parts called atoms. It is these parts of things that chemists study, and rearrange to create new products that make our lives that much better.

ATOMIC BREW:
THE MOLECULE AND I

A molecule is the smallest part of anything that exists as that thing. You cannot see molecules, but everything in the world is made up of them. The best way to understand this is to imagine yourself shrinking way, way down until you become one. If you were a molecule of something on a tabletop, a salt crystal (one grain of salt) on the table would look like a mountain to you. If you were a molecule of water, you would be the last, littlest part of a drop. The last part of that water drop to evaporate would

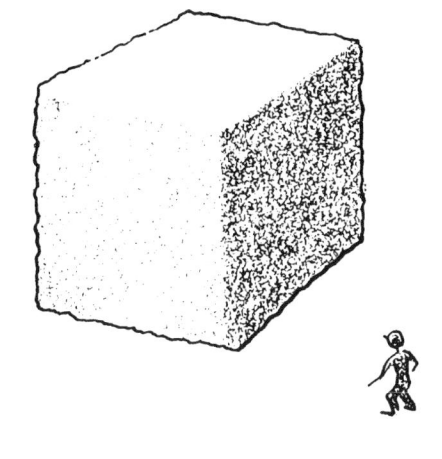

be you. Now you have a good idea of how small molecules really are. But, while molecules are small, the parts that make them up are even smaller. These very small parts that form molecules are called atoms.

If you were a molecule of oxygen, you would be made up of two of these very small parts, or atoms. You would need two atoms of oxygen, because one atom of oxygen does not behave like oxygen.

A substance with only one kind of atom is called an element. Oxygen, hydrogen, nitrogen, and carbon are all elements. (See "Periodic table of the Elements" and "Your Diamond Ring? Just Another Carbon Copy!") If you were an element of nitrogen, you would be made up of only nitrogen atoms. If you were an element of carbon, you would be made up of only carbon atoms. You could not be anything else.

Atoms of different elements come together to make different molecules. A molecule of water is made up of three atoms. If you were one atom of oxygen, you would have to be joined by two friends representing hydrogen atoms to make a molecule of water, because water has two atoms of hydrogen and one atom of oxygen. You would now be a substance, made up of two (or more) different elements, called a compound. Water, carbon dioxide, and sugar are all examples of compounds. As a molecule, or small bit of matter, you could exist in three possible forms. Chemists would identify you as one of the three states of matter: solid, liquid, or gas.

If necessary, a scientist, or chemist, could again split you apart, using electricity, into your original parts or atoms. Now you would no longer be water but three separate atoms, two hydrogen atoms and one oxygen atom. The very smallest part of you that could ever exist as water would be a molecule.

Oxygen

CHARTING THE ELEMENTS

A special table known as the Periodic Table of the Elements can help you better understand atomic chemistry. Dmitri Ivanovich Mendeleyev, a Russian chemist, put together the first table of the elements in 1869. He left some spaces in it so that, when new elements were discovered, they could be placed on the chart. In a modern version (see Periodic Table of the Elements chart) the seven rows numbered at the left and running across the table, called periods, tell the number of orbits the electrons take in each of the elements. Period-one elements have only one orbit, period-two have two orbits, period-three have three orbits, etc.

Each element on the chart has a number (atomic number) and a letter symbol as well as an atomic weight. Find oxygen on the chart (period 2, column 16/6A). The atomic number of oxygen is eight. This shows that there are eight protons in the nucleus of the atom. Notice the

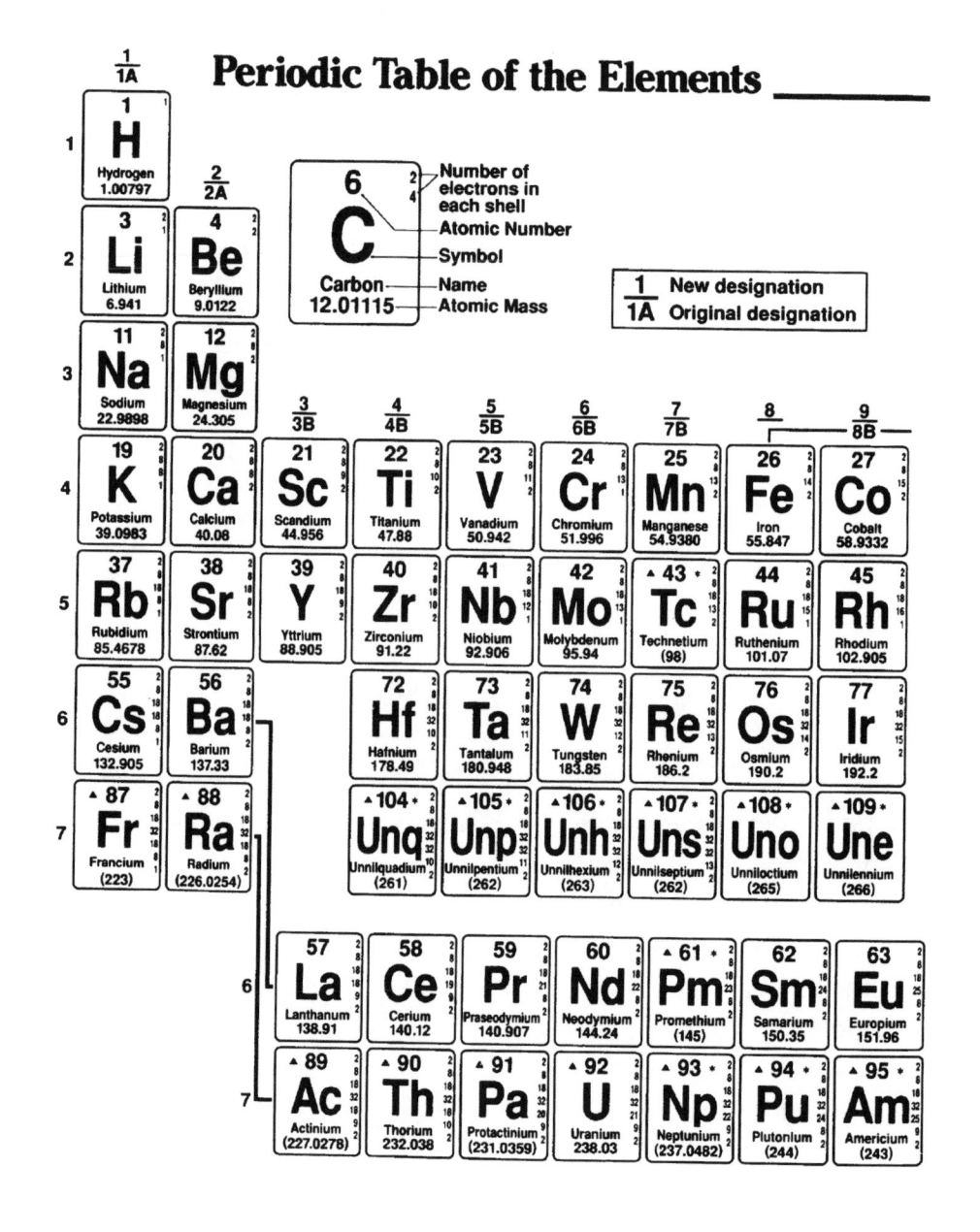

Periodic Table of the Elements _____

numbers two and six on the right side of the box. They add up to eight. The two numbers, one on top of the other, represent the number of electrons in the first orbit (2) and in the second orbit (6) of the element oxygen. The number of electrons orbiting the nucleus of an atom is the same as the number of protons in the nucleus.

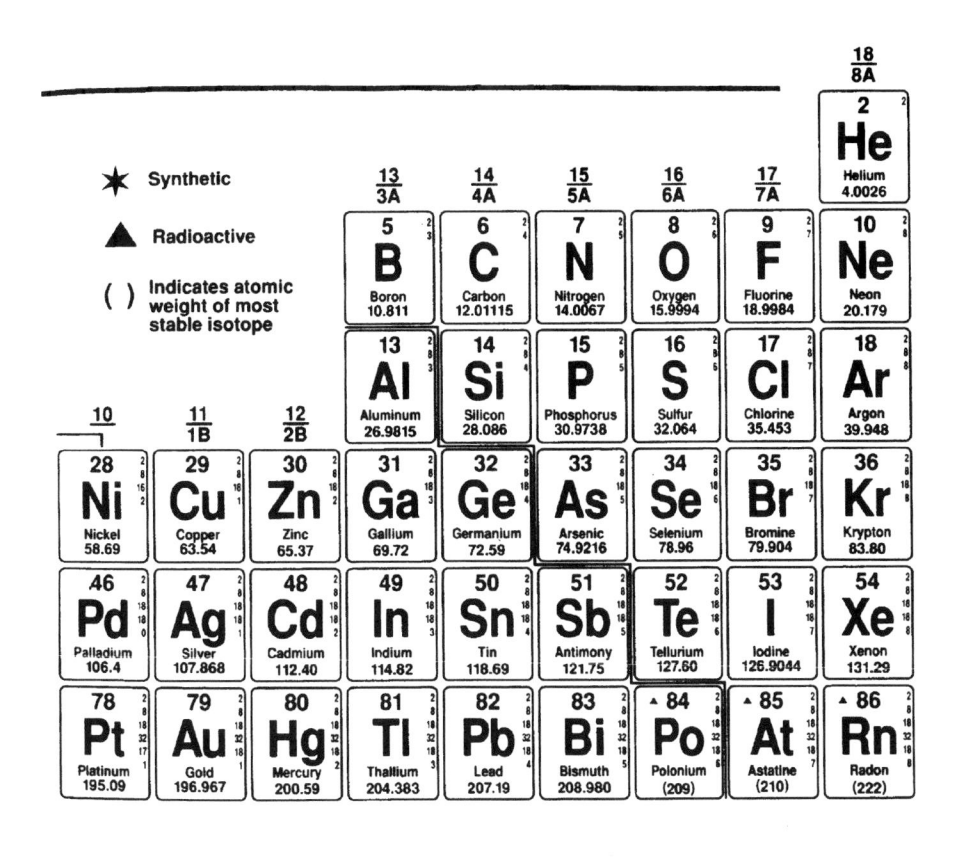

ATOM UP!

Everything on the earth is made up of atoms. They are the smallest part of any element, and the atoms of each element are different. If you were to take all the electrons in each element and *add 'em up*, you would get different (atomic) numbers. Now, you know why we titled this section "Atom Up!"

Each atom has a central point, or nucleus, made up of neutrons and protons. Some atomic parts contain electrical charges: the protons in the nucleus contain *positive* electrical charges, but the neutrons contain no charge (they are electrically neutral). Spinning around the nucleus, however, are even tinier parts called electrons. These have a *negative* electrical charge. These positive and negative electrical charges between electrons and protons are what keep the atom whole and together.

Hydrogen atom

It helps to think of the nucleus of an atom as a ball, and the electrons as smaller balls circling it. Chemists sometimes call the paths the electrons take around the nucleus "shells." Better yet, think of the nucleus of the atom as the sun and the electrons as circling, or orbiting it as its planets. The orbiting planets are attracted to, or pulled toward, the sun just as the electrons are to the nucleus of the atom.

Atomic Orbits

An easy way to start learning about atoms is to make a model of one. Although electrons and protons are not clay balls (in fact, electrons are fast-moving, electrically charged particles that move faster than you can say "atom"), making a clay model will help you understand what can be a very difficult idea.

You need:

4 colors of modeling clay wide-mouth jar lid
newspaper (to cover work area)

What to do:

Spread some newspaper over your work area. Select any two colors of clay. We'll use red and blue. Now, make two red clay ropes and a blue rope, rolling them out with your hands. These will show the orbits, or shells, or paths the electrons will take around the nucleus.

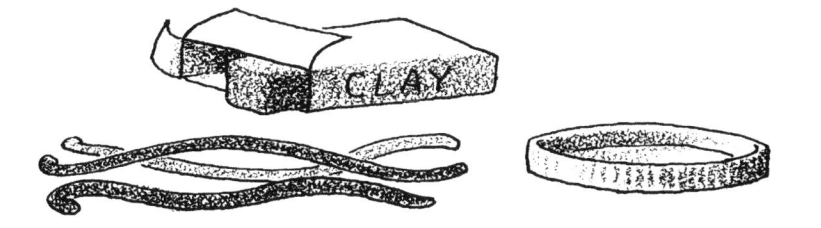

Make certain that you make the ropes long enough to make complete circles inside the jar lid. Press the first red rope against the inner rim of the lid. Follow it with the blue rope, pressed in next to the red. (When you finish your model, it will have a target pattern.) Now press another circle of red in next to the blue rope; then place a blue "bull's-eye" piece of clay in the middle. When you finish, flatten the clay with your fingers.

Next, make a "yellow" clay ball and stick it on the "bull's-eye." Make two smaller (green) balls and stick these to the outside of the blue bull's-eye, one on each side and in a straight line with the larger ball. Then place eight more green balls in four groups of two on the outer edge of the red ring.

What happens:
You now have made a usable atomic model!

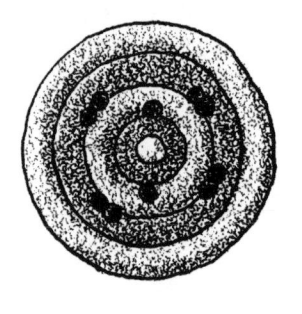

Why:
Atoms can have no more than seven orbits, or paths, and only so many electrons can fit into each orbit. The larger ball in the "bull's-eye" represents the nucleus of the atom. The two smaller balls on the outer edge of the blue circle show that there are only two electrons in the first orbit. The second orbit, the edge of the red ring, has eight green balls around it, showing that only eight electrons can be in its orbit.

The third orbit of the model (outer edge of the blue clay circle, not filled) can have up to eight more green balls, or electrons, if it is the last orbit, but up to eighteen, if it is not the last. An important thing to remember is that, after the first orbit, each orbit in turn must have eight electrons before another orbit is started.

What now:
Look at the Periodic Table of the Elements and identify the model you have made; then add balls, or electrons, to your atomic model to make other elements.

Isomers are essentially compounds, or atoms of two or more elements that chemically unite. Although they have the same number and kinds of atoms as other compounds, they are arranged differently. Scientists have taken compounds and chemically rearranged their molecules to form isomers and make new products. Detergent, paint, gasoline, and aspirin, products we use every day, are but a few examples of products made by this process.

Isomer Patterns

Now, challenge your brain power. See how many isomer models you can make. Try this with friends. It makes a great brainteaser!

You need:
6 paper clips
paper and pencil

What to do:
Take one paper clip. Place it in front of you. You have made your first pattern. Can you make any more with just the one clip? Select two paper clips and place them end to end to form a chain. Use the same two clips and place one on top of the other to form a cross. How many patterns can you make with these two clips?

Add another clip to the two to make three. How many patterns can you make now, using the added clip? Now add another clip to make

four, then five, then six. How does increasing the clips by one increase your chances for making new patterns? Hypothesize, or guess, how many patterns you can make before each activity. Write down your estimate, or guessed number, and draw each pattern you are able to make.

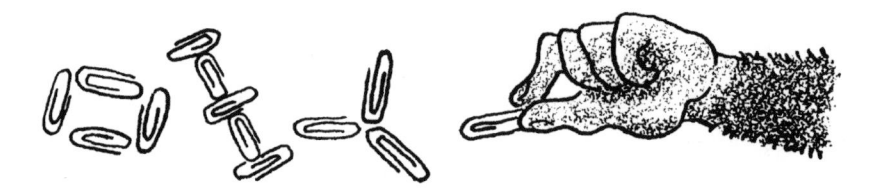

What happens:
Every time you add one more paper clip, you are able to make more new patterns.

Why:
This experiment is based on a study of probability; in this case, how many patterns you can make in each activity. The more paper clips, or elements, you have to work with, the greater the number of patterns you are able to make. The number of possible patterns increases faster than the number of clips you add.

PENCIL PUSHER

Most pencils have six flat sides. Number the sides by writing 1 through 6 on them. Place a book on a table and roll the pencil towards it until it stops. What are the possible chances that a certain number will come up?

By chance, each number will come up equally; in mathematics, we say the outcome is "equally likely." Are there any variables, or things that could affect how many times a certain number side on the pencil could come up?

Molecules in Motion

You can demonstrate the movement of molecules in solids, liquids, and gases in a simple way.

You need:
a small box lid (or flat box with short sides)
marbles (or any other small spheres, or balls)
scissors

What to do:
Place a layer of marbles, or balls, in the lid so that they are jammed close together. Move the lid back and forth slowly. Now, take some of the marbles out of the lid and move the lid back and forth again, faster than you did when more marbles were in it.

Take more marbles out of the lid and move it at an even greater speed than before.

Finally, cut a hole in each side of the lid and shake the lid again, and again.

What happens:
As the marbles get fewer and fewer, they spread out more easily. Some leave through the holes in the lid.

Why:

The "packed marbles" at the start show molecules in a solid substance. This explains why these substances are hard. They move, but they don't move much.

A number of marbles taken out shows molecules in a liquid. They are farther apart and they move more easily.

Finally, the few marbles in the lid demonstrate molecules even farther apart and moving quite rapidly. This represents a gas.

The holes in the sides of the box show what happens when substances break away from substances: water boiling on the stove will turn to water vapor, or steam, and leave the pot. A drop of water left in a dish will evaporate. If one of its molecules is moving fast enough, it will move from the surface of the drop and into the air.

When an ice cube is heated, it changes from a solid form into a liquid state, and then into a gas. The molecules of water never change, but the forms the substance takes do change; for example, from ice to water to vapor.

The Water Factory

In this experiment, you'll become a wizard of chemistry. You'll distill water, or take salt out of it, and you won't need a lot of expensive chemistry equipment to do it. Impossible, you say! Try it and find out.

You need:
a small clear jar with lid, half-filled with water
use of microwave (adult help recommended)
kitchen mitt, pot holder, or dish towel
a spoon
salt

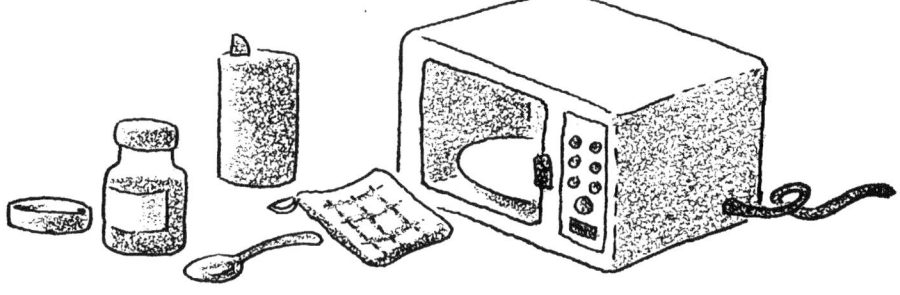

What to do:
Drop a few grains of salt into the jar of water. Stir it with a spoon and take a taste. The water should taste salty; if not, add a few more grains of salt. Put the jar of salt solution in the microwave (without lid) for about 90 seconds, or until the water comes to a boil.

Boiling Water

Do not touch or remove the jar from the microwave! The water is scalding hot!

Carefully reach in with a mitt or folded dish towel and hold the jar while you screw on the lid. (Better yet, get an adult to do it for you.) After the jar has thoroughly cooled, unscrew the lid and taste the water drops under it or on the sides of the jar.

What happens:

The water drops on the sides of the jar or under the lid do not taste salty.

Why:

The boiling water in the closed jar makes steam (water vapor) that collects as condensation (water drops) that forms on the sides of the jar or under the lid. Salt is a compound that will not leave the water (in steam) when boiled, so the salt is removed from the steam. This is a good way to purify water.

What's the Solution?

Chemists study suspensions and solutions—what are they all about? Try this simple experiment and find out.

You need:

2 large wide-mouth jars, half-filled with water
2 tablespoons (30 ml) salt
2 tablespoons (30 ml) soil
a hand lens
a spoon

What to do:

Add the soil to one jar of water, the salt to the other. Stir both. Look through your hand lens at both jars.

What happens:

The particles of soil appear to be hanging in the water. Because of their weight, the larger soil particles settle to the bottom of the jar first, followed by the medium particles, and then the smaller ones. The particles of salt in the other jar have disappeared, or dissolved.

Why:

The soil did not dissolve, or mix and disappear, into the water, because soil and water are composed of molecules of different types. These different molecules cannot chemically combine. The soil and water are what chemists call a "suspension" because the soil particles spread, or become suspended, throughout the water and then later settle to the bottom of the jar, or come out of suspension. But water and salt do combine. The salt dissolves, or seems to disappear, in the water. Its particles (crystals) do not fall to the bottom of the jar. This is an example of a solution. Chemists call the solid molecules that become part of a solution, such as salt, a "solute," and the liquid molecules, such as water, a "solvent."

Chromatography: Watercolor

Chemists needed a way to separate substances such as dyes and chemical mixtures into their separate parts. In this experiment, we'll mix two different food colors and see if we can bring them back. This is a simple version of what chemists call "chromatography."

You need:
red and blue food coloring
medicine dropper
a small container
2 white napkins or paper towels
newspaper
a cup of water

What to do:
Mix 2 to 3 drops each of red and blue food coloring in the same small container. Put the two napkins together and place them on top of the newspaper. Pour the colored mixture in the center of the napkins. With the medicine dropper, squirt water on the food coloring and try to separate the colors.

What happens:
The colored mixture separates into purple (red-blue) and light blue areas.

Why:
The water acts as a solvent, dissolving the food coloring solution. Because the colors dissolve at different rates, they separate into circular colored areas as the solvent travels through the absorbent, sponge-like napkins.

Fluttering Flatworm Marathon

Enter these fantastic paper flatworms in a marathon, or race, and see which one wins. It's all based on molecules, too!

You need:
paper towel strips, cut about ½ inch (1 cm) wide
    (as many flatworms as you wish to race)
a medicine dropper (if you're racing with friends, you
    may want to provide a dropper for each)
water

What to do:
Fold the strips back and forth, accordion-style. Line them up evenly on the kitchen counter. Load the medicine dropper(s) with water. Let a few drops of water fall on the ends and middle of the paper strips and try to extend, or stretch, the worms across an imaginary finish line.

What happens:
The paper worms seem to flutter and turn.

Why:
The thousands of open holes in the paper fill with water. This "capillary action" expands, or makes larger, those parts of the paper. As the paper expands, it moves, and so do your flatworms!

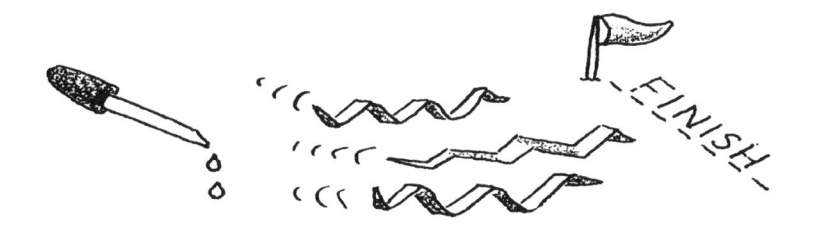

Tip of the Iceberg

If all the icebergs in the seas were to melt, would the sea level rise? This very simple experiment will give us the answer, and it's based on a very important compound chemists study—water!

You need:

a glass   6 to 8 ice cubes
warm water

What to do:

Place as many ice cubes as you can into a glass; then fill the glass to the brim with warm water. Wait.

What happens:

When the ice cubes melt, the water does not overflow.

Why:

The ice cubes simply displaced the water in the glass, or the amount of ice that melted was exactly equal to the mass of the ice cubes below the water. Like the ice cubes in the glass, the main part of an iceberg is under water. If all the icebergs were to melt, as did the ice cubes in our experiment, the sea level would remain the same.

Air Is Real

How do you know air is real? Since it is invisible, you certainly can't see it. Can you prove it really exists? The following experiment will give you the answer. Roll up your sleeves for this one!

You need:

a stiff rubber pad or plastic lid   a deep basin or pot almost filled
a glass of water (clear plastic   with water
  is best)   a medicine dropper

What to do:

Fill the glass with water. Put the waterproof pad over the mouth of the glass. Hold it in place with your hand. Now, carefully turn the glass upside down and place it under the water in the pot or basin until it is completely under the surface. Do not remove the pad until the glass is completely under the water and touching the bottom of the pot.

Observe the water level in the glass. Tilt the glass to one side and carefully place the empty medicine dropper under it. Squeeze the dropper. Remove the dropper from the pot and squeeze the water out of it. Repeat what you did before (squeezing the empty dropper under the glass). Do this several times. You'll know you're doing this experiment correctly when, after squeezing the dropper, you see bubbles entering the glass of water.

What happens:

Air bubbles move up the inside of the glass, and the water level in the glass gets lower.

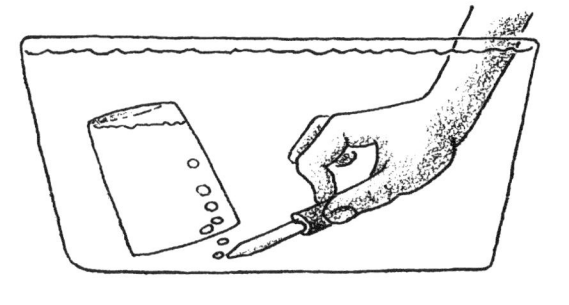

Why:

Air was in the medicine dropper when you squeezed it. The bubbles on the side of the glass were the air forced out of the dropper. As you "pumped" air into the glass with the dropper over and over, you saw the water level in the glass go down. Since the air had to go somewhere, it displaced some of the water, forcing it out of the glass. Now you know that air is real. It takes up space.

Dry Goods

Molecules of air can even stop paper from getting wet in a glass of water.

You need:
a small glass
a napkin or paper towel
a glass bowl
water

What to do:
Crumple the paper and place it in the bottom of the glass. Make certain it is tight so that the paper will not fall out. Fill the bowl with water. Now, turn the glass upside down over the bowl and lower it until it touches the bottom of the bowl. Lift the glass straight up out of the bowl. Continue to keep it upside down as you dry around and inside the rim of it. Now, take the paper out of the glass.

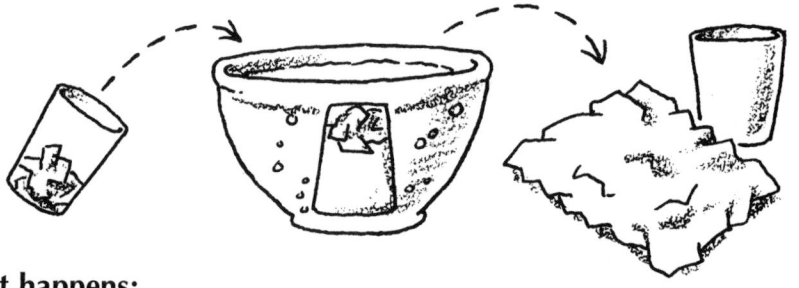

What happens:
The paper inside the glass remains dry.

Why:
When the glass is pushed into the water, the molecules of air do not escape but instead are pressed together and act as a shield between the water and the paper. Some water enters the glass but not enough to wet the paper. The molecules of air take up enough space to block it.

Very Berry Litmus Paper

Here is your chance to make your own litmus paper to test for acids and alkalis, called bases. It's done with berries and it's very berry easy!

You need:

½ cup of berries (blackberries, blueberries, or strawberries)

small strips cut from white construction paper

a small bowl

a fork

water

a teaspoon

paper towels

What to do:

Remove any stems and place the berries in a bowl. Crush the berries with the fork until they look like jam. Add a little water to thin the juice. Dip the paper strips in the juice and spoon the juice over them until they are well coated. Slide the strips between your thumb and finger to remove the pulp. Place the strips on paper towels to dry When they are dry, pick off any big pieces of pulp or berry skins you missed and your Very Berry litmus paper is ready for use.

WHAT DO THE COLOR CHANGES MEAN?

Purple blackberry litmus turns pinkish-red in acids and deep purple in alkali compounds, or bases. These strips work best for litmus testing, for they show the most change.

Purple blueberry litmus turns reddish-purple in acids and light bluish-purple in bases.

Pink strawberry (although not as noticeable as the other two) turns bright pink in acids and light pinkish-blue in bases.

Thoroughly confused? Not to worry! We can tell you how to remember this easily: the paper that has more red in it is reacting to acids, while the paper that has more blue in it is reacting to bases.

Litmus Lotto

Are you ready to test your homemade Very Berry litmus paper? By dipping the paper into different solutions, you can find out if the substance is acid or alkali (a substance that can dissolve in water and weaken acids). When we test how much acid or alkali a substance has, we say we are testing for the pH of that substance.

You need:

2 homemade Very Berry litmus strips
2 small containers, one with lid
3 tablespoons dishwashing liquid

½ cup water
¼ cup vinegar
paper and pencil
some newspaper

What to do:

First read "What do the color changes mean?" before continuing. Put the water and dishwashing liquid into the container with a lid, close it up and shake to mix well. Put the vinegar into the other container. Dip strips of litmus paper into the solutions. Hypothesize, or guess, if the color change will show whether that solution is acid or alkali. Write down the name of the solution (dishwashing liquid and vinegar), and record your answers. Now dry the strips of litmus on the paper towels (about five minutes) and label them as to what solutions they were dipped into and what color changes were noticed. Was your hypothesis, or guess, correct?

What happens:

The litmus dipped into the vinegar has more red in it. The litmus dipped into the soapy water has more blue in it.

Why:

Vinegar is acetic acid but soapy water is an alkali compound, or base. The berry-colored litmus paper are positive tests to determine which substances are acids or bases.

Note: Keep containers, litmus paper, pencil and paper for the next experiment.

223

More Litmus Lotto

Are you ready to do some more testing with litmus paper? Basically, you'll be doing the same thing as you did in "Litmus Lotto" but with different substances.

You need:

2 homemade Very Berry litmus strips
½ cup water, with 2 or 3 squirts of window cleaner with ammonia (*Be careful! This solution can be harmful! Dispose of it carefully when finished!*)
¼ cup lemon juice

Handle carefully

What to do:

Dip the litmus strips and record your guesses and the results of the test as you did under "Litmus Lotto."

What happens:

The litmus that was dipped into the lemon juice will have more red in it, but the one that was dipped into the window-cleaner ammonia will show more blue.

Why:

Lemon juice is another acid, called citric acid, but the ammonia solution is an alkali compound. Can you guess what other fruits may have citric acid, and test your hypothesis?

pH Power

Use your Very Berry litmus paper again to test your tap water, soil, swimming pool or pond water, even your saliva (spit)!

You need:
homemade Very Berry litmus strips
containers (small jars, paper or Styrofoam cups, margarine tubs)
testing samples:
  backyard soil with water
  tap water
  local pond, lake, or river water
  saliva
  whatever else you like

What to do:
Dip the strips of litmus paper into the samples. (See "What to do" under "Litmus Lotto.")

What happens:
The strips will change color depending on whether the samples are more acid or alkali.

Why:
The litmus papers are positive tests for the acids or bases in substances. (See "What do the color changes mean?")

Put Out the Fire

Make your own fire extinguisher with a few materials you can find around your house.

You need:

a large, wide-mouth jar with lid	a large nail
2 cups water	hammer
3 tablespoons (45 ml) baking soda	a spoon
½ cup vinegar	a small jar

What to do:
First, on a rock outside or on an old workbench or board, turn the lid of the large jar over, and with the hammer and nail pound a large hole through it. (*Get adult help, if needed!*)

Pour the water into the large jar. Add and mix in the baking soda. Fill the small jar with vinegar

and gently place it, without a lid, into the large jar, making certain that the vinegar jar does not spill its contents. Screw the *punctured* lid onto the large jar. *Turn the lid away from your face and tip the jar toward the sink.*

What happens:
A foamy liquid spurts out of the hole in the lid.

Be careful handling jar

Why:
Baking soda (sodium bicarbonate) puts out fires when used in soda-acid fire extinguishers. In your homemade version, the vinegar (acetic acid) mixes with the baking soda to produce the carbon-dioxide gas (CO_2) that smothers fires.

The Gas Guzzler

A car is called a gas guzzler when it wastes gas. In this experiment, gas wastes water. Try it and see!

You need:

a square piece of coffee filter,
  about 4″ (10 cm)
3 teaspoons (15 ml) baking soda
  (sodium bicarbonate)
a shallow bowl of water

a rubber band
a tall, narrow jar filled
  with water
permanent marker pen
magnifying hand lens

What to do:
Place the baking soda in the middle of the square of the filter. Gather the filter together to make a pouch and fasten the top with a rubber band. Place the baking soda pouch in the tall jar of water and place your hand over the opening. With your hands in place on the bottom and the top of the jar, turn the jar upside down and place its opening in the bowl of water. Remove your hands. Mark the water line on the jar. Watch the glass jar with the hand lens. Be patient; you must wait at least an hour for results.

What happens:
Bubbles rise from the pouch in the bottom of the jar to the top of it. Some bubbles cling to the sides of the jar. Within an hour, the water drops slightly, but noticeably, below the marked water line.

Why:
As the baking soda in the pouch is dissolved by the water, it produces carbon dioxide gas (CO_2). This gas needs room in the jar, so it displaces the water, or forces some of it out of the jar, lowering the water level.

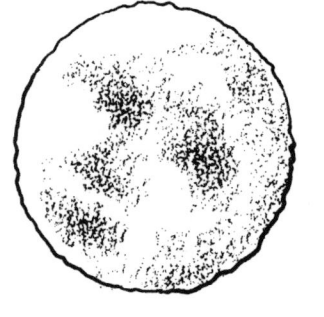

Blue Moon Rocks

You'll think you've stepped out on the moon when you grow this crystal garden. Make certain you cover your work area with newspapers so you won have crystals growing everywhere!

You need:

a frozen-food tray
paper towels
a disposable cup
3 tablespoons salt

3 tablespoons water
3 tablespoons laundry bluing
a spoon
a magnifying hand lens

What to do:
Place a folded paper towel in the bottom of the tray. Crush the second paper towel and place it on top. In the disposable cup, mix all the ingredients together and slowly spoon the mixture over the paper. With the hand lens observe what happens.

What happens:
Blue bubbly crystals instantly appear in the container. (For a full garden, it will have to set for at least **24 hours**.)

Why:
The salt solution with the bluing becomes saturated until no more can dissolve. As the water is soaked up by the paper towels and evaporates, the salt left behind forms new crystals around the powdery bluing.

The Diamond Mine

Alum is a type of mineral or chemical salt that puts the pucker into some pickles, making your mouth feel as if it wants to close up. It looks and feels very much like table salt (sodium chloride), but while table salt in a microscope looks like ice cubes, with flat sides, alum crystals have many angular sides, or facets. Try making your own clear alum crystals and you'll think you've discovered a diamond mine.

You need:

small bottle of alum (available in the supermarket)
a disposable cup half-filled with warm water
a spoon

a small jar
a piece of nylon thread
pencil
a magnifying hand lens

What to do:
Slowly and carefully pour the alum into the cup of water, stirring as you pour, until no more will dissolve. You'll know when the solution is saturated because you'll hear the alum grains scratching on the bottom of the cup and you'll see some floating in the water. If you put your finger in the cup and touch the bottom, you'll be able to feel the undissolved crystals. Keep the solution in the cup **overnight**.

The next day, pour the water into the jar and tie one end of the nylon thread around a large piece of hardened alum crystal you'll find in the bottom or on the sides of the cup. (Be patient with this. If you've ever threaded a sewing needle, you'll understand what we mean. It's

hard to tie the fine nylon thread around the small alum crystals.) Wind and tie the thread around the middle of a pencil and place the pencil over the jar mouth so that the alum dangles low in the water. Keep the jar in a protected place for **several days** and observe the crystals from time to time.

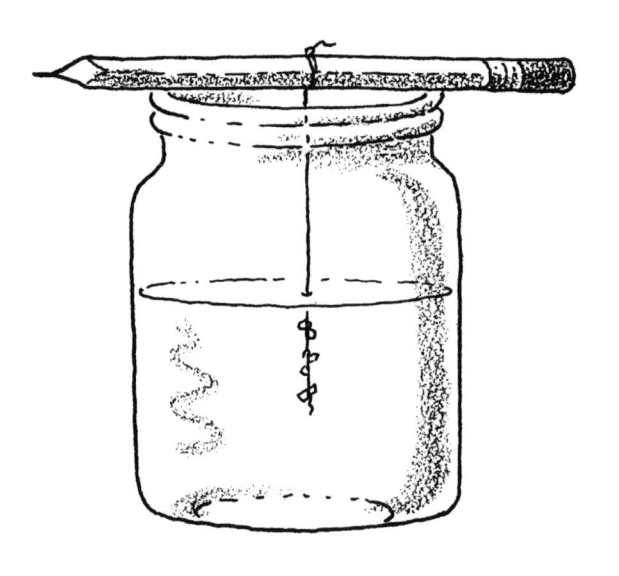

Note: Save the other alum crystals on the bottom of the paper cup and set them to dry on a paper towel. Place them on a dark piece of construction paper and study them with your hand lens. Save these shiny, many-sided alum crystals for "The Gem Show?'

What happens:
If you hold the thread up to the light and view the alum crystals, you'll see what appears to be many shiny brilliant gems.

ABOUT CRYSTALS

Crystals can be grown from a string tied to a pencil and placed across a cup or glass, or scraped with a spoon from the sides and bottom of the container. Keep the crystal solutions in a warm, sunny window. The longer the crystal solution is left to evaporate, the larger the crystals will be.

Store your crystals in a dry place and be careful handling them. If your hands are wet or damp, it is best to use tweezers or a plastic spoon.

Why:

Again, the crystals are formed by dissolving enough solutes or solid substances (alum) in the solvent or water to make a saturated solution. Then the cooled solution causes the alum molecules on the string to build on one another. Crystals will continue to form on the crystal string until all of the solution evaporates.

ROCKY MOUNTIANS

Watch these beautiful rock salt crystals climb on the sides of a string and turn into sparkling mountains of diamond-like cubes. Follow the instructions as in "The Diamond Mine," but replace the alum with ¼ cup of rock salt. Use a strong string dangling from a pencil to catch the growing crystals. Don't rush this one! Great mountains of crystals may take as long as two to four weeks to grow.

CHAPTER SEVEN
SIMPLE SPACE & FLIGHT
EXPERIMENTS

YOU'RE ON THE AIR

Yes! You're definitely on the air in this chapter. You'll learn about the principles of flight, or Bernoulli's law. Once you understand this, you'll know what keeps aircraft in the air.

Besides constructing many types of airfoils, or models of an airplane wing, you'll learn about air currents and how they circulate around and act on a plane's surface. This circulation of air, both fast and slow, lifts the airplane up into the upper atmosphere.

In addition, you'll construct toy helicopters, rotary motors, flying propellers, and real cardboard plane models that fly.

With a few simple materials, and a little effort, you'll be on the air in no time.

Ruler's Uprising

This is one ruler that will be uplifted, even do a back flip! And it's all due to Bernoulli's principle.

You need:

a strip of light cardboard, about ruler-width and half its length	ruler
	pencil
	scissors
tape	table

What to do:

Place the cardboard strip on the ruler so that it is touching one end and extends toward the middle. Push the strip upward a bit to form a slight arch, or curve, about an inch (1.5 cm) in height. Tape both ends of the strip to the ruler.

Place the ruler on a table and balance it on the pencil. The ruler should extend about three inches (8 cm) off the edge of the table.

Now, blow a steady stream of air over the top of the cardboard strip and down the length of the ruler. If nothing happens, or if the ruler just moves down the table on the pencil, adjust the balance point of the ruler on the pencil and try again.

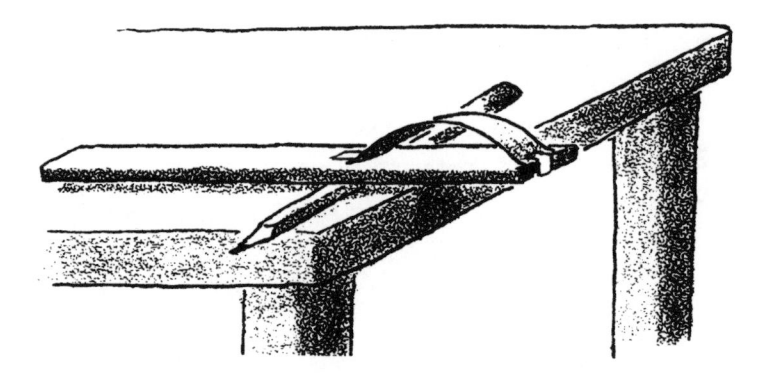

What happens:
The ruler rises, springs up, and does a back flip.

Why:
Bernoulli's principle is used when a plane lifts into the air. The same principle applies to our cardboard wing, or airfoil, taped to the ruler.

The air traveling over an airplane or cardboard wing has to travel farther and faster, so the pressure over the wing is less. Because the flow of air is slower on the wing's flat underside, it produces greater pressure and forces, or pushes, the aircraft upward.

Blowhard

Blow hard and recreate Bernoulli's Principle of Liquid Pressure. Simulate, or copy, an airplane's wing in this simple but uplifting experiment.

You need:
a strip of paper

What to do:
Place one end of the paper just
below your lower lip and
blow hard over the top of it.

What happens:
The paper rises and flaps in the air.

Why:
Again, a fast-moving flow of air passes over the top of the paper, producing lower pressure, while the slower airflow beneath the paper causes greater pressure. The difference is the cause of the lift, pushing the strip of paper upward.

Let's Wing It!

Do you love experiments? This one's a breeze! Design an airplane wing, or airfoil, and see how it reacts to a rapid air stream.

You need:

notebook paper   large paper clip
tape   adult help, to straighten clip

What to do:

Two pieces of notebook paper, about 4 by 5 inches or 11 by 14 cm. (You can also cut a sheet of typing paper into quarters, use two now, and keep the other two quarters for the next experiment.) Keep one piece of note paper flat and form a slight arch, loop, or hill on top with the other, as shown.

   Tape the curved piece of paper to the outer edges of the flat piece, and you have made a copy of an airplane wing, or airfoil.

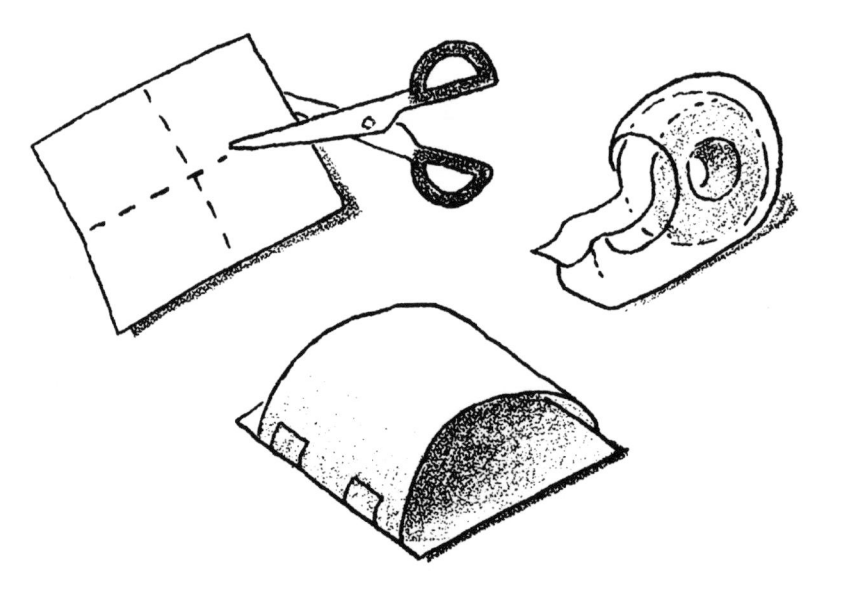

Now, carefully straighten a large paper clip (adult help may be needed) and poke it through the middle of both pieces of paper. Bend the clip slightly underneath, if needed, to hold the paper.

Gently but rapidly, blow some air *over* the short, front side of the air-foil, followed by blowing again just *underneath* it. Be careful to blow only for short periods, and to rest in between blowing (your body needs air, too!).

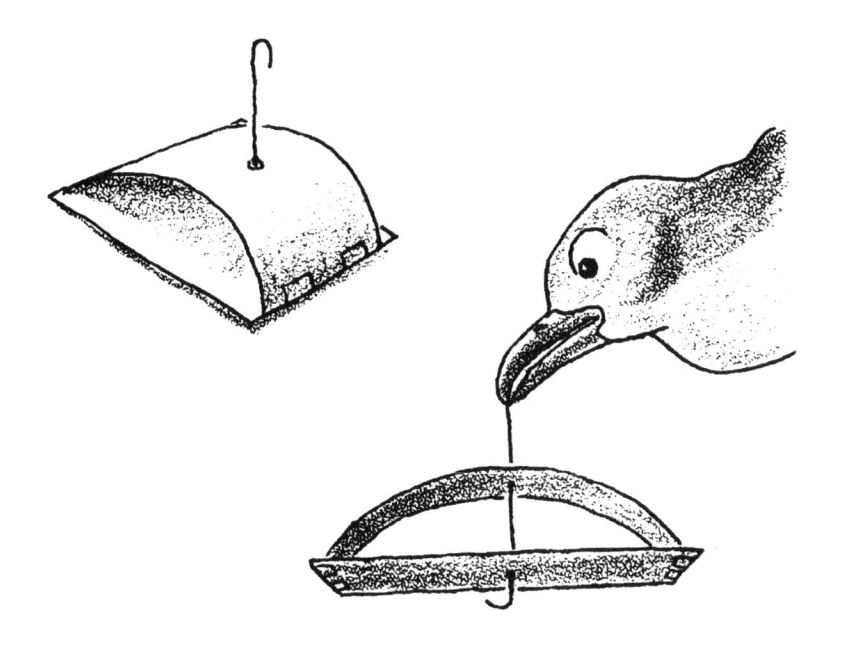

What happens:

When you blew a short burst of air over the curved side of the airfoil, it lifted; however, no movement was noticed when blowing a stream of air under the wing.

Why:

Again, Bernoulli's principle explains it. The lower air pressure on the top of the wing and the greater pressure on the bottom caused lift. (See "Ruler's Uprising.")

Foiled Again!

This time we're going to start rolling, and then square off, and find out what happens.

You need:

notepaper   straightened paper clip
tape   from "Let's Wing It!"

What to do:
From a notebook, take a small sheet of paper and roll it into a cylinder or tube, and tape it. Take another piece of paper, fold it in half, then open and fold each end to the center crease. Shape the creased sheet to form a box. Tape that, too.

   Again, have someone poke the straightened paper clip into the middle of each shape and test each separately. Make certain the hole is large enough so the airfoil slides up and down the paper clip.

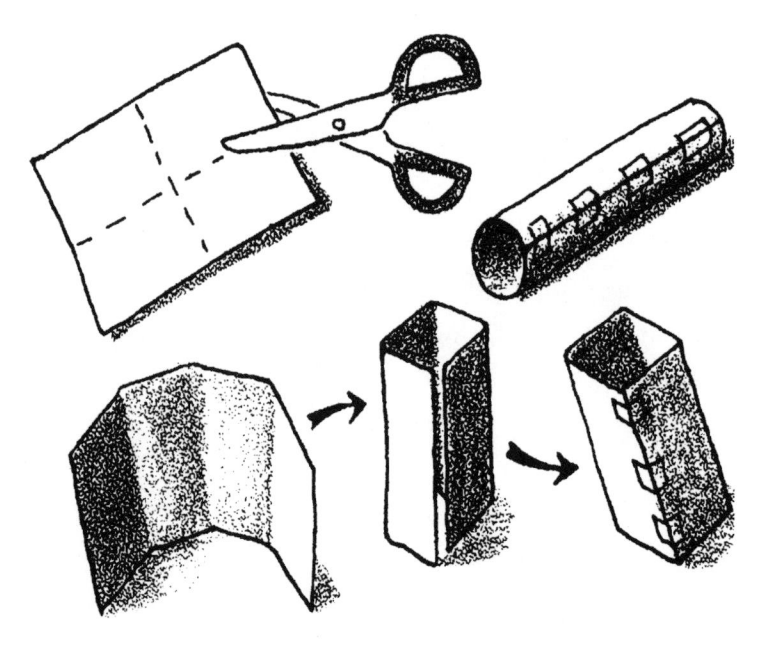

As you did in "Let's Wing It!," blow over the top of each shape and then under it. Again, remember to rest between blowing. Did you notice any difference in the movements between the airplane foil, the cylinder, or the box? Do you think how an airplane wing is designed is important?

What happens:
The cylinder airfoil rises very little, while the box wing does not move at all.

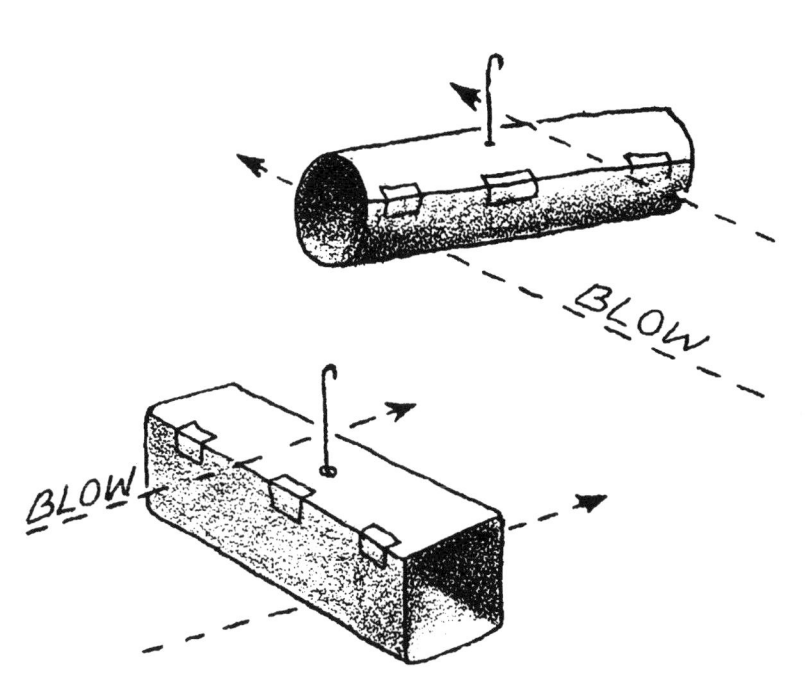

Why:
The push of air against a wing of a plane is called drag. Instead of helping the plane move smoothly through the air, it breaks up or blocks the airflow, so it holds the plane back.

This is why the design of an airplane wing is so very important. Our first airfoil created a smooth flow of air around the wing, while the curves and angles of the cylinder and box caused much drag, or breaking up and blockage of air.

Whirlybird

In the next two experiments, you'll become an expert on helicopter flight. With a simple pencil and piece of light cardboard, you'll duplicate the effect of the spinning blades, or rotor, of a helicopter.

You need:

scissors

a pencil with an eraser

thumbtack

a strip of light cardboard about 1¼ x 16 inches (3 x 40 cm)

What to do:

Place the middle of the cardboard strip on the top of the pencil eraser and press the tack through the strip to attach it. Make certain the tack is in tightly, as you bend the two ends of the strip upward from the middle. Your rotor, blade, or cardboard strip should have a slight V-shape at the eraser.

You are now ready to launch your model. This experiment can be done inside or outside the home. For best results, it can be launched from a height, such as a deck or staircase.

Because high places can be dangerous, ask an adult to help—you'll want someone to witness your big launch anyway!

To do the launch properly, rapidly roll the pencil between your hands and release it. Be certain you roll and drop it the same way each time you conduct the experiment. (It should spin and turn as it drops downward.)

Do this many times, conducting many trials, before you decide how your model helicopter performs, or flies.

What happens:
With practice, your model helicopter with the cardboard strip rotor should turn and spin and whirl through the air as it gently floats downward.

Why:
Like an airplane, the rotors, or wings, of a helicopter are an airfoil and are designed to catch the slower-moving air under them rather than the fast-moving air over them.

These crowded or dense air molecules cause the rotors and the craft to be pushed upward.

The small side rotor on the tail end of the helicopter stops what is known as torque, balancing and keeping the whole craft from turning, while the main rotor helps the craft to lift and turn, according to its position.

Although our cardboard/pencil model with its rapid hand-spin thrust does not lift the model very much, it still reduces the fall rate as it descends.

Twirly-Whirlies

Twirly-what? Whirlies! In "Whirlybird," we made a simple pencil-and-paper helicopter-like toy. Now, let's replace that straight and simple blade with a circular pinwheel-and-cross rotor. Will the design of the different rotors make your model stay up in the air longer? Turn and fly better?

Do longer or wider rotors make a difference? Let's try different shapes, sizes, and widths of rotors to find out what works best.

You need:

3 pencils	light cardboard
scissors	thumbtacks

What to do:

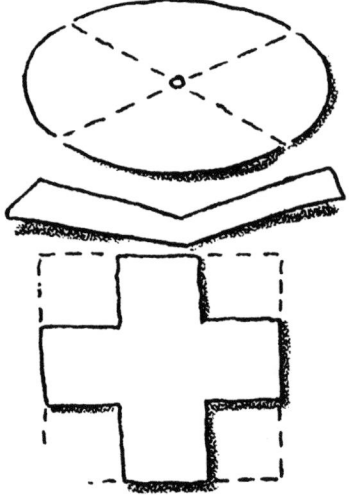

Cut a circle between 4½ and 8 inches (11–20 cm) in diameter from the light cardboard. Cut four slits opposite each other in *toward* the center, but leave the center uncut. Fold one side of each slit to form a pinwheel.

Next, cut a strip 2 by 8 inches (5 x 20 cm) long and fold the strip in the center to form a V. Last, cut a 6-inch (15 cm) square of cardboard and cut out 2-inch (5 cm) squares from each corner to form a cross. Turn the cross ends up.

Now, tack the middle of each cardboard rotor to the top of a pencil eraser. Make certain the thumbtack is securely in place on all three models.

To launch, rapidly roll a pencil between your hands and release it. Again, see "Whirlybird" for help and hints!

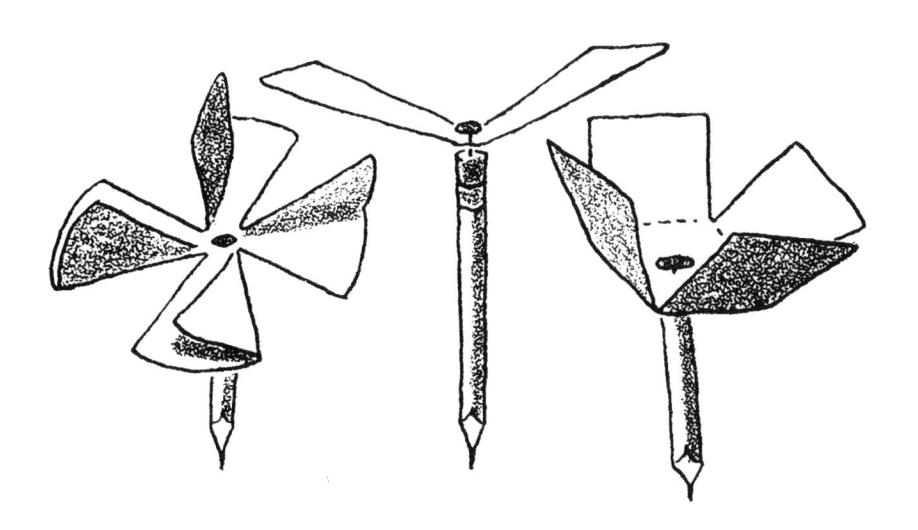

What happens:

With our test models, the 2 by 8 inch (5 x 20 cm) strip worked fairly well but was somewhat clumsy. The pinwheel airfoil was very clumsy, did not turn or rotate, and fell to the ground without catching the air currents. However, the 6-inch (15 cm) cross rotor flew very well, with smooth and gentle spinning, or rotation, as it softly fell to the ground.

Why:

The cross rotor was probably more like a real helicopter's airfoil than the other models. The wide blades with the four upturned ends, when rotated by hand, caught the denser, closer air underneath it and reduced the rate of drag from air holding it back as it fell to the ground. See "Whirlybird."

What now:

Do this same experiment, but see if you can make a perfect airfoil, or helicopter rotor, by adjusting the variables——other things that can affect spinning and flight.

For example, will longer or wider rotors make a difference? Or heavier or lighter paper or cardboard? Will making a drive shaft or spinning launcher help? In the next experiment, we'll find out!

Rotor Motor

You can make a jet-propelled, helicopter-like rotor, or blade, whirl, using nothing but 100 percent balloon power.

You need:

cardboard paper towel tube
2 large oblong balloons
one ¼-inch wooden dowel,
  18 inches (45 cm) long

scissors
paper clip
tape
a helper

What to do:

Ask an adult to help by using a sharp scissors tip to punch two holes completely through the tube, through both sides, at a point midway along its length. The holes need to be exactly opposite each other so that an inserted dowel will fit right across. Place the dowel through the holes in the tube and turn, or rotate, the tube on the dowel many times until it spins freely.

Next, blow up one of the oblong balloons, twist and clip it, and carefully tape it to one end of the tube. (Be sure to fasten it well.)

Blow up the second balloon, twist and clip it, and fasten it to the other end of the tube, making certain the balloon opening is facing opposite the first balloon.

Now, get ready for the action! To do two things at once, you'll need the help of your assistant.

While your helper carefully takes the paper clip off one of the balloons and holds the end of it closed, you do the same—and, at a given signal, both of you release your balloons.

What happens:
As soon as you release the balloons, the tube whirls and spins.

Why:
The rush of air from the balloons mounted on opposite ends of the tube pushes them forward, turning the tube around the dowel. The air being expelled by the balloons causes this push. Sir Isaac Newton's third law of motion explains it best: for every action there is an equal and opposite reaction. The reaction of the balloons is to move forward. What would happen if the two balloons were placed on the dowel with their neck openings in the same direction?

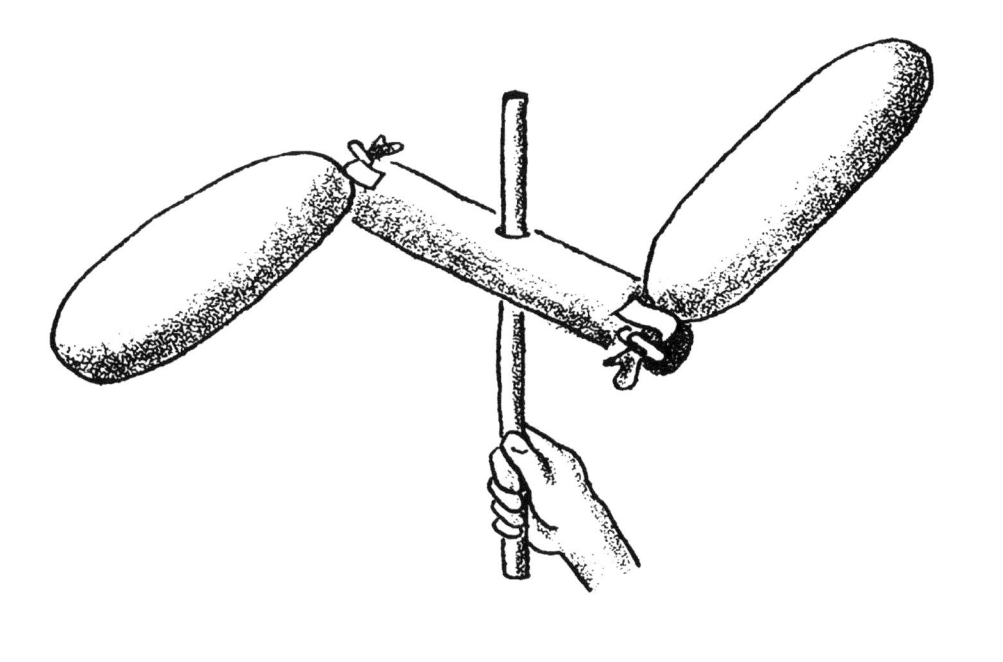

I'm Banking On You!

Would you like to make the kind of instrument that helps pilots determine an airplane's position in flight? The *artificial horizon* will tell you whether you are flying level, or banking, or tilting, right or left. You're bound to crash in on the fun.

You need:

shoe box lid
plastic sandwich or freezer bag
2 permanent markers
  (different colors)
scissors

short bolt with nut,
  or other fastener
paper hole punch (optional)
tape
ruler

What to do:

Flatten and cut the ends off the shoe box lid and cut the flat, rectangular piece of cardboard in half. Cut one of the halves an inch (3 cm) shorter (1).

Cut a 3-inch (8 cm) square from the plastic bag. With one of the marker pens, draw a straight line across the center of the piece (2).

Now, cut a 2¾-inch (7 cm) circle from the center of the longer piece of cardboard and tape the clear plastic piece with the line on it to one side. Again, make certain the line is centered in the middle (3).

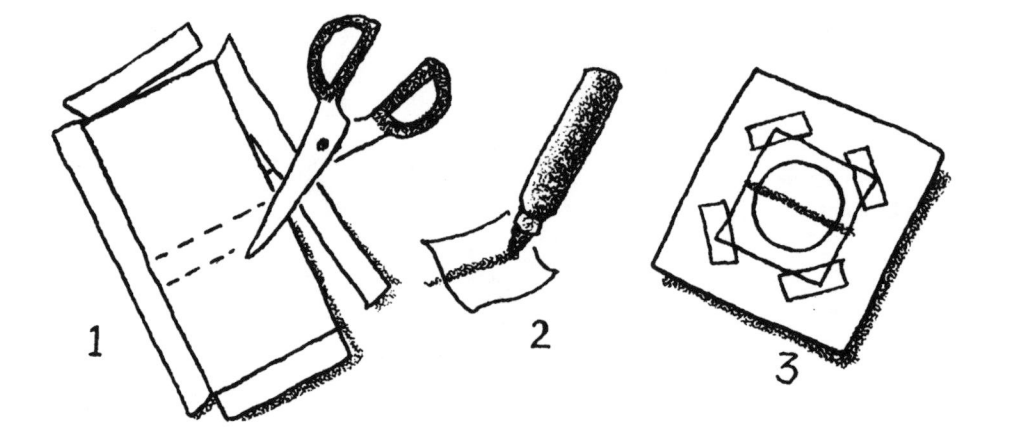

On the second, shorter piece of cardboard, draw a different-colored line. It should be in the center, so as to divide it. Now draw a 90-degree straight line vertically or straight up from the center of the other line. You should have what looks like an upside down T.

Last, place the two cardboard pieces together—the window-lined piece on top of the inside shorter T-piece. Make certain both lines are matched up with each other.

Have someone punch a hole in the top center pieces of the cardboard, as you would a hanger on a picture, and position the bolt and nut (or fastener) in it.

The back (shorter) piece should move freely back and forth, much like a pendulum on a clock. Your flight instrument is now ready to be tested.

The line you drew on the plastic window represents the wing, while the cardboard with lines attached to the window shows the horizon, the line between the earth and sky.

Hold the attached longer piece level with the floor and slowly but gradually tip the instrument to the right and then to the left.

What happens:
When tilting, if the horizon line is below the wing, the airplane is headed upward. If the line is above the wing line, the plane is angled downward.

Why:
A real artificial horizon helps a pilot navigate accurately even if he or she cannot see ahead. It tells the pilot whether the plane is going up, down, or flying level.

The instrument shows two lines, one of which represents the horizon, the other the wing. The horizon line is balanced by a gyroscope or a spinning wheel that keeps the horizon line level with the real horizon. This instrument is so accurate that it keeps the two horizon lines steady, even if the airplane is not.

Note: Your artificial horizon must be matched up, line for line, carefully in order to register correctly, to give you an accurate reading.

Meter-Made

Make an aneroid barometer, which is similar to an airplane's altimeter (altitude meter). Although your liquidless barometer won't measure altitude above sea level, it will teach you the highs and lows of air-pressure changes.

You need:

16 oz. wide-mouth jar   scissors
straw   ruler
tape   clay
large balloon

What to do:

Cut the neck off the balloon and make a one-inch (3 cm) cut on its side. Open it up and stretch it over the mouth of the jar, as you would spread skin over a drum. It should be put on tight, but not *too* tight. Done correctly, it will not slip off the mouth of the jar but will form an airtight seal.

Next, place the straw in the middle of the balloon skin and carefully and gently tape it.

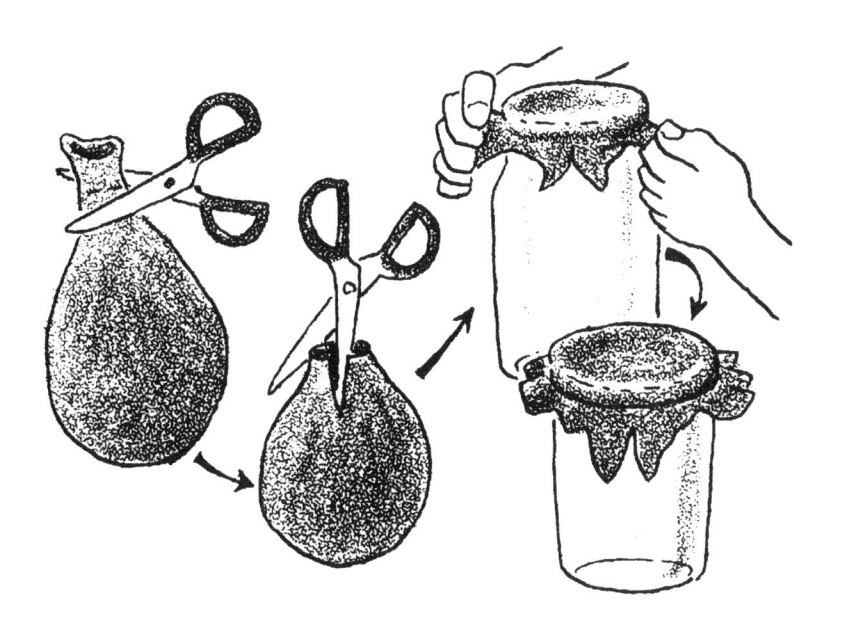

Last, form a ball with the clay and stick the end of the ruler with the lower numbers into it. The clay will form a stand for your ruler-scale. Place the ruler close to the straw and record any numbered up and down movements.

What happens:
The straw will move up or down to record any air pressure changes in the jar.

Why:
When the straw moves upward on the ruler, the pressure is higher; when it falls, the pressure is lower.

The aneroid barometer you made is similar to an airplane's altimeter, but it has no liquid in it. Too, unlike the airplane's device, it only shows altitude changes above sea level.

As a plane ascends, or climbs, the air pressure becomes less and is recorded as a drop on the altimeter. Air pressure at sea level exerts a greater force and affects all things on Earth.

Note: In order to show accurate barometric pressure changes, keep your barometer safe and undisturbed in a sheltered area for an extended, or long, period of time.

A Prop-er Engine: A Wheel Deal!

Modern jet planes use a mixture of fueled, hot, compressed rushing air to turn a series of wheeled fans on rods, or axles (called turbines).

This compressed, or flattened and pressed, air is then forced out of the plane's tail and it pushes, or thrusts, the craft forward. Early turbo-prop planes used propellers and turbines to do the same job, but not as well as modern jet crafts. Find out how early jet-prop planes worked in this simple, easy and fun experiment—it's a wheel deal!

You need:
one medium cup with
  plastic lid (from fast food
  place, save yours!)
lump of clay (size of a large marble)
rubber band

cardboard
scissors
ruler
straw
tape

What to do:
Cut a rectangular section in the middle side of the cup that extends halfway down its sides. Poke a hole in the middle of the bottom of the cup and cut the flap off the straw hole in the plastic lid.

Draw two circles 3 inches (8 cm) in diameter on the cardboard and divide each into eight parts, like circles used for teaching fractions.

Next, make ¾ cuts on the lines in the circles and bend the sections back and forth to represent the blades of a fan. Use tape to reinforce cuts and repair any tears.

Poke holes in the middle of the circular fans and push the straw through them. Each fan should be in the middle of the straw and about 2 inches (5 cm) from the other.

Fit the fan-and-straw assembly through the bottom hole of the cup while securing the plastic lid and straw into the top. Test the assembly to see if it turns easily. If not, cut larger holes to accommodate the straw, so that it will turn freely.

To make the propeller, cut a 1 x 5-inch (2.5 x 13 cm) propeller-shaped piece out of the cardboard.

Cut small slits into the center of each side and gently bend each part in opposite directions. This will give the propeller its third-dimensional shape.

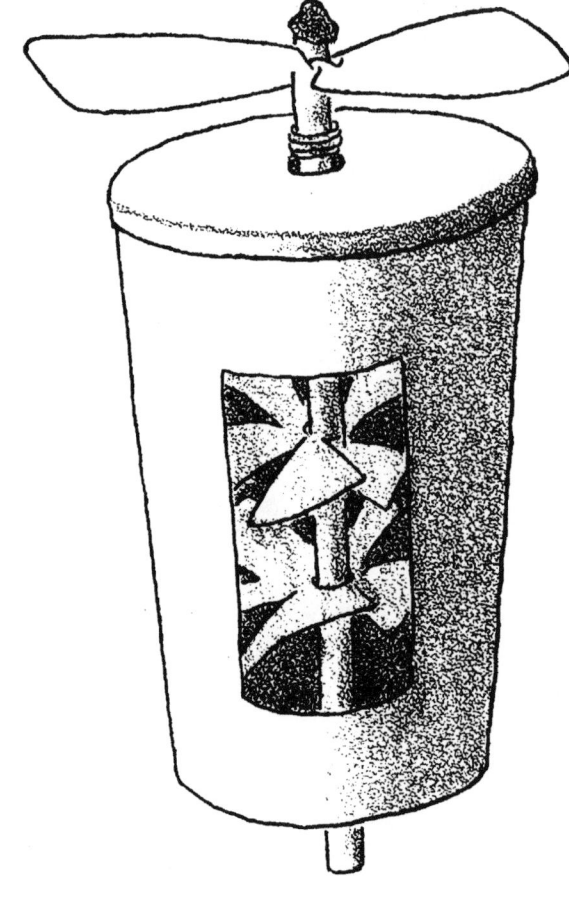

Assemble the propeller by wrapping the rubber band around the straw securely, where it pokes up through the lid. This will act as a buffer between the propeller and the lid, so that the propeller will stay forward and turn more freely. Next, place the propeller on the end of the straw (it will be necessary to poke a hole in the middle of the propeller), in front of the wrapped rubber band.

Finally, secure the propeller in place by shaping a nose for your plane out of clay and pushing it into place on the straw in front of the propeller.

Now you are ready to test your model jet prop. Blow a steady stream of air to the sides of the propeller and watch what happens.

What happens:
By blowing a stream of air to the sides of the propeller, the compresser-turbine fanned parts are turned around.

Why:
Although our experiment turboprop model is fun to make and test, it does not necessarily show how a real turboprop works. Our model essentially was made to show how the movement of turbine parts is needed in the jet-propulsion process. In a real turboprop engine, the turbines turn the propellers, while in our model it is the propeller that turns the turbine parts.

Again, in a modern jet engine, incoming air at the front of the plane is compressed, or squeezed together, by engine parts. The jet's fuel is ignited or burned in a chamber and the hot gases are blown out of the rear of the plane. The thrust, or the forward push of the plane, is explained by one of Newton's three laws of motion, put forth in the year 1687, that every action has an equal and opposite reaction.

Index